THE SENSE OF A BEGINNING

The Sense of a Beginning

Theory of the Literary Opening

Niels Buch Leander

MUSEUM TUSCULANUM PRESS

The Sense of a Beginning: Theory of the Literary Opening
By Niels Buch Leander

Consultant: Brian Russell Graham
Copy editor: Jordy Findanis
Layout, composition, and cover design: Janus Bahs Jacquet
The book is set in Inka B 10/14
Printed in Denmark on 100g Munken Lynx paper
by Narayana Press, www.narayana.dk
ISBN 978 87 635 4386 6

Cover illustration: Michelangelo Buonarroti, *The Creation of Adam* (before restoration), Vatican City, Sistine Chapel, center of the ceiling. ©2017 Photo Scala, Florence.

This book is published with financial support from
E. Lerager Larsens Fond
Landsdommer V. Gieses Legat
Lillian og Dan Finks Fond

Museum Tusculanum Press
Dantes Plads 1
DK-1556 Copenhagen

www.mtp.dk

Contents

To my family

It is written: "In the beginning was the Word!"
Here I falter! Who can help me continue?

GOETHE, *Faust*

PROLOGUE

How to Begin

The beginning is always the chief thing in every process
PLATO, *Republic*

Beginnings are so central and so complex that in ancient times they required their own god. The two-faced Janus looking both back and forth in time was the Roman god of beginnings whose dual outlook was designed to ease the temporal complexity of any initiation.[1] January, the first month of the year, is still named in honor of this intricate god who both remembers the year that passed and looks ahead to the year to come.

If this god of beginnings helps smooth transitions, his efficacy does, however, come at a certain price. A modern interpretation will not fail to recognize that the god's particular perspective also endows him with a doubtful character: you cannot see his two faces at the same time; he might be deceitful or—as we tellingly say—double-faced. We may have to depend upon him, yet we know that there is something cunning about him. We may need him, yet we know perfectly well that he is ambiguous.

It is the objective of the present book to reveal the Janus-headed nature of fiction through a study of the literary opening. A novel's first lines mark the transition from the reader's own world to a narrated world—a transition from the reader's reality to a textual reality. This transition is, however, so uniquely complex that in the process the reader will have to embrace a certain "deception." The opening will have to say as *much* as

1 Janus was also the god of prefaces and prologues, which is why it seems even more appropriate to evoke him here. For more on Janus, see Denis Hollier, *Against Architecture: The Writings of Georges Bataille* (Cambridge, MA: MIT Press, 1989).

possible and as *little* as possible in order to lure the reader into the textual reality. As I argue in chapter 1, the ability to accept such a deception is, all the same, pivotal in the human ability to understand beginnings in life in general—and literary beginnings therefore play an instrumental role in making us apprehend reality.

Beginnings are in this sense more important than endings, I claim. Admittedly, we note a symmetry between beginnings and endings in so far as an ending marks the reversed transition from the narrated world back into the reader's world. Yet, from a formal point of view, this symmetry breaks down. For one thing, endings have conventionally been marked metatextually by "The End," "La Fin," or "Explicit liber"; the book has ended. This Latin term for ending, "explicit," says it all: the exit of the narrative can be explicit—and should be clearly marked. In contrast, the literary beginning—the "incipit"—does not conventionally have its own metatextual marker. Typically, a novel simply begins. A number of implicit, paratextual markers will naturally sustain the beginning, but otherwise we simply have to trust that the beginning is the beginning.

Janus head stamped on a Roman bronze coin (diameter 32 mm, weight 28.44 g) from around 200 BC. Wikimedia Commons.

And as in the case of Janus, our trust in the beginning only works fully when we somehow accept that we are simultaneously being "deceived."

If the literary beginning is rarely explicitly marked, it tends instead to rely upon implicit indications and conventions that can serve to smooth the transition into the textual reality. Often, the reader will have to be presented with a beginning that is recognizably a beginning. It can therefore be claimed that the literary beginning will relate more naturally to particular literary conventions and, above all, to the universal and archetypal incipit "Once upon a time," as I discuss at greater length in chapter 2. Yet, the literary beginning is two-faced also in this sense: it cannot avoid relating to prior conventions of beginning, yet this is also precisely what prompts a quest for finding innovative loopholes in the conventions.

The beginning is therefore privileged indeed. First, it marks the place where the transition between text and reality is most distinct. Second, the complexity of this transition makes the text relate more directly to prior conventions of beginning than the rest of the text, accentuating the intertextual relation between one beginning and another, as examined in chapter 3 and 4. Moreover, the opening sets off our mind in a certain direction, which inevitably influences the lines that follow and thus shape our entire reading experience. As the German author Martin Walser puts it, "the novel is always a game, but the first line irrevocably shows how the game should be played."[2] In this sense, the beginning is unique by being the only literary component that is available at all time during our reading experience, even at its conclusion.

From considerations of these three textual relations—"hors-texte" ("outside-the-text"), intertext, intratext—it is evident that the literary beginning is more than a mere prelude to the work itself; it is no less than the most central place to observe a work's literariness. As I show in more detail in chapter 2, the beginning is simply "the literary place *par excellence*," as the Italian author Italo Calvino claims.[3]

It is therefore astonishing that literary criticism in English has dealt very little with the literary opening. In fact, my book project started with my own surprise at the lack of critical works on the subject.[4] Since the dawn of time, people have reflected theologically and philosophically on beginnings, as will be discussed in the first chapter. Yet, despite obvious parallels between cosmological concepts like 'origin' and 'conception' and the ones used to describe literary creation, literary critics have not

2 Martin Walser, "Erfahrungen mit ersten Sätzen oder Aller Anfang ist schwer," in *Vormittag eines Schriftstellers* (Frankfurt: Suhrkamp, 1994), 162. Unless otherwise noted, all translations from non-English sources are my own.

3 Italo Calvino, "Appendice: cominciare e finire," in *Saggi 1945–1985*, ed. M. Barenghi (Milan: Mondadori, 1995).

4 As the narratologist James Phelan exclaimed when asked: "There's not that much on beginnings period" (in an e-mail to Professor Harry E. Shaw).

concerned themselves much with openings. Occasionally, articles on literary openings have appeared in English, but always as rather isolated and singular contributions to the discipline, for instance when elucidating a particular text or the methods of a certain author. This book can therefore lay claim to being the first comprehensive study in English of the modern literary opening.[5] Yet, this fact calls for explanation rather than celebration: such a lack of critical works on the opening is no less than baffling, especially when we think of the increasing importance of the participatory reader both in modern literary criticism and in the commercial book market.[6] One of my ambitions in this book is therefore also to uncover possible reasons for this neglect of the literary opening.

We could hardly explain this neglect by arguing that no one has ever urged literary scholars to examine openings further. As early as in 1943, the renowned medieval scholar Ernst Curtius deplored the lack of "evident ordering principles and a comprehensive exposition of beginnings."[7] In 1979 one of the leading narratologists of the German-speaking tradition, Franz Stanzel, notes that "the problem of theme/rheme arrangement [in the opening] has scarcely been examined by narrative criticism," assessing with full confidence that "the question would be a very rewarding area for future research."[8] In 1980 the Romance scholar Victor Brombert started collecting some of the central considerations in an article, pointing out that "the field of opening signals still remains fairly uncharted territory."[9] Nearly fourty years after Brombert's article, this assertion still holds true, despite the discipline's strengthened interest in conventions of reading during the past decades. One exception is the

5 The only full-length study of the opening to appear in English is A. D. Nuttall's *Narrative Beginnings from the Epic to the Novel* from 1992, which focuses on literature from Homer until 1850. The present study focuses on the development from 1850 up until the present day. Nuttall's book as well as a study on openings in a medieval context, D. Vance Smith, *The Book of the Incipit: Beginnings in the Fourteenth Century*, Medieval Cultures, vol. 28 (Minneapolis, MN: University of Minnesota Press, 2001), will be discussed in chapter 1.

6 Modern manuals for aspiring writers cannot emphasize this strategic position strongly enough. In their handbook *So You Want to Write*, Piercy and Wood devote a long chapter to "The Importance of Beginnings," knowing the modern reader's impatient and impulsive consumption. Marge Piercy and Ira Wood, *So You Want To Write: How to Master the Craft of Writing Fiction and the Personal Narrative* (Wellfleet, MA: Leapfrog Press, 2001). At the world's largest bookseller, amazon.com, readers have access to precisely the opening, which they can view before committing to purchasing a book.

7 Ernst Robert Curtius, "Mittelalter-Studien," *Zeitschrift für Romanische Philologie* 63 (1943): 246.

8 Franz Karl Stanzel, *A Theory of Narrative*, trans. Charlotte Goedsche (Cambridge: Cambridge University Press, 1984), 164.

9 Victor Brombert, "Opening Signals in Narrative," *New Literary History* 11, no. 3 (1980): 493.

volume *Narrative Beginnings* from 2008 edited by Brian Richardson and to which I contributed.[10] Anthologies of opening lines have appeared, in print as well as online, but only with the carefree perspective of book lovers cherishing their favorite novels, not as a tool for critical insight.[11]

Whenever the topic of openings is mentioned, one work does however spring to mind: Edward Said's early work *Beginnings* from 1975.[12] Yet, people seem to have forgotten that this monumental work fails altogether to address the question of a work's concrete opening, establishing instead a theoretical inquiry into the authorial process of beginning. In fact, Said only broached the topic of literary openings three times in this some four hundred-page study.[13] As I discuss in more detail in chapter 3, *Beginnings* is not centrally concerned with literary openings, but rather with leveling an attack on authoritative, "dynastic" relations in the literary field. It is therefore paradoxical that the authority of Said and the sheer monumentality of his book may have had the adverse consequence of having pre-empted further critical interest in the question of openings. In a sense we as critics seem "to have ended with Said's beginning," as Vance Smith fittingly puts it.[14]

Yet, the presence of Said's book hardly explains altogether why the field of openings appears to have been so oddly neglected in Anglo-American criticism in contrast to, for instance, French criticism, as is one of my central points throughout this book. Could part of the explanation also be found in the methodological problem of *delimiting* such a study? To be sure, all books begin. The critic is naturally faced with a potentially infinite pool of openings. Could one ever examine openings in a comprehensive fashion without relying on a somewhat arbitrary selection of beginnings?

This methodological worry is—as I discuss below—genuine. Yet, we notice that critics have not refrained from discussing *endings*, which of course would be subject to the same methodological concern. A central work in modern literary criticism is thus Frank Kermode's *The Sense of an Ending* (1967), which is representative of a quite extensive literature on

10 Brian Richardson, ed., *Narrative Beginnings: Theories and Practices*, Frontiers of Narrative (Lincoln: University of Nebraska Press, 2008).

11 See the appendix to this book for references to anthologies and critical articles.

12 Edward W. Said, *Beginnings: Intention and Method* (New York: Basic Books, 1975).

13 Ibid., 43–46, 84, 89. In these three passages, Said discusses the openings of *The Prelude* and *Paradise Lost* and the opening of *Huckleberry Finn* as well as the narrative frames of Conrad's *Heart of Darkness*.

14 D. Vance Smith, *The Book of the Incipit: Beginnings in the Fourteenth Century*, Medieval Cultures, vol. 28 (Minneapolis, MN: University of Minnesota Press, 2001), xii.

endings, such as David Richter's *Fable's End: Completeness and Closure in Rhetorical Fiction* (1974), D.A. Miller's *Narrative and Its Discontents* (1981), Marianna Torgovnick's *Closure in the Novel* (1981), and Peter Brooks's *Reading for the Plot* (1992).[15]

These works do not fail to mention the beginning, but they all, in one way or the other, subordinate the beginning to the sway of the ending. Just as Kermode has his "recursive reading" and Brooks his "anticipation of retrospection," Torgovnick claims that "in novels, as in lyrics, the process of closure often begins with the work's first lines."[16] The import of the beginning is thus almost systematically negated by being reduced to an effect of the *telos* (the Greek term for endings, which is important to Aristotle's *Poetics*). The beginning can in this way never be read in its own right, not even as setting up the fundamental conditions of the reading process.

The peculiar lack of works on beginnings is thus further underscored by the strong presence of works on endings. Noting that these works furthermore tend to undo the beginning, I argue in chapter 3 that considerations of beginnings and considerations of endings are not at all complimentary. There is instead an *ideological* schism that divides beginnings and endings. I thus observe that while the Anglo-American critical tradition tends to negate the opening in the work's teleology, French critics have more readily investigated and recognized the impact of the opening.[17] It is for instance also indicative that above-mentioned Curtius and Brombert, who called for further research into openings, were both Romance scholars, Brombert for instance drawing on discussions from the French criticism of Louis Aragon and Raymond Roussel. My study of the beginning thus aims *en route* to illuminate a central aspect of the great divide between Anglo-American and French criticism.

One of the presuppositions underlying my book is thus that, from a critical point of view, beginnings and endings tend to mutually exclude or annihilate each other, not compliment each other. As a consequence, an interest in beginnings will rest on a particular vision of literature that tends to challenge the teleology of the work. When Yves Navarre in

15 Frank Kermode, *The Sense of an Ending* (New York: Oxford University Press, 1967); David H. Richter, *Fable's End: Completeness and Closure in Rhetorical Fiction* (Chicago: University of Chicago Press, 1974); D.A. Miller, *Narrative and its Discontents* (Princeton, NJ: Princeton University Press, 1981); Marianna Torgovnick, *Closure in the Novel* (Princeton, NJ: Princeton University Press, 1981); Peter Brooks, *Reading for the Plot: Design and Intention in Narrative* (Cambridge, MA: Harvard University Press, 1992).

16 Torgovnick, *Closure in the Novel*, 10.

17 I will elaborate on the schism between French and Anglo-American criticism in chapter 3, the Epilogue and the Appendix.

his book *Premières pages* (First Pages) (1983) titles all chapters "chapter 1," he does so in a conviction that "in chapter 2 starts the terrible lie of an established, structured, orderly work."[18]

Since it is a common conception that modern literature is more conscious of its own mode of opening, I devote chapter 3 to a study of modernist beginnings. Somewhat paradoxically, modernist texts seem both to lack recognizable beginnings and to see beginnings as a unique space of experimentation. Close attention to historical changes in the stylistics of openings will, however, elucidate these inconsistencies and show how much of modernism's uncompromising, yet contradictory character can be seen in the period's perception of the beginning.

The historical survey of the modernist opening in chapter 3 will furthermore illustrate my suggestion in chapter 2 that openings are expressions of historical variations that can be identified by the literary critic. Literary history has had notorious difficulties in being truly *literary*, tending instead to slide into sociological or materialist considerations of historical periods. Literary history has, to put it bluntly, been quite disappointing when it comes to explaining formal shifts historically. However, focus on a concrete formal unit such as the opening provides a means of observing changes in the fundamental literary categories. The eminent Russian critic Jurij Tynjanov thus claims that a central literary concept like "influence" can "only be affirmed when identical functions bring about identical or analogous formal elements."[19] As I show, the opening provides precisely such a formal element that can be compared synchronically as well as diachronically by the literary historian.

I mentioned above that the beginning is two-faced insofar as it serves two functions: it needs both to say as *much* as possible and as *little* as possible. That is to say, the literary opening serves in the first place to prepare for, and expose, that which follows and it must provide sufficient information for the story to unfold. The opening of Henry Fielding's *Tom Jones* (1749) is thus presented as "containing as much of the birth of the foundling as is necessary or proper to acquaint the reader with in the beginning of this history."[20] Yet, an opening must not only inform—it also has to lure and draw in its reader. This is most frequently achieved

18 Yves Navarre, *Premières pages. Roman* (Paris: Flammarion, 1983).

19 This is what Jurij Tynjanov calls an "auto-function." "On Literary Evolution," in *Readings in Russian Poetics: Formalist and Structuralist Views*, ed. Ladislav Matejka and Krystyna Pomorska (Ann Arbor: Michigan Slavic Publications, 1978), 68.

20 This is the title of the book's first chapter. Henry Fielding, *The History of Tom Jones, a Foundling* (London: A. Millar, 1749).

by withholding or suppressing information, which means that this secondary function often works directly against the opening's expositional function. To the reader, the opening thus represents both what I call an *exposition* and an *exposure*.

A text's particular 'mode' of opening will depend largely on how these two faces of the opening play off against each other. In my view, a major reason for the critical interest in the opening therefore lies precisely in determining the tension and oscillation between these two opposing functions of the opening. By thus comparing different modes of opening, my claim is that we may begin to conjecture about historical changes in the formal and cosmological outlooks that underlie them.[21]

One methodological complication regarding this task, however, is that an opening has no clear demarcations. As already mentioned, an opening is never explicitly marked. We do have a number of paratextual indications, such as title, title page, etc., that may assist us in locating the beginning of a text.[22] Yet, even these paratextual indications may sometimes play a direct textual role: a title may, as in the case of *Tom Jones*, be part of the opening; a preface may, as in the case of Italo Svevo's *Zeno's Conscience* (1923), be the actual opening.[23] Though, for the most part, readers possess an intuitive notion of where the text begins and tend to locate the beginning of a text quite uniformly.

Where the beginning *ends* is, however, far more difficult to say. Is the opening simply the first line, the *incipit*? Or is it rather the first three lines, the first paragraph, the first page, or even the first chapter? The most clear-cut criterion would be simply to consider the *incipit*, e.g. the first line. Yet, even this criterion may not always be entirely straightforward. If the first line is an exclamation like "Tschah!," as is the case in Guy de Maupassant's *Pierre and Jean*, should the second line not also be taken under consideration in order to determine the source of this exclamation? At the other end of the spectrum we find Marie NDiaye's *Comédie classique* (Classical Comedy) (1987), whose 124 pages are written as one long sentence; the entire novel is in fact one first line![24] Rather than pursuing a definitive, clear-cut definition of the length of an opening, I will therefore propose a flexible, yet pragmatic answer: an opening ends

21 I am fully aware that establishing a history of the beginning also perpetuates the narrative structure based on beginning, middle, and end.

22 For a thorough examination of these paratextual elements, see Gérard Genette, *Seuils* (Paris: Seuil, 1987).

23 Italo Svevo, *La coscienza di Zeno* (Bologna: L. Cappelli, 1923).

24 Marie NDiaye, *Comédie classique* (Paris: P.O.L., 1987).

when the reader has obtained the most elementary information about the spatial and temporal positioning of the narration. This may be achieved in the first line, but only rarely.

What is clear from this definition, and from this prologue in general, is that I shall principally look at literary openings from the point of view of their *reception*—not their *conception*. The opening is what leads the reader from a private reality into a textual reality and it is therefore concretely located at the beginning of the book. The place in the actual manuscript that the author *began writing* a book will not be taken into consideration in my study, fascinating as that question may be in other respects, for instance in the so-called "critique génétique," or genetic studies, which has become quite a large discipline in the French literary field. I shall, however, be the first to admit that the reception of a text cannot take place without at least a consideration of its conception. A text is laid out in the knowledge that it will be read in a particular order. Any opening will therefore be conceived with an understanding that the reading is supposed to begin precisely there. Although I focus mostly on how the opening appears to the reader, I therefore occasionally allow myself to discuss how an author imagines the reader to receive the opening.

If modern, commercial writers are keenly aware of the importance of an enticing opening for the subsequent success of their product, our present study cannot simply presuppose that literary openings always take full advantage of their privileged position. Some openings, even by—at the time—bestselling authors, are simply unmemorable, or even ordinary, for instance those by otherwise respected writers like Fyodor Dostoevsky and Henry de Montherlant.[25] In contrast, Samuel Beckett's openings are all analytically self-aware and superbly crafted.[26] I will principally be concerned, however, with how an opening connects the reader with the work and therefore less concerned with evaluating the sheer artistic quality of openings. Hence, I will deliberately shun the

25 Openings by Dostoevsky, *The Idiot*: "Towards the end of November, during a thaw, at nine o'clock one morning, a train on the Warsaw and Petersburg railway was approaching the latter city at full speed." *Crime and Punishment*: "On an exceptionally hot evening early in July a young man came out of the garret in which he lodged in S. Place and walked slowly, as though in hesitation, towards K. bridge." Openings by Montherlant, *The Bachelors*: "On this cold evening of February 1924, towards seven o'clock, a man appeared... " Fyodor Dostoevsky, *The Idiot* (London: Penguin, 1955 [1868–1869]); Fyodor Dostoevsky, *Crime and Punishment* (New York: W.W. Norton, 1989 [1866]); Henry de Montherlant, *Les Célibataires* (Paris: Grasset, 1934).

26 As can be seen simply from the title of the novel *Comment c'est* (How It Is), which in French is nearly homophonous with the verb to begin, "commencer." Samuel Beckett, *Comment c'est* (Paris: Minuit, 1961).

temptation to establish a sort of "canon" of the most elegant or most striking openings and instead focus on the literary effect of a vast variety of openings, good or bad.

I will therefore avoid approaching openings from the perspective of a bibliophile who revisits a cherished book through the emblem of the first line, as is the most common approach. Instead I have collected and catalogued openings from a great variety of authors and periods in order to draw as much comparative interest from them as possible. The problem is of course that all books begin, which means that my study faces a potentially infinite corpus. While the selection of a corpus is always a major methodological question, in this study it seems so much more pressing. A large number of novels must be considered for reaching a reliable level of generalization. Needless to say, however, the interest lies not in the statistics themselves, but in the texts. I suspect that there may simply be no steadfast method for finding the perfect balance between the statistical weight of a large number of texts and the elucidation of individual analyses. Instead I will use criticism's two faces, generality and particularity, to pursue how openings enter into dialogue with each other and convey literature's earnest sense of a beginning.

CHAPTER 1

To Begin with the Beginning: A Cosmology of Openings

Men can do nothing without the make-believe of a beginning
GEORGE ELIOT, the opening of *Daniel Deronda*

The Ambiguity of Genesis

In the beginning was a syntactical ambiguity.[1] As Genesis opens with God's creation of the universe, the syntax of the divine word immediately erupts into theological debate. Hebrew does not contain punctuation, and from the original it is therefore not clear whether the first verse of Genesis is a complete sentence or a temporal subordination. Does the Bible open with:

(A) In the beginning God created the Heavens and the Earth.

or instead with the subordinated clause:

(B) When God began to create the Heavens and the Earth...

which would make either Genesis 1.2. or 1.3 the main clause?[2]

The syntax of this opening line becomes terribly important, for it changes our entire conception of God's powers. If Genesis opens with

1 Parts of this chapter were published in Niels Buch Leander, "To Begin with the Beginning: Birth, Origin, and Narrative Inception," in *Narrative Beginnings: Theories and Practices*, ed. Brian Richardson, Frontiers of Narrative (Lincoln: University of Nebraska Press, 2008). I thank the University of Nebraska Press for the permission to reuse material from this publication.

2 This debate is discussed in further detail in Claus Westermann, *Biblischer Kommentar: Altes Testament: Genesis 1–11* (Neukirchen-Vluyn: Neukirchener Verlag, 1974).

The phrase "Incipit Vita Nova," meaning "a new life begins," appears in the first line of Dante's poem "La Vita Nuova," published in 1295. This illustration elegantly ties together natural and textual beginnings. Aubrey Vincent Beardsley (1872–1898), *Incipit Vita Nova* (1893), pencil, pen, black ink and bodycolour on brown paper. Wikiart.

an independent sentence, God is seen to create the universe out of nothing—a pure *creatio ex nihilo*. If, on the other hand, the first verse is a subordinated clause, it appears that the universe already consisted of chaotic matter, which God then turned into order and shaped the universe into life.

Genesis provides an illustrious example of a concurrence between a textual beginning—the Bible—and the description of an external beginning—the Judeo-Christian cosmology. The textual beginning describes a beginning; in this case, nothing less than the beginning of the universe. In this chapter, I examine these relations between textual beginnings and regular beginnings, with special attention to the way in which literary beginnings present and relate to cosmological beginnings. This is an important relation because, in the opening sentence, a book could be said to perform a "genesis" of its own. Indeed, "incipio"—the biblical "in the beginning"—is precisely what has induced the term "incipit," the Latin and now French term for the opening sentence of a literary text. Literary works *must* begin and do so by establishing the parameters of a narration of which the reader is not cognizant. Literary openings are in this sense radically inaugural and at face value resemble cosmologies more than quotidian beginnings. In the Aristotelian tradition, for instance, it is the logical boundaries of the work—beginning and end—that establish a "cosmological" parallel that renders artistic mimesis possible.[3]

In order to assess this "cosmological" facet of literary openings, I both examine beginnings conceptionally and show how different literary openings establish themselves as beginnings. As the debate about Genesis illustrates, the way we present a beginning shapes the way we conceive of it. This in turn reveals a fundamental rift in our approach to beginnings: Must a credible beginning be absolute? Or do we, quite the opposite, trust a beginning only when it openly declares its dependence upon premises and preceding existence? This question cannot be answered altogether synchronically, but is subject to considerable historical variation. In the case of Genesis, for instance, the consensus amongst theologians and biblical commentators has shifted with time from the *creatio ex nihilo* of line (A) above towards the idea of line (B) that creation must in any case presuppose the prior existence of matter.[4] How the literary opening reflects such historical variation will be touched upon in this chapter and pursued in more detail in chapter 3.

The old distinction between art and nature has caused scholars to distinguish between "artificial" and "natural" beginnings. This vocabulary, however, has the unfortunate consequence of insinuating that beginnings in art do not really take place. Strictly speaking, "artificial" means "made as a copy of something natural,"[5] a meaning which a scholar like A.D. Nuttall accepts when he asserts that "the formality of an artificial opening necessarily simulates the validity and force of natural beginnings."[6] But it would be misleading to think of beginnings in art as mere replicas; books really do begin. In the following I argue that if a literary opening echoes a "natural" creation or cosmology, it does not principally do so

3 See page 23 for further discussion of the Aristotelian approach.

4 See Westermann, *Biblischer Kommentar: Genesis 1–11*: 150. A twentieth-century commentator, W.R. Lane, even claims that "both translations [i.e. Genesis 1.1 as independent clause or as a subordinated clause] presuppose preexistent material which was transformed by creation." William R. Lane, "The Initiation of Creation," *Vetus Testamentum* 13 (1963): 72. To complicate matters, at the time the Old Testament was written, there was, philologists have shown, no conceptual distinction between chaos and the absence of matter. Matter simply could not be without form; matter was order. Consequently, Genesis 1.1 could not at its conception have caused any ambiguity: the genesis would necessarily be absolute. Only from Augustine's Aristotelian theology (AD 354–430) emerges the idea that amorphous matter can exist, which makes a semantic distinction between (A) and (B) possible. Cf. Augustine, *The Confessions of St. Augustine*, trans. E.B. Pusey (London: J.M. Dent & Sons, 1907).

5 "Artificial," in *Concise Oxford Dictionary* (Oxford: Oxford University Press).

6 A.D. Nuttall, *Openings: Narrative Beginnings from the Epic to the Novel* (Oxford: Clarendon Press, 1992), 23.

by way of imitation or simulation. Rather, it obtains its own authority to speak by dissenting from established natural beginnings.

The Combinational Cabala: Mode of Creation vs. Mode of Beginning

In the light of the sustained, syntactico-theological debate about the first verse of Genesis, it is not surprising that the first ever "formal" analysis of a textual opening was performed on precisely Genesis. In 1612, the German mystic Jacob Böhme sketched the power of the combinational cabala in his work with the rejuvenating title: *Aurora.*[7] An entire section of his book is entitled "An exposition of the first verse of the first chapter of Genesis, according to the language of Nature." Those who think that this title resembles that of a twentieth-century formalist essay will be even more surprised to learn that the section consists in what we would call a "semantic" analysis based on the texture of the words of Genesis: The section is nothing less than a phonetic analysis of the Old Testament's opening lines.

Böhme's curious exposition will, however, disappoint any linguistically conscious modern reader. Böhme based his analysis on the German Bible, completely unperturbed by the fact that "God's word" necessarily sounds different in the original Hebrew. Furthermore, by using a translation of the Bible, Böhme had already determined central parts of his interpretation, for instance by taking the contentious first verse straightforwardly as an independent sentence (A) and not as a subordinated clause (B).

This, however, brings Böhme in line with most cabalistic thinkers who endorse the Neoplatonic vision that God's attributes never manifest themselves. Without knowable attributes, God—also called "Ein-Sof," meaning "without end"—can only appear as nothingness.[8] When Böhme and the cabbalists read the first verse of Genesis as an independent sentence, their conception of the *creatio ex nihilo* thus takes a peculiar twist. If God created the world out of nothingness, and He himself is nothingness, He must have created the world out of Himself.[9]

7 Jacob Böhme, *The Aurora* (London: Watkins, 1960 [1612]).

8 Harold Bloom, *Kabbalah and Criticism* (New York: Seabury Press, 1975), 24–25.

9 It appears somewhat ironic that the cabalists in this way use an Aristotelian syllo-

If, however, we compare Böhme's cabalism and the two diverging orthodox interpretations of the first line of Genesis, we notice one thing: that the effectiveness of these interpretations depends little on *how* they explain the world's creation. Although they differ, the overall function of each interpretation is to articulate that the world *had* a beginning. It is more important to say that the world *began* than to say how it was created. This can in fact be observed in all creation myths, as Pettazzoni's classic work on the subject reveals: "What is of the greatest importance is that there should be a myth of beginnings, which may or may not be a myth of creation, but which cannot possibly be done without, for on this myth, be it what it may, the very existence of the universe and of mankind depend in any case."[10] Even in cosmologies, the mode of *creation* is generally less important than the mode of *beginning*. A beginning has the ultimate explanatory authority because, unlike creation, it seems both to escape experience and to define actual events. In a sense, a beginning contains this explanatory power precisely because it does not need to explain *itself* in the way that a creation does. This paradox also stresses the potential of the textual opening because the textual opening will always be more concerned with its mode of beginning than with any mode of creation.

The Relation between Literary Openings and Cosmologies

How, then, do literary openings and cosmologies relate? J. Hillis Miller has claimed in one of his later works that the literary opening is a "miniature, secular, all-too-human version of God's 'Let there be light'—in Genesis."[11] Although I agree that the inaugural potential of a literary

gism to subvert the Aristotelian distinction between cause and effect. Harold Bloom says "'cause' and 'effect' are always reversible, for the Kabbalists regarded them as linguistic fictions, long before Nietzsche did," *Kabbalah and Criticism*, 25. This unorthodox cabbalistic perspective will enlighten my discussion in chapter 3 of the modernist and postmodernist vision of creation. For the moment, I note that Derrida discusses Böhme in his essay on Valéry and cites Hegel for stating that "in the Aurora, Böhme starts from the qualities." Jacques Derrida, "Qual Quelle – les sources de Valéry," in *Marges de la philosophie* (Paris: Minuit, 1972), 338–39.

10 R. Pettazzoni, "Myths of Beginning and Creation Myths," in *Essays on the History of Religion* (Leiden: E.J. Brill, 1954), 27f.

11 J. Hillis Miller, "Literature as Virtual Reality," in *On Literature* (London and New

opening is significant, I wish to maintain here that we must be more precise when describing this analogy. I therefore turn to analyzing a number of literary openings which in one way or another reflect the biblical opening.

Hillis Miller rightly observes that a surprisingly great number of novels open by means of a beam of light or an open window, which he then construes as a reflection of the *fiat lux* ("Let there be light") of Genesis.[12] In order to determine the nature of this frequent literary *fiat lux,* let me first juxtapose two openings, one by Charles Dickens, which Hillis Miller himself mentions, and one by Edmond Jaloux, written roughly a century later:

> The first ray of light which illumines the gloom, and converts into a dazzling brilliancy that obscurity in which the earlier history of the immortal Pickwick would appear to be involved...
>
> CHARLES DICKENS, *The Pickwick Papers* (1836)

> Never had I seen such a luminous day: the earth knew not what to do with the sun, one was bathing in pure alchemy, everything turned to the philosopher's stone. Every passer-by looked like a prospector; sifting the streams would have revealed gold nuggets. Even the shade was a pool of rays.
>
> EDMOND JALOUX, *L'Age d'or* (The Golden Age) (1926)

In *The Pickwick Papers* an initial beam lights up the nearly primordial gloom and sets the history of the "immortal Pickwick" in motion. It is deliberately unclear who is speaking; the tone is impersonal, the grammatical subject is the ray of light, separated from its main predicate by subordinated predicates. Yet the omniscience of the narrator is evident from the way that the first ray is singled out and the entire history of Pickwick grasped. However, herein lies also, I claim, the irony of this opening. By choosing the verb "convert," the opening overtly plays with religious nuances and parodies Pickwick's god-like status with the adjective "immortal."

In *L'Age d'or* (The Golden Age), the perspective has shifted to a first-person narration, a form that had become much more frequent in the beginning of the twentieth century. With its many alliterations in the original French, the language is by design poetic, and the tone mythical

York: Routledge, 2002). In this text, Hillis Miller discusses the literary opening rather casually as the opening of a virtual reality.

12 Ibid., 25. Hillis Miller seems here to have forgotten his analysis of *Bleak House* from 1959 in which the light is dimmed. I discuss this analysis below.

and wondrous. Something is clearly in the making, the fecundity being accentuated by numerous water metaphors, "bathing," "streams," "pools." Yet, the perspective of this creation is intriguingly reversed, just as the syntax of the first sentence is reversed and highlights the negation "never." Indeed, it is not the sunlight that gives life to the planet, but instead the earth that produces the sunshine. At the center of the wonder stands the philosopher's stone, the profane substance that can transmute the essence of things.

It seems fair to say that the *fiat lux* of Genesis is reflected in these literary openings. However, contrary to Hillis Miller, I maintain that the literary *fiat lux* functions not simply as a "secular miniature" of Genesis, but rather as a reaction or rejoinder to it. The literary *fiat lux* does not evoke Genesis in order to borrow some of its authority; rather it establishes its own authority precisely by imitating Genesis's structure and rearranging it with a certain irony.[13] By exposing the need to strive for its own authority, the literary beginning does admit to a certain conceptual vulnerability, yet this transformative wit is also a way to assure its own credibility as a beginning.

Even if the above openings do reflect the *fiat lux*, openings far from always imitate this performative act of creation. I could for instance juxtapose two other scene-setting openings by Dickens and Jaloux, which evoke cosmology even in the absence of any *fiat lux*:

> London. Michaelmas term lately over, and the Lord Chancellor sitting in Lincoln's Inn Hall. Implacable November weather. As much mud in the streets, as if the waters had but newly retired from the face of the earth, and it would not be wonderful to meet a Megalosaurus, forty feet long or so, waddling like an elephantine lizard up Holborn Hill.
>
> CHARLES DICKENS, *Bleak House* (1852–53)

> The rain fell behind the windows, steadily and continuously, and rue Cernuschi gently shone under the autumn sky. An anemic light entered the room and swept across the distinct furniture.
>
> It was one of those gloomy and almost impersonal days, when life appears only through layers of fog and moisture, gray, vague, and melancholic, like those gelatinous and colorless anemones

13 I discuss this use of irony further in chapter 2.

> lining the bottom of the sea. Standing against a window, Simone de Clausel looked at the endless water.
>
> EDMOND JALOUX, *Le Démon de la vie* (The Demon of Life) (1908)

Bleak House opens by providing specific spatial and temporal indications ("London," "Michaelmas") as was so common in nineteenth-century fiction. However, this temporal precision is at odds with the opening's succession of tenseless noun phrases.[14] Even when the series of noun phrases ends, the verb phrases fail to settle the tense since they are in the conditional mood ("as if the waters had," "it would"). In this way, Dickens's opening tries to establish itself outside time. A reversal to cosmology then takes place with the withdrawal of the waters, leaving the earth in the hands of prehistoric animals before finally recreating London.

A. D. Nuttall has argued that the opening of *Bleak House* is a "reversed Genesis," thereby arguing that even this reversal of Genesis is itself ultimately reversed.[15] Unlike Hillis Miller in his reading of *The Pickwick Papers*, Nuttall is not so receptive to Dickens's play with religious connotations. Genesis 1.9–10 does talk of God separating the waters from the earth, but, as the presence of dinosaurs makes clear, the cosmology of *Bleak House* is not that of a Christian cosmology. Dickens writes instead on a background of new sciences like paleontology and the nascent evolutionary theories of the Victorian period.[16] It is striking, for instance, that all terms with potential religious connotations instead evoke the secular. The "Lord" at the center of the reversed creation is hence the "Lord Chancellor," the second highest ranking of the "Great Officers of State" in Britain. "Michaelmas" is not the religious feast in honor of the archangel who announced that knowledge will flourish amongst those who will not be saved, but could refer instead to the autumn term in the university system or in the legal system.[17]

Jaloux's *Le Démon de la vie* (The Demon of Life) evokes a similar rever-

14 A succession that A. D. Nuttall is even prepared to call "modernist." Nuttall, *Openings*, 195.

15 Ibid.

16 Which may also explain why Dickens makes a mistake when he describes a megalosaurus's walking like a lizard: a megalosaurus is a biped and walks more like a human being. As background information, Charles Darwin's *Origin of the Species* appeared soon after, in 1859. Charles Darwin, *On the Origin of Species by Means of Natural Selection* (London: J. Murray, 1859).

17 According to the Old Testament, Michael is the Jews' archangel who announced the salvage of Israel; "At that time thy people shall be delivered, every one that shall be found written in the book. … But thou, O Daniel, shut up the words, and seal the book, to the time

sal to a primordial unification of waters and earth—or possibly to a city under the Deluge. The light is weakened, anemic, or literally "bloodless." The phonetics of this term "anemic" seems to lead to the central image of the colorless and gelatinous sea anemones that have covered the bottom of the sea since the dawn of time. The water is here "impersonal" and hides "life," as if God's creation has not yet materialized or is inaccessible. One person does, however, appear, Simone, a reminder of St Peter's pre-Christian name, Simon, the fisherman.

An oddity about Jaloux's opening is that all four sentences quoted here could be shifted around arbitrarily; all four sentences could in fact have been the opening sentence ("The rain fell...," "An anemic light...," "It was one...," "Simone..."). This may emphasize the monotony of the atmosphere, but as a critic it is difficult not to see it as a technical deficiency. Jaloux's opening does not seem to define a clear logic of beginning; it does not have one sentence that sets the others in motion. Instead the sentences unconfidently keep using the indefinite article, "a," as if they do not trust their own beginning. Dickens and Jaloux both use the trope of cosmological beginning; the principal difference in their literary efficacy is, however, that Dickens employs the trope to justify the use of definite articles, thereby taking its own myth of beginning seriously by presupposing the objects' existence. This is a formal consideration, which fundamentally changes the conditions of the beginning.

As already mentioned, Hillis Miller holds the literary opening to echo the *fiat lux* of Genesis not just by frequently reproducing the primal light, but through the trope of the window.[18] Since obviously no window appears in Genesis, Hillis Miller must be thinking of the window as a symbolic passage of light. The window certainly features prominently in innumerable openings—in the modernist period, for instance, in such central novels as D.H. Lawrence's *Women in Love* (1920), Virginia Woolf's *To the Lighthouse* (1927), and *Mrs Dalloway* (1925).[19] What may sustain Hillis Miller's idea is that the window is often illuminated by a beam of light, as we see in the openings by the experimental modernist Valery Larbaud:

> The sun jumps right through the blades of the shutter; It feels

of the end: many shall run to and fro, and knowledge shall be increased." The Book of Daniel in the Old Testament, XII 1–4.

18 Hillis Miller, "Literature as Virtual Reality," 32.

19 D.H. Lawrence, *Women in Love* (New York: Quality Paperback Book Club, 1920); Virginia Woolf, *To the Lighthouse* (London: L. & V. Woolf at the Hogarth Press, 1927); Virginia Woolf, *Mrs Dalloway* (New York: Harcourt Brace and Company, 1925).

> good to be able to leave the window open all night at the beginning of November.
>
> VALERY LARBAUD, *Amants, heureux amants* (Lovers, Happy Lovers) (1923 [1921])

> All of a sudden, the reflection from the parlour's glazed door swept by the sand of the courtyard before our feet.
>
> VALERY LARBAUD, *Fermina Marquez* (1911)

In both these instances, however, the window does not support the trope of light. The brutality of the sun light is on the contrary *alleviated* by the narrator. In the first instance, the direct and otherwise unswerving light is regulated by the slatted shutter and, in the second instance, the light is reflected from the parlor and into the very heart of the human dwelling—the courtyard—where it even throws itself at the feet of the narrator. Rather than borrowing the authority of the divine light to open the novel, windows and doors rather emphasize the human manipulation and subjugation of that light in the resolve to begin.

The window, however, is used precisely to support the idea of the opening as a threshold. Rather than marking the absolute beginning of the *fiat lux*, the window serves as a narrative "Janus-head" looking both back and forth—or inside and outside. Rather than imitating an absolute beginning, the window indicates a deliberate transition from one sphere to another. Two openings that exemplify this phenomenon are D.H. Lawrence's *Women in Love* (1920) and Le Clézio's *The Interrogation* (1963):[20]

> Ursula and Gudrun Brangwen sat one morning in the windowbay of their father's house in Beldover, working and talking.
>
> D.H. LAWRENCE, *Women in Love* (1920)

> Once upon a little time, in the dog-days, there was a fellow sitting at an open window.
>
> LE CLÉZIO, *Le Procès verbal* (The Interrogation) (1963)

In both examples, the window smoothes the entry into the literary work by marking a natural threshold between the reader's outside-world and the fictional universe that is now being introduced. The window moreover creates a frame around the protagonists, as if it were a *tableau vivant* that

20 Lawrence, *Women in Love*; Jean-Marie Gustave Le Clézio, *Le Procès verbal* (Paris: NRF Gallimard, 1963).

could accompany the reader in the reading. In *Women in Love*, the window bay finally serves to initiate the novel's central theme by emphasizing the threshold between the secluded house of the protagonists' father and the outside world that awaits them as they fall in love.

It is furthermore important to notice that both *Women in Love* and *The Interrogation* exhibit a temporal structure which does not evoke Genesis, but rather another well-known structure: the classic fairytale opening "once upon a time." In *Women in Love*, "one morning" is a neat way of combining a novelistic realism with the temporal structure of "once upon a time."[21] Le Clézio imitates the classic opening more directly, but adds the diminutive "toute petite" ("little"), which strikes the reader as rather odd. The odd diminutive seems moreover to function in two conflicting ways: First, the diminutive adds a redundancy, which enhances the puerile aspect of the fairytale opening. Yet the diminutive simultaneously lessens the fantastic and grandiose aspect of the storytelling and prepares the reader for a common quotidian tale, further confirmed by the mundane "dog-days."

From these examples, I maintain that the evocation or imitation of Genesis simply functions like the evocation of other familiar structures such as "once upon a time." The familiarity of the chosen opening component serves first of all to allow an opening to clear its own space and establish a relation of credibility vis-à-vis the reader. In all the above examples, this imitative practice does not venerate the established opening phrase, but rather tends to reduce it to a "cliché," in the sense both of a trivial formula and a stereotype for generating openings.

Certainly, God's *fiat lux*—"Let there be light"—accentuates that beginnings depend on an illocutionary act. Beginnings are not performed *by* language, as some theorists would say, but they are certainly performed *in* language. "In the beginning was the Word [*logos*], and the Word was with God," as St Johns Gospel opens. This performative aspect is present in all beginnings because they depend on an authority in order to be accepted *as* a beginning.[22] Unlike "holy scriptures," whose authority within a sect or religion is never questioned, the literary beginning, however, will have to obtain its authority in order to begin. It can obtain this authority in a number of ways. One obvious way is to borrow its authority from an already existing, authoritative beginning such as the Bible's and through the trope of cosmological creation establish the necessary literary myth

21 I discuss the function of the opening "once upon a time..." at length in chapter 2.

22 The performativity of beginnings will be discussed in chapter 2.

of beginning. I have shown, however, that a literary opening rather searches for its own authority by appealing to a familiar structure, which it transforms creatively in order to appeal concurrently to the reader's credulity and curiosity.

The analogy between cosmology and a book's inaugural power is therefore not as straightforward as one would expect. The literary analogy with Genesis turns out to be more accurately a rivalry or a revision of it. The specificity of the literary beginning stems rather from a combination of eagerness and hesitation in the struggle against the creative weight of preceding authorities. We remember for instance how Goethe's *Faust* is impeded by the opening of the Gospel:

> It is written: 'In the beginning was the Word!'
> Here I falter! Who can help me continue?

This intimidation is of course subject to historical variation. In modernist "books of hours" such as Rainer Maria Rilke's *The Book of Hours* (1899) and Paul Valéry's *Alphabet* (1924–29),[23] we therefore observe more explicitly the intrinsically palimpsestic quality of literature, which tries to outmaneuver the metaphysical weight of the literary creation by duplicating it.[24] Even if cosmological creation myths no longer have their foundational property, a text will have to create a beginning of its own.

The Natural Beginning and the Authority of the Literary Opening

The question is now whether a literary text, if it tends to subvert the weight of cosmologies, could instead establish its authority by locating other beginnings. If, for instance, we revert to the ancient Greek conception of narrative, we notice that Greek reason views narratives as committed to "begin at the beginning." The famous *logos* that we associate with the Greek sense of rationality simply refers to the presupposition

23 Rainer Maria Rilke, *Das Stunden-Buch* (Teddington, Middelsex: The Echo Library, 2008 [1899]); Paul Valéry, *Alphabet* (Paris: LGF – Livre de Poche, 1999).

24 Gérard Genette was the first to suggest this palimpsestic quality of modern literature, see Gérard Genette, *Palimpsestes. La littérature au second degré* (Paris: Seuil, 1982).

that a narrative takes a certain direction.[25] Using the *logos* requires that the speaker be committed to speaking "straight" and to telling how the "whole thing" started.[26] It is only by beginning at the beginning that a speaker will be able to summarize what happened in a way that will present the chain of events in its various dimensions without leading anyone astray. Conversely, it is only through the decision not to hide or distort anything that a speaker will be able to set out from the premises of the affair itself and avoid obfuscating the narrative by beginning with his or her own perspective. In other words, a narrative involves explaining how the current situation *came about*, or as Hesiod puts it in his *Theogony* (800–700 BC), the current state will need to be presented in the light of its "natural" beginning.[27]

Hesiod's line extends itself into Aristotle's celebrated thoughts on the structure of tragedy in the *Poetics*. Having described "a whole" as "that which has a beginning, a middle and a conclusion," the *Poetics* defines a beginning as "that which itself does not of necessity follow something else, but after which there naturally is, or comes into being, something else."[28] In other words, the beginning cannot be deduced from what preceded it. The middle and the conclusion, however, should follow from the beginning, and nothing else should follow the conclusion. This logical demarcation of the artwork precisely sets up a "cosmological" parallel that renders mimetic representation possible. A plot must therefore not begin "from a random point"[29]—the beginning ought to be "natural."[30]

The Greek appeal to "natural" beginnings may seem both rational and commonsensical, yet to begin at the beginning is not as simple as it sounds. As the Greeks themselves were aware,[31] the commitment to

25 Rémi Brague, "Le récit du commencement. Une aporie de la raison grecque," in *La Naissance de la raison en Grèce: Actes du colloque de Nice mai 1987*, ed. Jean-François Mattéi (Paris: PUF, 1990), 23.

26 Ibid., 24.

27 Hesiod, *Theogony*, in *The Theogony, Works and Days, and The Shield of Heracles* (Stilwell, KS: Digireads, 2008), v. 156, 203, 408, 25, 52.

28 Aristotle, *Poetics*, in *The Norton Anthology of Theory and Criticism*, ed. Vincent B. Leitch (New York: W.W. Norton & Company, 2001), 96.

29 Ibid.

30 Aristotle's ultimate interest, however, lies in the *telos*, in the "final cause" and its means of persuasion as effected through emotion and style as well as through argumentation. The *logos* thus ultimately serves the artwork's resolution: "The end is most important of all" (ibid., 95), which explains Aristotle's deep preoccupation with patterns of resolution like *peripeteia* (resolution by reversal of the protagonist's position) and *anagnorisis* (resolution by the protagonist's recognition of his or her fate). I will discuss resolution and *telos* below in chapter 2 and 3.

31 Brague, "Le Récit du commencement," 29.

finding a "natural" beginning involves a conceptual obstacle. Going back to a state of affairs prior to the present involves *logically* restoring things as they *physically* were. This exercise is not easy—and for two reasons: first, it would practically require the speaker to relinquish his or her present perspective. Yet, it is only through the present perspective that the speaker will be able to focus on the direction and move through the sequence of events as they happened. Second, when locating a beginning one could theoretically extend the search infinitely backwards.

It is therefore also significant that in the *Theogony*, which is both a cosmogony and a description of the birth of the various gods, Hesiod uses the superlative of "first" only twice.[32] In this way he singles out two beginnings of fundamental importance: The first superlative beginning is when Hesiod began his career as a poet: "this word [*logos*] first the goddesses said to me" (l. 24) and the second is when the muses are asked to explain how the cosmos first began from primal chaos (l. 115–16), quite similarly to Genesis in its second interpretation, "When God began to create the Heavens and the Earth...." In Hesiod's textual middle ground between allegory and mythology, both superlative beginnings accentuate the narrative mediation and the interdependency of beginning and narration, which is also manifest in the opening of the *Theogony*:

> From the Heliconian Muses let us begin to sing, who hold the great and holy mount of Helicon...
>
> HESIOD, *Theogony* (~700 BC)[33]

The Infinite Regress of the Beginning

The conceptual obstacle in tracing "the beginning" as an analogy to a cosmological beginning is addressed by Paul Valéry in his famous, but often misread aphorism "In the beginning was the fable" (1929):[34]

32 Hesiod, *Theogony*, v. 24 and 116.

33 This analogy is further heightened by the fact that Hesiod himself is from Ascra at the bottom of the Helikon Mountains: his own origin marks the beginning of the narrative.

34 Paul Valéry, *Œuvres*, ed. Jean Hytier, vol. I, Pléiade (Paris: Gallimard, 1957), 394. Valéry continually altered this opening in provocative ways, for instance in the opening of *Alphabet*, which reads, "In the Beginning was the sleep" and the ironic "In the Beginning was the joke" (written in 1907 in his notebooks, *Cahiers IV*, and quoted by the *Petit Robert*

> In the beginning was the fable
>
> Necessarily. For what was is spirit and has no properties that are not spiritual;
>
> So, if you imagine going back to the 'beginning', you can only imagine it by stripping yourself, at each step back a little more, of what you know from experience, or at least by more and more sporadic testimonies. And you are obliged to conceive these more and more distant pictures, to supplement them more and more by your own production of personages, events and spectacles.
>
> In the end, there's only you. It's all stemming from you: pure fable.

By recasting the opening of St John's Gospel with "fable" rather than "logos," Valéry insinuates that God's definitive illocutionary act of creation rests conceptionally on a "fable" in the sense of both an instructive story and a creative lie.[35] Tracing a beginning becomes a fable or a narrative, which will depend on a willingness to "strip" oneself ("se dépouiller") of accumulated experiences and to "peruse" oneself (a different meaning of "se dépouiller") in order to locate elements that can make up for the ever fading representation of the past moment. In the end, then, nothing is left but the individual's "production" of the past that makes up characters, events, scenes, thereby giving the word "representation" its full theatrical meaning: the past is staged in the mind. In other words, the beginning does in fact "begin" only when we begin to imagine it.[36]

The presumed firmness of the past is hence illusory because it is *necessarily* contingent upon the present, as indicated in the incomplete phrase "Necessarily" that opens Valéry's aphorism. A beginning does not secure a constancy or a foundation, but on the contrary leads only to the individual's present potentiality: the pursuit of a secure beginning only leads to a creative beginning. Valéry finds that every thought of an origin will inescapably contain the present moment as its reference frame; we always look to the origin to explain something present to us in this very

under the entry "fable." See the entry "Fable," in *Petit Robert*, ed. Josette Rey-Debove and Alain Rey (Paris: Dictionnaires Le Robert, 1994).

35 According to the *Petit Robert*, "Fable," a fable can mean both: 1. Fictive narrative whose intention is to express a general truth 2. False anecdote. The English word "fib" is for instance an abbreviation of the obsolete expression a "fible-fable."

36 "L'origine est, en tout, imaginaire." Paul Valéry, *Cahiers*, vol. XXIII (Paris: C.N.R.S.), 592. Cf. "origine est une illusion." Paul Valéry, *Œuvres*, ed. Jean Hytier, vol. II, Pléiade (Paris: Gallimard, 1960), 1451.

moment: "All thought of the origin of things is only a reverie of their present disposition, a way of degenerating reality, a variation on what is."[37]

The strangely vocative "necessarily" from "In the beginning was the fable" reappears in Valéry's reflection on Edgar Allan Poe's *Eureka*. Here Valéry affirms that a beginning is *necessarily* established by coincidence, by an imaginative coincidence of all and nothing:

> As for the idea of a beginning—I mean an absolute beginning—it is necessarily a myth. Every beginning is coincidence; we should develop here some sort of contact between everything and nothing. In trying to think about it, we find that every beginning is a consequence—every beginning ends something.[38]

A beginning cannot be absolute—that would be a "myth," a "fable"—because it consists in the span between full existence ("everything") and an imagination of nothingness ("nothing").[39] Imagining a beginning will however necessitate that something else comes to an end. A beginning will not be a foundation, but instead follows from and completes another enterprise.

In several respects, Valéry's analysis of the beginning anticipates the explicit twentieth-century critique of origins, which contemporary readers will tend to associate with the rise of literary theory and, more particularly, with the poststructuralism of Michel Foucault.[40] In *Les Mots et les choses* (*The Order of Things*) from 1966, Foucault shows how beginnings taken as origins have become unexpectedly indeterminate as they only highlight the finitude of human potential.[41] Locating an origin will naturally help to fill in the gap between the present and the past,

37 "Au sujet d'Eurêka" in Valéry, *Œuvres*, I: 863.

38 Ibid., 863–64. This text is clearly meant to be read in relation to the above aphorism, as it ends by reiterating: "As for [the] origin [of the Universe],—IN THE BEGINNING WAS THE FABLE. There it will always be," 867, trans. Sandy Pecastaing in "Poe and the Myth of Origin," *International Journal of Humanities and Cultural Studies* 1, no. 3 (2014).

39 Or as Hegel would have expressed it: "The beginning therefore contains both, being and nothing, is the unity of being and nothing; or is non-being which is at the same time being, and being which is at the same time non-being." Quoted in George Steiner, *Grammars of Creation* (London: Faber and Faber, 2001), 196.

40 We notice that Valéry does not ask what a beginning is, but instead how we think of one. "What is in effect required of us to think of this origin?," "Au sujet d'Eurêka," Valéry, *Œuvres*, I. In his *Beginnings*, Edward Said draws heavily on Foucault in precisely this respect. I discuss Said later in chapter 3, in the section "Said's Beginnings: The Elusive Opening."

41 In the chapter "The Retreat and Return of the Origin," in Michel Foucault, *The Order of Things: An Archaeology of the Human Sciences*, trans. Alan Sheridan, Routledge Classics (London: Routledge, 2001), 358–71. (French title: "Le Recul et le retour de l'origine," in *Les Mots et les choses* (Paris: Gallimard, 1966.)

yet, in this recuperative project, the origin itself typically recedes still further. In the attempt to bring knowledge closer to its own inception, the recovery of the beginning will therefore tend to alienate us, just as Valéry describes it.

According to Foucault, eighteenth-century philosophy still imagined an origin to be a sort of "tableau" based on what he calls the "ideal genesis" of representation. From the nineteenth century, however, "such an orgin is no longer conceivable."[42] Instead, human beings can only locate their origin "against a background of the already begun" and the origin therefore fails to constitute a true beginning:

> [Man] is never contemporaneous with that origin which is outlined through the time of things even as it eludes the gaze; when he tries to define himself as a living being, he can uncover his own beginning only against the background of a life which itself began long before him.[43]

By making us rely upon events that necessarily precede the knowledge of the individual, origins instead endow us with a sense of belatedness, which ultimately encumber our own potential for radical beginnings.

Valéry also describes this alienating belatedness in a small, little-known manuscript from 1921, where Orpheus's mythical creativity sets off only when the past fades and becomes inconceivable:

> Orpheus's Beginning
>
> – I was born without knowing it, without wanting it, in a time which has become fabulous, and which is so old that it passes for not having been. This is how time is aging: not only is it no longer, but it is no longer conceivable and it seems impossible that it ever was so.[44]

Orpheus does not know his origin, his birth, which has instead entered into the time of fables. His origin lies entirely outside time; it belongs not just to a time that no longer exists, but to a time that is no longer even conceivable. This was precisely Foucault's expression—the origin is no longer conceivable. Yet in the void exists also the conditions of future conception, or as Valéry expresses it: "This inconceivable chaos is ordered by my intention to conceive. I myself have shuffled the cards

42 Foucault, *Les Mots et les choses*, 340.

43 Ibid., 341. Translated in Foucault, *The Order of Things*, 350.

44 Paul Valéry, "Commencement d'Orphée," in *Lake Collection* 9.2 (University of Texas at Austin, Harry Ransom Center, 1921).

in order to rearrange them."[45] It is when we lose the sense of origin that we endeavor to initiate our own beginnings.[46]

Differentiating Origins from Beginnings

This discussion of Valéry and Foucault points to the necessity of differentiating *origins* from beginnings more generally speaking. Indeed, when we think of beginnings, we may not have noticed that two directly opposed ideas are in play: on the one hand, a beginning can be thought of as a capacity to initiate something new. A beginning in this sense serves as an internal indication of change, which helps to underline the agent's essential freedom and potential, no matter how small the enterprise: "I begin to walk," "I begin this chapter," etc. On the other hand, a beginning can be read as the external event that originally constituted an object, situation, or being (e.g. "modernity began with the industrialization," "the beginning of the universe," etc.). A beginning thus traces and institutes an *origin*, thereby allowing us to make sense of the way that we, or something, ended up in the present place. Understood as origin, a beginning is intended to provide explanation. This in turn circumscribes our present potential: such a beginning is meant to *determine* the present situation.

In other words, beginnings confront us with, on the one hand, a radical contingency—through the will to act and conceive—and, on the other hand, a reassuring determinism—through the desire to explain and resolve. Part of the effectiveness of the opening of Genesis can in effect be explained by the fact that it contains both kinds of beginnings. God began creating the universe, but God's beginning is in the Judeo-Christian tradition also thought to be the beginning of the universe. In Genesis, God's active potential and the humans' passive explanation of the beginning of all things coincide.

Despite their divergent implications, these two aspects of beginnings—let me call them "a start" and "an origin"—are surprisingly easy to confuse, especially in English where "beginning" is both a noun (e.g. "the beginning") and a participle (e.g. "she is beginning"). After all, their major difference lies in its temporal positioning. A start could be seen as

45 "Au sujet d'Eurêka," Valéry, *Œuvres*, I, 863.

46 This idea is also proposed by Brooks, *Reading for the Plot*, 6. However, Brooks's account differs in important ways from mine, as I discuss in chapter 3.

what one day could constitute the origin of something or someone, just as God's start is taken as the origin of the human race. Origins could be described as insights into a previous moment's starting potentialities that were now 'closed' and determined by time's passing.

How closely these two aspects of beginnings—starts and origins—are associated is in fact a matter of considerable historical fluctuation. Indeed, eras with a limited belief in genuine change tend to conflate the distinction altogether. In the Middle Ages, for instance, the two aspects of beginnings seemed almost inseparable due to a readiness to encompass each and every conception under one instigating act of creation.[47] A start was consequently perceived more like an origin in present time as it did not indicate a window of change, but instead a continuation of a previous motion.[48] In contrast, modern writers tend to differentiate sharply between starts and origins, especially in the twentieth century where the differentiation was a prerequisite to a systematic critique of origins. In this way Foucault is careful to set apart origins from beginnings generally, which he instead characterizes as the *termini a quo* (e.g. temporal thresholds) of temporal events.

Beginnings and the Human Sciences

The distinction between these two forms of beginnings does in fact play a pivotal role in the formulation of the human sciences in the twentieth century. It stands for instance at the very heart of the poststructuralist rejection of a foundational, humanist interpretation. In the seminal text "Structure, Sign, and Play in the Discourse of the Human Sciences," Jacques Derrida associates the notion of origin closely with humanism's traditional metaphysical or "onto-theological" perspective.[49] The distinction between "start" and "origin" could therefore explain what Derrida in this text pinpoints as the fundamental divide in the human sciences. Whereas the human sciences traditionally sought interpretations that

47 Smith, *The Book of the Incipit*, xx.

48 From Augustine follows the idea that there is no fundamental distinction between past, present, and future. See "The Memory of the Beginning,"in Augustine, *The Confessions of St. Augustine*.

49 Jacques Derrida, "La Structure, le signe et le jeu dans le discours des sciences humaines," in *L'écriture et la différence* (Paris: Seuil, 1967), 427.

served as origins and thus put "an *end* to the [interpretative] game," the alternative mode of interpretation, which Derrida clearly advocates, is no longer concerned with reassuring origins, but attempts instead to go beyond humanism by "affirming the game."[50] Beginnings that do not "end" semantically are hence used anti-theologically.

The theoretical approach to literary openings is in this respect just as important and illustrative as any other beginning. Members of the so-called Geneva School of the 1950s and 1960s have for instance attempted to relocate origins in literature by seeing them in the extratextual form of authorial consciousness.[51] It is in this light that the central member of the Geneva School, Georges Poulet, in his *Le Point de départ* (The Point of Departure) interprets Paul Valéry as a whole cosmological system: "Just as there was in Genesis a fabulous first moment which was that of creation, there must at each instant [according to Valéry] be another absolute beginning; one where ... the mind, resuming consciousness, finds itself in the presence of all that it can make exist."[52] Poulet's friend and heir, Hillis Miller, was in fact the first American to write on literary openings when in 1958 he wrote a chapter on the opening of Dickens's *Bleak House*, which I discussed above.[53] Hillis Miller's analysis is not as such a stylistic one, but focuses instead on the spatial and temporal location of the reader. In accordance with Poulet's phenomenological criticism, Hillis Miller treats the opening of *Bleak House* as an origin, as a mental moment gathering momentum and spreading through the rest of the novel: "The entire novel seeks to explain, by a retrospective reconstruction going counter to the forward movement of the novel, how the world came to be in the befogged, mud-soaked, fragmented, and decomposed state presented in the initial paragraphs."[54] The initial detachment of characters and spaces serve as pieces that simply need to be put together: "In a sense all the novel is present in the initial moment and is only explicated or pieced together by the events which follow."[55] From Poulet's and Hillis

50 Ibid., added emphasis. The game of beginning is precisely what Derrida practices in his analysis of Francis Ponge's short poem "Fable": "By the word by begins this text / in which the first line tells the truth."

51 For further details see my encyclopedia entry on Poulet: Niels Buch-Jepsen, "Georges Poulet," in *Encyclopedia of Modern French Thought*, ed. Christopher John Murray (New York and London: Fitzroy Dearborn, 2004).

52 Georges Poulet, *Le Point de départ* (Paris: Plon, 1964), 13.

53 J. Hillis Miller, "Chapter VI: Bleak House," in *Charles Dickens: The World of his Novels* (Cambridge, MA: Harvard University Press, 1958). It is worth noting that Hillis Miller's book is dedicated to Poulet.

54 Ibid., 168.

55 Ibid.

Miller's vocabulary we sense that the literary work is treated almost theologically—the opening is really an authorial genesis.[56] As was clear from my own analysis of *Bleak House*, Hillis Miller and Nuttall are not receptive to Dickens's ironic play on religious connotations. Instead the work is seen as a perfect parallel to cosmological creation, which elevates, first, the work to a world unto itself and, second, the author to a creating consciousness of a conspicuously theological kind.

It is in this context that Derrida's anti-theological vocabulary should be read. We tend to think of Derrida, Foucault, and also Barthes as essentially anti-biographical theorists, but their anti-theological vocabulary indicates that we should think of them principally as anti-phenomenological thinkers.[57] The central schism in twentieth-century human sciences can thus be explained as a controversy over how to understand beginnings. Valéry and later Foucault, Derrida, and other theorists of the human sciences wish to separate the connotations of "origin" from the concept of "beginning" in order to release the present human potential through its own beginnings. The ironic consequence is, however, that by making this sharp distinction they need to take the human dependence upon origins seriously. The beginning that they envisage is precisely based on a renunciation of the dependency upon origins. Foucault, for instance, portrays origins as both alienating and inescapable, a frustrating dynamics that will elicit human creativity.[58] The renunciation of the origin is in this way a narrative that sets new beginnings in motion.

The Make-Believe of a Beginning

Through this analysis of beginnings, I hope to have illustrated that there can be no beginning independently of the particular narrative we bring

56 The Geneva School is of course not the first to propose this idea of the authorial genesis. Wordsworth's *Prelude* (1798–1850) is typically interpreted in this way, for instance by Nuttall: "The matter of The Prelude is the growth of the poet's mind ... In this, Genesis and the poem's inception can be one." Nuttall, *Openings*, 144. Unsurprisingly, Marcel Proust was a central source of inspiration to the Geneva critics.

57 A closer inspection of Barthes's manifesto-like "Death of the Author" reveals for instance that the notion of author is not to be dismissed altogether. Rather, the notion is to be freed from theologically loaded concepts such as "origin." Roland Barthes, "La mort de l'auteur," in *Œuvres complètes II*, ed. É. Marty (Paris: Seuil, 1994 [1968]). I discuss Barthes in more detail in chapter 3.

58 For example see Foucault, *Les Mots et les choses*, 340.

to it. In the recent past one can hardly discern a beginning from the event itself: "I started reading this book" is at times indistinguishable from "I am reading this book." Yet, the beginning labels the event, and this is crucial because epistemologically speaking we never describe an event as such, but always present an event by employing a certain description. Sartre is therefore only half right, or half wrong, when in his *Nausea* (1938) he writes that "in life there is never any beginning."[59] In life there are temporal events, but a beginning is an event subjugated to a certain description that needs to be established. That does not imply that beginnings are pure fictions; they exist in time, but simply cannot be located independently of us.[60] It is, for instance, not enough to explain a beginning by means of the temporal interval between a beginning and an end: that interval simply cannot be defined without the description of the interval itself. In other words, a beginning requires a supporting narrative, which can describe the beginning *as* event. On the logical plane, it can be observed that a beginning already contains narrative components because, as analytic philosophers have shown, sentences that include beginnings will automatically be narrative sentences.[61] When undertaking a beginning, we must therefore begin not at "the beginning," but with the description with which we wish to place the event.

"To begin at the beginning" is therefore at best a useless tautology. When the befuddled white rabbit in *Alice in Wonderland* asks where to begin his account, and the King of Hearts very gravely orders him to "begin at the beginning ... and then go on till you come to the end: then stop," we easily pick up on this tautological humor.[62] Despite the evident truth of the king's suggestion, the rabbit is no better off: because where does the account indeed begin? Under what description does the account, and hence its beginning, fall? Without this descriptive component, the beginning eludes us—just as it did Valéry and Foucault. A beginning simply cannot be understood in itself, or as Hegel puts it, a beginning is "an unfulfilled immediacy which cannot be analyzed [*Nichtanalysierbar*]."[63] In other words, a beginning is what philosophers call an epistemological

59 Jean-Paul Sartre, *La nausée* (Paris: Gallimard, 1938), 57.

60 I here argue against Nuttall who claims that beginnings can be located independently of us. Nuttall, *Openings*, 201–8.

61 Arthur Danto, *Analytical Philosophy of History* (Cambridge: Cambridge University Press, 1965). 157. "Each of these terms, to be true of an event E-1, logically requires the occurrence of an event temporally later than E-1, and sentences making use of such terms in the obvious way will then be narrative sentences."

62 Lewis Carroll, *Alice in Wonderland* (New York: Norton, 1992 [1865]).

63 Hegel, quoted in Steiner, *Grammars of Creation*, 22.

"primitive"—a building block, which cannot or should not be scrutinized, and on which other knowledge is therefore constructed.

For this reason, the inaccessibility of the beginning and its dependency on a narrative component do not discard the human reliance on beginnings. On the contrary, "Men can do nothing without the make-believe of a beginning," as we learn in the first line of George Eliot's *Daniel Deronda* (1876).[64] Let us look more closely at Eliot's striking opening:

> Men can do nothing without the make-believe of a beginning. Even Science, the strict measurer, is obliged to start with a make-believe unit, and must fix on a point in the stars' unceasing journey when his sidereal clock shall pretend that time is at Nought. His less accurate grandmother Poetry has always been understood to start in the middle; but on reflection it appears that her proceeding is not very different from his; since Science, too, reckons backwards as well as forwards, divides his unit into billions, and with his clock-finger at Nought really sets off *in medias res*. No retrospect will take us to the true beginning; and whether our prologue be in heaven or on earth, it is but a fraction of that all-presupposing fact with which our story sets out.
>
> GEORGE ELIOT, *Daniel Deronda* (1876)

Eliot's *credo* does not dismiss the human belief in beginnings; on the contrary, it is the very impossibility of arriving at a "true beginning" that prompts us to believe even more firmly in beginnings. We cannot be taken to the true beginning, but will have to rely on an "all-presupposing fact" that will set everything in motion. To Eliot, all human inquiry is "obliged to start with a make-believe unit" in order to measure other things and get its interpretation under way. In this way, all human endeavor in fact shares some of its structure with literature, namely its narrative aspect. All modes of inquiry rely on their own narrative of beginning, and literature's more explicit reliance on make-believe therefore helps to conceptualize beginnings in general. What Eliot makes clear is that a beginning's *foundational* quality cannot be separated from its *fictional* quality. The designation of a beginning is a requirement of narrative, but a beginning in itself requires a narrative.

64 George Eliot, *Daniel Deronda* (New York: Modern Library, 2002 [1876]).

Birth and the Complication of the Natural Beginning

Greek reason may recommend locating a "natural" beginning, but as I have shown, the designation of such beginnings is highly problematic. In fact, I claim that literature has always shown resistance to the "commonsensical" approach to beginnings. If we revert to the oldest example of a critical assessment of a specific literary opening, we notice, for example, that it addresses precisely this problem of "natural" beginnings. In his *Ars Poetica*, Horace defies the Greek *logos* and eulogizes Homer for opening *in medias res* with:

> Sing, goddess, of the Wrath of Peleus's son Achilles
> HOMER, *The Iliad* (~800 BC)

To Horace what makes Homer the greatest of poets is precisely that "he doesn't ... begin the Trojan War from the twin egg (*ab ovo*) [i.e. the conception of the twins Clytemnestra and Helen]."[65] Inception does not begin by conception. To Horace, the *midway* becomes instead the very measure of the whole work: the poet "tells his fables and mixes truth with falsehoods in such a way that the middle squares with the beginning and the end with the middle."[66] Horace's symmetrical dictum resounds throughout the history of composition, from Pierre de Ronsard's poetological advice "begin in the middle" to the famous opening of Dante's *Divine Comedy* (1307–21):[67]

> Halfway through the journey of my life

In the Horacian line of thought, poetry should precisely show that the laws of art are unlike the laws of nature; this entails that the beginning of a poem should never fuse with an established beginning in nature.

So accepted was Horace's principle that Lord Byron's resolve to "begin at the beginning" in his *Don Juan* (1819–1824) could be nothing but deeply polemic:

65 Horace, *Ars Poetica*, in *The Norton Anthology of Theory and Criticism*, ed. Vincent B. Leitch (New York: W.W. Norton & Company, 2001), 127. Moreover, Homer *tells* the Muse where to begin; he is not told to begin himself.

66 Ibid.

67 Pierre de Ronsard, *From a Brief on the Art of French Poetry*, in *The Norton Anthology of Theory and Criticism*, ed. Vincent B. Leitch (New York: W.W. Norton & Company, 2001 [1565]). He further asserts that "great poems never begin at the first of the action." Dante, *Inferno*, trans. Allen Mandelbaum (New York: Bantam Books, 1982).

> Most epic poets plunge "in medias res"
> (Horace makes this the heroic turnpike road),
> ...
> That is the usual method, but not mine –
> My way is to begin with the beginning[68]

Lord Byron therefore opens by "narrating somewhat of Don Juan's father / And also of his mother, if you'd rather."

Yet, the problem about beginning "with the beginning" is that even birth and conception, which we think of as the most "natural" of beginnings, quickly turn *artificial* rather than *natural*. Intuitively, it seems natural to begin one's life story with an account of one's birth. But, as Georges Perec explains in his semi-biographical text *Je suis né* ("I am born") (1990), there is in fact something deeply implausible about beginning a text with "I am born."[69] To see what Perec means, let us look at the humor involved when Dickens's David Copperfield begins his narrative in precisely that way:

> I am born. Whether I shall turn out to be the hero of my own life, or whether that station will be held by anybody else, these pages must show. To begin my life with the beginning of my life, I record that I was born (as I have been informed and believe) on a Friday, at twelve o'clock at night. It was remarked that the clock began to strike, and I began to cry, simultaneously.
>
> CHARLES DICKENS, *David Copperfield* (1849–50)

Dickens's opening looks like a number of realist biographical narratives which situate themselves through the time of the birth. A couple of examples are Alphonse Daudet's *The Man With the Golden Brain* (1860) and Marcel Pagnol's *My Father's Glory* (1957), with almost identical structures despite their historical disparity:

> I was born in a small town of the old Swabia, at the court-clerk's office, on a sunny day at Pentecost.
>
> ALPHONSE DAUDET, *The Man With the Golden Brain* (1860)

68 "Canto the first: VI–VII," Lord Byron, *Don Juan* (London: John Lehmann, 1949), 21.
69 "Georges Perec, *Je suis né* (Paris: Seuil, 1990).

> I was born in the town of Aubagne, beneath the goat-crowned Garlaban, in the days of the last goatherds.
>
> MARCEL PAGNOL, *My Father's Glory* (1957)

The structure—birth place and time of the birth—is so familiar that we immediately recognize it as an indication of an autobiography. Yet, the narrative need not be a "real" autobiography; the narrative could be a piece of fiction, which lends its authority from the familiarity of the opening phrase.

The complication about beginning with "I am born" clearly stems from the use of the present tense. Although it is standard in French to use the past participle about one's birth, "Je suis né," it seems deeply illogical because the past participle is the same as the present tense with an adjective. It is this logical inconsistency that Dickens plays on. By beginning with "I am born" in the absence of temporal and spatial indications, Dickens manages to blend an almost abstract birth with the humor involved in imagining that one could be present at one's own birth. When the second line therefore evokes uncertainty about who the hero of the narrator's life will be, we also sense the presence of the narrator being born in the process and who now wonders whether the narration which in the third line turns into past tense will ever move ahead as expected and recapture the present tense. The birth appears to be double: the narrator tells the tale of his birth ("I was born on a Friday"), but the narrator is also born to us as readers in present time.

The humor and implausibility of the opening passage lies in the fact that one cannot be present at one's own birth. The information that one will have of the birth could of course never have been obtained firsthand, and the narrator mitigates the provocative opening by adding, quite reasonably, that his information about the birth has been obtained through others. The irony continues, though, as the information he conveys is not a precise, spatial, and temporal information, but the rather "useless" information that he was born "on a Friday" (few people, after all, know what day of the week they were born on). The rather implausible coincidence that Copperfield started crying exactly as the clock struck twelve furthermore accentuates that the tale of his birth is reported through others and may not be entirely accurate. Through this inaccuracy the tale gains symbolic power; the birth may not serve as a beginning in itself, but when the clock strikes twelve at the moment of birth, the birth is supported structurally by the beginning of a new day. The authority of the birth is hence undermined by the assertive beginning, which corresponds with Copperfield's fatherless status, born exactly at twelve o'clock, "at Nought," as Eliot wrote in the opening of *Daniel Deronda*, and whose witnesses to the birth need to be asserted rather than taken for granted.

What the opening of *David Copperfield* shows is that even in saying "I," we rely upon previous tales, which together constitute our individuality. Without explicitly acknowledging these tales, we readily accept that we are the continuation of the individual who according to the record of our parents, or the registry office, was born at that precise time and in that precise place.[70] This was part of the insight of Valéry's "Orpheus's Beginning," discussed above, which challenges the standardized and informative "I was born" by opening with "I was born without knowing it..." This identity of the narrating subject is, however, at the center of narrative theory, to such a degree that Alain Robbe-Grillet in his analysis of Robert Pinget's *Mahu* (1952) claims that "a book always begins with 'I was born'."[71] But Robbe-Grillet's surrender to these three words is not unproblematic. In his view, "the novel paradoxically ends in a whole collection of possible openings, which all begin with these three words, but in the end degenerate into a cacophony of shrieks, stammering, and incomplete sentences." Although "je suis né" ("I am born") is paradigmatic, this mode of opening not only stagnates but self-destructs: "Once again everything is to be redone."

This disintegration expresses a revolt against the idea that the textual beginning should serve as an origin by evoking a birth. Although Dickens's opening shows an awareness of the artificiality of opening with a birth, it has nevertheless become emblematic of a traditional novelistic structure that politely begins by introducing the character through the social setting of a birth. J.D. Salinger's *The Catcher in the Rye* (1951) sets off precisely by evoking the exhaustion of Dickens's opening and reminds us of the social connotations of talking about one's birth:

> If you really want to hear about it, the first thing you'll probably want to know is where I was born, and what my lousy childhood was like, and how my parents were occupied and all before they

70 Umberto Eco, "Fictional Protocols," in *Six Walks in the Fictional Woods* (Cambridge, MA: Harvard University Press, 1994).

71 Robert Pinget, *Mahu ou le matériau* (Paris: Minuit, 1952). See Alain Robbe-Grillet's analysis of Pinget's novel, "Un roman qui s'invente lui-même," in *Pour un nouveau roman* (Paris: Minuit, 1963 [c. 1961]), 111–12.

> had me, and all that David Copperfield kind of crap, but I don't feel like going into it.
>
> J. D. SALINGER, *The Catcher in the Rye* (1951)

Here the rejection of "that David Copperfield kind of crap" precisely ensures the unsentimental authenticity of Salinger's narrator, who refuses to tell the reader about his parents because they are "touchy as hell." This breach of the Dickensian courtesy becomes the frame that sets the tone of Salinger's novel. The historical shift is also of great consequence. David Copperfield explains his origin, but plays with the logical inconsistency of the perspective, which makes his birth ironically natural. Salinger's novel treats the origin as forbidden or unreliable, which has the consequence that the novel is firmly placed in the verifiable present, which is also symptomatic of the historical periods to which Dickens and Salinger belong.

From the opening of *David Copperfield* we sense that there is something paradoxically abrupt about talking about one's beginning. The search for a natural beginning very easily turns inconsistent and therefore humorous, as we are further reminded by one of the most brilliant openings in literary history, that of Laurence Sterne's *Tristram Shandy* (1759) where the narrator begins by recounting how he was even *conceived*:[72]

> I wish either my father or my mother, or indeed both of them, as they were in duty both equally bound to it, had minded what they were about when they begot me.
>
> LAURENCE STERNE, *Tristram Shandy* (1759)

Sterne's opening is clearly positioned in the polemic about the Horacian dictum because Tristram soon exclaims: "right glad I am, that I have begun the history of myself in the way I have done; and that I am able to go on, tracing everything in it, as Horace says, ab Ovo."[73] But of course Tristram has not proven that a story can successfully begin *ab ovo*. Rather he has taken the *ab ovo* dictum *ad absurdum*, thereby demonstrating that the true *ab ovo* beginning appears instead to begin *in medias res*.[74] It is important to realize, however, that the absurdity involved in the opening

72 Laurence Sterne, *The Life and Opinions of Tristram Shandy* (London: Penguin, 1967 [1759]).

73 Ibid., 4.

74 The play on the absurdity of the narrative perspective is exploited even further by Carlos Fuentes when, in *Cristóbal Nonato*, the narrator is not even born at the beginning of the story. Carlos Fuentes, *Cristóbal Nonato* (Mexico City: Fondo de Cultura Económica, 1987).

scene stems not from Tristram's narrative mode, but from his explanatory mode. As Nuttall has argued, Tristram's initial disorientation is established by commencing the retrospective counter-flow of explanation before the narrative flow has properly begun.[75] Furthermore, the humor of the absurdity should not be forgotten; the humor precisely means that we as readers do not take the absurdity entirely seriously.

The absurdity of the narrative perspective in *David Copperfield* and *Tristram Shandy* does of course rely on the fact that they are both first-person narratives. It is clearly the presumed certainty of Copperfield's and Tristram's narrations that appears absurd: because *how* could they know?[76] One way that a first-person narrative can deal with the birth of the narrator without resorting to humor is by presenting the past through layers of uncertainty, for instance when the narrator of Jules Vallès's *L'Enfant* (*The Child*) (1878) asks about his birth:

> Was I nourished by my mother?
>
> JULES VALLÈS, *L'Enfant* (1878)

In contrast, third-person narratives deal more easily with the birth of the protagonist, as in these examples:

> There was a baby born named Ida.
>
> GERTRUDE STEIN, *Ida* (1941)

> His birth was irregular, and so he passionately loved regularity, the inviolable, commandment and taboo.
>
> THOMAS MANN, *The Tables of the Law* (1943)

> The first thing the midwife noticed about Michael K when she helped him out of his mother into the world was that he had a hare lip.
>
> J.M. COETZEE, *Life and Times of Michael K* (1983)

In such third-person openings, birth serves not just as the beginning of the narrative, but also typically as the naming of the protagonist.

When we consider the status of the natural beginning, we must therefore remember the notion of narrative perspective. A narration will always be narrated and the narrator will inevitably take on a perspective.

75 Nuttall, *Openings*, 158.

76 Compare with the opening of *Præludier* (Preludes) by Peer Hultberg: "Imagine that, isn't it peculiar, but when I was born I was entirely covered by black hair." Peer Hultberg, *Præludier* (Copenhagen: Gyldendal, 1990).

Even an "objective" narrator adopts a perspective, namely that of an objective narrator, which restrains what can and what should be told. In other words, any narrator has not just a story to tell, but also a way of telling it. The belief in literature's dependency on natural beginnings seems to rest on a neglect of this fundamental difference between the narrator's story and the way that it is presented. The "internal" perspective of the narrator cannot conform to the "external" perspective of the event. The problem in the case of natural beginnings like birth and conception is that they necessarily belong to the "external" perspective, and the reason why we laugh at the openings of *David Copperfield* and *Tristram Shandy* is that they mix the external perspective of birth or conception—which we believe can be verified by observation—with the internal perspective of the narrator who reports the event. Pointing out the discrepancy between these two perspectives may in fact be one of literature's greatest achievements.

I have shown that, throughout literary history, the biological beginning has always been viewed with a great deal of suspicion and skepticism. The literary insight into narrative perspective has indicated an epistemological difficulty of explaining a beginning, which is accentuated in the case of biological beginnings, or as Milton's Adam in the Garden of Eden ponders:

> For Man to tell how human Life began
> Is hard; for who himself beginning knew?[77]

The search for such biological beginnings will only end up in a dependency on other narration. Each beginning will not only have to be narrated, but will be a narration in itself. Whereas the "natural" beginning of birth and conception ends up seeming rather artificial, humorous and deliberately ironic, a beginning that *limits* the perspective of the first-person narrator to the present seems sincere and intuitive, as in the case of the opening of *Jacquou le Croquant*:

> The farthest back I remember is 1815, the year where the strangers came to Paris...
>
> EUGÈNE LE ROY, *Jacquou le Croquant* (1899)

In this case, the first memory of the narrating consciousness also becomes the opening of the novel. This limits the opening's dependency on

77 John Milton, *Paradise Lost: Authoritative Text, Sources and Backgrounds, Criticism*, A Norton Critical Edition (New York: W.W. Norton, 2005), VIII, 250–51.

second-hand sources, and the explicit indication of the narrator's limits opens for a different standard of reliability.

The reason for these perspectival complications is that modern literature, especially with the rise of the novel, tends to tell the tale of one single individual. From Cervantes's *Don Quixote* (1605–15), the novel has had to adapt to the challenges of narrating life-stories, as if the individual is now a world in itself, needing its own cosmology. The problem, however, is that a life is not narratively cohesive. Aristotle, for instance, praises Homer precisely for not recounting all the things that happen to one person.[78] His explanation is that "a plot is not unified, as some suppose, if it concerns one single person. An indefinitely large number of things happens to one person, in some of which there is no unity. So too the actions of one person are many, but do not turn into a single action" (1451a). Nevertheless, modern literature, with its more subjectivist outlook, tends precisely to situate an individual within a plot and therefore investigates alternative ways of establishing unity—the unity that *David Copperfield* and *Tristram Shandy* deal with in ironic ways.[79]

Conclusion: The Beginning of a Story Is the Story of a Beginning

The textual openings analyzed in this chapter tend to run counter to recognized, authoritative beginnings. This I see as a clear indication that the authority of textual beginnings depends not on a simulation of naturalness, but on an evocation of *familiarity* meant to appeal to the expectations of the reader. We saw, for instance, that the openings that evoke Genesis do not do so in order to borrow its authority, but rather because the cosmological beginning provides a familiar platform for

78 Aristotle, *Poetics*, 1451a.

79 This has earned *Tristram Shandy* the label as an important precursor to the modernist novel. I save a thorough discussion of the modernist novel for chapter 3. At this stage, however, it is important to indicate that modernism frequently exhibits an explicitly anti-Aristotelian attitude (e.g. Fernando Pessoa, "Notes on a Non-Aristotelian Aesthetics," in *Always Astonished: Selected Prose* (San Francisco, CA: City Lights Books, 1988). Yet, the modernist novel in fact agrees with Aristotle with regard to the disunity of the single-person plot; the difference is simply that this disunity is not shunned, but intensely explored. One could therefore also add that the modernist novel treats the opening of the novel as a "start," not as an "origin," according to the distinction I made earlier in this chapter.

presenting the text's own specific terms of fictionality. The echo of origin that we often find in literary openings is therefore not an imitation of the primordial creation, as Nuttall and Hillis Miller suggest. Rather, such echoes mark the instigation of a newborn relation between text and the reader. If echoes from "natural" beginnings resound in literary beginnings, it is only because they can be heard by the reader.

This is supported by the fact that unmediated beginnings are unknowable, as shown in this chapter. Even our own beginning cannot be ascertained without relying on other narratives—and in this regard Racine's exclamation "what I know best is my own beginning" would be misleading if read literally.[80] The inscrutability of beginnings instead calls for them to be narrativized, and in my analysis of Valéry I illustrated how a present start could be understood only as the abstract notion of origin begins to dissipate. One's fundamental approach to beginnings—whether one sees them as "starts" or as "origins"—has profound epistemological and ideological consequences, which can be traced in the central twentieth-century divide in the humanities between "theorists" and "philologists." Nevertheless, even a beginning that altogether defies the notion of origin will nevertheless have to establish its authority on an alternative narration. Therefore, when Virginia Woolf writes in *The Waves* (1931) that "if there are no beginnings and endings there are no stories," we must not forget that the opposite also holds true.[81] If there are no stories, there are no beginnings.

The beginning of a story, whether cosmological or literary, will then also have to be the story of a beginning, a phenomenon that John Barth deliberately plays on in the opening of his *Lost in the Funhouse*:

> Once upon a time there was a story that began.
>
> JOHN BARTH, *Lost in the Funhouse* (1969)

Without this narrative aspect of beginnings, an infinite regress would develop. As I showed in my discussion of Valéry, the search for a beginning could extend infinitely backwards until the beginning becomes entirely unrecognizable and ineffectual. It is this infinite regress that Tristram Shandy explores through the absurd location of the moment of conception. Ultimately, only the origin of the world would do unless something

80 Racine, quoted as epigram by Louis Aragon, *Je n'ai jamais appris à écrire ou les incipit* (Paris: Skira, 1969).

81 Virginia Woolf, *The Waves*, annotated and ed. Molly Hite and Mark Hussey, A Harvest Book (Orlando, FL: Harcourt, 2006). Quoted in Danto, *Analytical Philosophy of History*, 155.

stops the regress. And this something, I claim, can only be a narrative structure, which mediates the otherwise inaccessible beginnings.[82]

My contention is therefore that "natural" beginnings are in fact "artificial" in the sense that they, like literary manifestations, depend on narrative components. I therefore recommend that we do not distinguish in essence between artificial and natural beginning, but rather between beginnings that are *internally* grounded and beginnings that are *externally* grounded, which I will pursue further in the next chapter. This does not imply, as Nuttall fears, that natural beginnings are being reduced to mere "cultural fictions" that we read *into* the world, but never *off* it.[83] In fact, Nuttall simply sets up a false dichotomy. When, for instance, we read the clock to indicate "1 o'clock," then "2 o'clock," etc., that does not entail that time passes independently of us. Likewise, we read beginnings into the world on the basis of real events since these help us structure an otherwise unsystematic collection of events. The narrative component that we add serves to enhance our ability to trace and define temporal beginnings and it is therefore a fundamental instrument in our understanding also of the natural world.[84] In this sense we comprehend life as if it were a fiction, but that does not of course in any way turn it into a fiction. It is simply that, as George Eliot puts it in her opening of *Daniel Deronda*:

> Men can do nothing without the make-believe of a beginning.
> GEORGE ELIOT, *Daniel Deronda* (1876)

82 I here argue against Nuttall, *Openings*, 210.

83 Ibid., 195.

84 Kant's noumenal philosophy proposes a similar explanation of beginning. See his "Third Antinomy" in Immanuel Kant, *Prolegomena to Any Future Metaphysics*, Revised ed., Cambridge Texts in the History of Philosophy (Cambridge: Cambridge University Press, 2004). Cf. Paule Levert, *L'Idée de commencement* (Paris: Aubier, 1961).

CHAPTER 2

Initiating the Contract of Fiction: A Theory of Openings

The beginning, which is a god established in men, maintains all things

PLATO, *Laws* 775e

The Bait and the Performativity of Literary Openings

One of the most fascinating words in the French language is the verb "amorcer." Literally the verb means to put on bait—or more dramatically to load a weapon. Most frequently, however, the verb is used in its figurative sense where it means "to initiate" or "to begin." That this concrete verb can gain such figurative meaning suggests that any human endeavor begins with a kind of enticement and requires a means to lure someone in. To begin in this context involves both a subject that attracts and an object to attract.

This extraordinary verb overtly recognizes what I have previously called the "deceitful" nature of beginnings: the beginning is bait. The verb accentuates quite clearly that any beginning depends on an interaction—and in the literary scenario, the interaction in question is of course that between the author and the reader. The beginning of a book is a "threshold," as the opening of Edmond Jabès's *The Book of Questions* (1963) tells us, and we as readers must be led on to ask "what happens on the other side of this door?"[1] The literary opening must therefore not only provide information enough to initiate the story; it must also

1 Edmond Jabès, *Le Livre des questions* (Paris: Gallimard, 1963).

"seduce" its reader into this form of communicative interaction. In other words, the beginning is, as Henry Fielding writes in his opening of *Tom Jones*, a "bill of fare to the feast"—it should both inform us and tempt us. In fact, as I show in this chapter, literature is characterized precisely by a constant negotiation—or sometimes even *collision*—between the *informative* and the *seductive* principles.[2]

"Amorcer" thus illustrates my general contention in this chapter that the literary opening—like any beginning—always contains a performative aspect. The opening calls for a response, which the reader is then lured into giving. It is this crucial initial contact at the threshold of the book that sets up what I would call "the contract of fiction." The opening sets up the narrative parameters of fiction such as perspective, tone, and focus—and, as I shall argue later in this chapter, these initial parameters determine also the conditions for closure. In order to illustrate this performative nature, I shall focus first on different types of narration—heterodiegetic, homodiegetic, covert, overt, etc.—in order to discuss the performative signals of the literary opening. I then establish a sort of "taxonomy" of opening signals, which serves to show that the performative aspect is to be located most clearly in irony, which can be both textual and intertextual. In particular, I discuss the implicit or explicit relation to standard introductory formulae, such as "once upon a time..." I shall furthermore illustrate that a text may begin by indicating its status as fiction through the use of what I call "perspectival abruptness," which renders the opening unordered from a narrative point of view. My intention is to argue that the equilibrium between narrative structure vs. narrative amorphousness is indicated at the beginning, not just by determining temporal aspects such as the use of *in medias res* and other temporal techniques such as prolepsis and analepsis,[3] but by determining the use of pronouns and determiners, which locate the subjectivity of the narration. This is abruptness in the narrative *perspective*. I will begin by using Gérard Genette's classic distinction between homodiegetic and heterodiegetic narration and between covert and overt narration in order to locate the performativity of the literary opening.[4]

2 This distinction is inspired by Andrea del Lungo who points to the following four functions of the opening: To start the text (codifying function); to interest the reader (seductive function); to stage the fiction (informative function); to set the story in motion (dramatic function). Andrea del Lungo, *L'incipit romanesque* (Paris: Seuil, 2003).

3 Gérard Genette, *Nouveau discours du récit* (Paris: Seuil, 1983).

4 Ibid.

Homodiegetic Narration

The opening's performative aspect seems most obvious in what narratologists following Genette call an "overt homodiegetic narration"; that is, roughly speaking, a narrative with an openly declared narrator who takes part in the narrative itself. An extreme example of this kind of narration is J.D. Salinger's *The Catcher in the Rye*, in which the reader is directly addressed:

> If you really want to hear about it, the first thing you'll probably want to know is where I was born, and what my lousy childhood was like, and how my parents were occupied and all before they had me, and all that David Copperfield kind of crap, but I don't feel like going into it.
>
> J.D. SALINGER, *The Catcher in the Rye* (1951)

The opening line is surprising—and slightly contradictory. "Really" gives the impression that Holden, the narrator, knows and even has spoken with his reader, yet the conditional mood and the "probably" indicates that Holden does not after all know the reader. When Holden begins to refer to David Copperfield, it emerges that the reader is, after all, imagined—or "implicit," as the narratologists say. Salinger's opening therefore plays on the narrator's expectation of what an ordinary reader will expect to hear in a first-person narration. Holden talks intimately, but indecorously to the reader. His intractable voice scoffs at the ordinary readerly expectations, which in the end only increases the curiosity; what does Holden hide—and why does he hide it? This concealment of information is precisely what lures the reader on. Here the seductive principle thrives precisely by quelling the informative principle. The interaction between narrator and reader is immediate as the opening demands an almost direct response from the reader: "Can you accept that I begin in this way when I flout the conventional *modus operandi* of openings?" From a communicative point of view, Salinger's opening furthermore flouts what linguists call the "cooperative principle," and I later argue in further detail that literature is what it is precisely because it sometimes simply refuses to "cooperate." In fact, that characteristic is part of the very "contract" we have with fiction.

It is not difficult to see why homodiegetic openings exhibit its pragmatic quality most clearly. A first-person narrator can more openly demand a response from the reader, as if it were a question: Do you accept the terms of this narration? The reader is in this way *initiated* and is actively invoked to "open" the literary work through his or her imagination. One illustrative example of the contractual first-person, homodiegetic opening is the famous opening of Melville's *Moby-Dick*:

> Call me Ishmael.
>
> HERMAN MELVILLE, *Moby-Dick* (1851)

In this imperative, the narrator introduces himself directly and thereby calls for the reader's acceptance. The imperative works directly as a speech act and performs the role as a contractual conditional: if you accept to call the narrator by the given name, you have accepted the terms of the narration and you may enter the work.[5] This pragmatic contact—or, rather, contract—between the narrator and the reader functions in homodiegetic narrations like *Moby-Dick* and *The Catcher in the Rye* through an introduction of the narrator, whom the reader will first have to accept.

Heterodiegetic Narration

This aspect of the homodiegetic narration does not mean, however, that the pragmatic aspect of a literary opening cannot be explicit in a *heterodiegetic* narration, i.e. a narration in which the narrator does *not participate* in the action, which is more typically a third-person narration. Even if the heterodiegetic narrator is essentially *covert*, the pragmatic aspect of the opening can still be highlighted through the narrator's appeal to the reader's spatial imagination, for instance like the opening question of Le Clézio's *The Book of Flights*:

> Can you imagine that? A great airport building in the middle of nowhere, its roof stretched flat under the sky, and on this roof a small boy sitting in an easy chair is staring straight ahead. The air is white, buoyant, there is nothing to see.
>
> LE CLÉZIO, *The Book of Flights* (1969)

The question is not asked with the polite conditional "could," but with the indicative "can," which indicates that the appeal to imagination is also a question of capacity: *can* you imagine what the narrator tells you? The

5 J. Hillis Miller discusses this opening in a similar fashion in "Literature as Virtual Reality." However, I have previously shown my reservations towards his general line of thought.

boy is quickly turned into the narration's focalizer and through his eyes we see that there is in fact nothing to be seen. But the reader's role is here also explained through a metanarrative maneuver: the reader needs to accept the terms of the narration although strictly speaking there is "nothing to see." A novel is "a book of flights" in more than one sense; it is a flight of fancy, which requires something specific of the reader. The reader has to surrender blindly to the narration. Several novels make this condition clear to the reader, such as Irvin Faust's *Foreign Devils* and Wright Morris's *Cause for Wonder*:

> Well you cannot hold back any longer. Close your eyes, hold your nose, grab air and jump.
>
> IRVIN FAUST, *Foreign Devils* (1973)

> What led you, just now, to glance at this page? To make a beginning, right?
>
> WRIGHT MORRIS, *Cause for Wonder* (1963)

My examination shows that the appeal to the reader's spatial imagination is particularly frequent when the destination is exotic and unfamiliar to the implicit reader. As in the case of Le Clézio's *The Book of Flights*, novels that begin in a colonial setting, for instance, tend to employ the pragmatic, heterodiegetic appeal, here Paul Scott's *The Jewel in the Crown*:

> Imagine, then, a flat landscape, dark for the moment, but even so conveying to a girl running in the still deeper shadow cast by the wall of the Bibighar Gardens an idea of immensity, of distance, such as years before Miss Crane had been conscious of standing where a lane ended and cultivation began.
>
> PAUL SCOTT, *The Jewel in the Crown* (1966)

The authorial appeal to the reader's participatory imagination comes across as natural and continuous; the "then" in Scott's "Imagine, then" gives an impression of an imagination already activated; a reader who only needs to be drawn to the next image. In this sense, the "then" actually *dedramatizes* the burden of imagination because the process seems already to have begun. Yet, the "then" also gives the reader the impression of narrative *estrangement*: has the story already begun before I, the reader, started reading? So whose story is it in the first place? And who is its expected audience—am I as reader included and active in it? Although the burden of beginning is dedramatized, these accompanying questions conversely *dramatize* the opening, especially since they are crucial markers of the colonial setting with its complex dynamics of appropriation. The impression that the act of imagination is already well under way at the beginning further allows the opening to launch a number of bewildering elements, such as the gardens and the girl who may or may not be "Miss Crane." At the same time, the opening draws up an image of some of the central themes of the novel: the protected garden and the shadows that it casts at the boundary of "cultivation."

The complex "then" from the opening line of *The Jewel in the Crown* occurs also in John Cheever's *Bullet Park* (1969), which goes even further in its appeal to the participation of the reader:

> Paint me a small railroad then, ten minutes before dark. Beyond the platform are the waters of the Wekonsett River, reflecting a somber afterglow. The architecture of the station is oddly informal, gloomy but unserious, and mostly resembles a pergola, cottage or summer house although this is a climate of harsh winters. The lamps along the platform burn with a nearly palpable plaintiveness. The setting seems in some way to be at the heart of the matter.
>
> JOHN CHEEVER, *Bullet Park* (1969)

The opening maintains an odd balance between authorial informative precision ("the Wekonsett River," "this is a climate of harsh winters") and impressionism ("a nearly palpable plaintiveness," "in some way"). The overt narrator describes the initial setting quite elaborately, but nevertheless seems uninformed, or vague, with regard to the greater purpose of the description: "The setting seems in some way to be at the heart of the matter." Although the reader is evoked to help "paint" the railroad, the narrator suspects this to be the crucial place to begin. This discrepancy makes it unclear whether this opening is predominantly readerly or authorial. In my discussion of "perspectival abruptness" later in this chapter, I address the complexity of such indexical indicators as "then," which fail to make a clear semantic reference.

In the last five openings from the mid-twentieth century cited above,

	Homodiegetic	Heterodiegetic
Covert narrator	Rare	Frequent (e.g. Le Clézio)
Overt narrator	Frequent (e.g. Melville)	Rare

FIGURE 1. The narrator: covert/overt vs. homediegetic/heterodiegetic

the reader is directly addressed. Such an address is of course not uncommon in the history of literature; the eighteenth- and nineteenth-century novel would very often begin by addressing the reader. Think of Laclos's *Dangerous Liaisons*:

> We feel in duty bound to warn our readers that, despite the title and the editor's comments in his preface, we cannot guarantee the authenticity of these letters.
>
> CHODERLOS DE LACLOS, *Dangerous Liaisons* (1782)

Yet, there is an important difference. The opening of *Moby-Dick* is exceptional for its time because it is not a faux-author who appeals to the reader in a preface, but rather a narrator who appeals to the reader from "inside" the story, as it were, in order to establish the terms of the fictional world that the reader is to enter. This is what is so "modern" about Melville.

The Literary Act and the Contract of Fiction

As I endeavor to show, it is a historical phenomenon that twentieth-century novels tend to refer more frequently to the performative aspect of its opening. However, I claim that this is not because modern openings are *more* performative, but rather because they tend to exploit or expose its performativity more self-consciously. In fact, it is my general contention that all openings possess equal performative force; performativity is simply a defining feature of literature. When the reader is directly addressed, as in the above examples from the twentieth century, the "implicit" reader is being addressed: the actual reader will always have to enter into a pragmatic situation when beginning a fictional work. As Gérard Genette has shown, even the primordial opening "once upon a time" can analytically be reduced to two pragmatic functions.[6] The first function is in fact a request ("try to imagine that there was a time"), and the second is performative ("now I intend to cause you to imagine that there was a time").[7] I shall elaborate on these considerations of the formula "once upon a time..." in my subsection below dealing with the

6 Gérard Genette, *Fiction et diction*, Poétique (Paris: Seuil, 1991), 49–50.

7 In Algerian Arabic, the standard opening phrase literally goes "I've told you what's coming," thereby acknowledging directly a narrator and a listener.

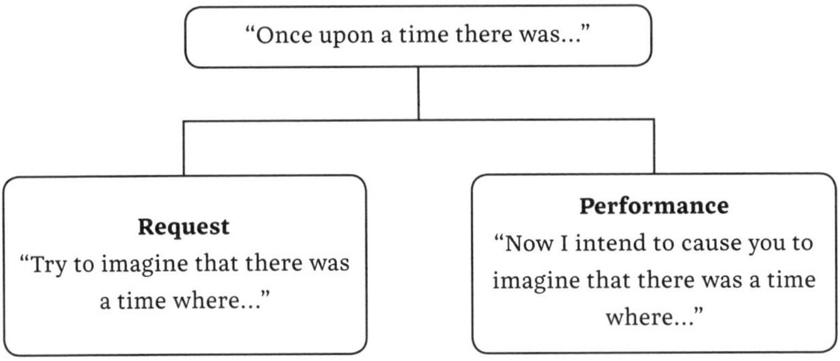

FIGURE 2. The performativity of the beginning

existential opening. This performative function is precisely what allows the reader to pass the threshold of the book and enter into the fiction.

This performativity of the opening could be expressed more generally—and more dramatically—by saying that to tell a story is to exercise a certain power. The opening is an impingement, and this is a situation which both parties—the author and the reader—will have to acknowledge. As Ross Chambers expresses it in his work on narrative "seduction": "The situation produced in the text proves subordinate to the situation produced by the text."[8] In other words, the narrative is always subordinate to the narration itself. This is simply a consequence of the way that language generally works, for as Paul Valéry concludes, language is *someone's act* before it is anything else.[9] Therefore, even in a heterodiegetic narrative—and even if it be covert—there is an underlying pragmatic contact between an "I" and a "you," which renders the opening performative. As Ford Madox Ford says: "Life [does] not narrate,"[10] *someone* does.

Valéry's idea that language is to be seen first and foremost as an act has since become a widely accepted view in the philosophy of language, with the so-called speech act theory developed in the 1960s and 1970s under the influence of notably J. L. Austin and John Searle.[11] It has now become commonplace in the humanities to talk of "speech acts," but in the literary field a speech act has often had an almost revelatory or

8 Ross Chambers, *Story and Situation: Narrative Seduction and the Power of Fiction* (Minneapolis: University of Minnesota Press, 1984), 45.

9 Valéry, *Cahiers.*

10 Ford Madox Ford, *Critical Writings*, Regents Critics Series (Lincoln: University of Nebraska Press, 1964), 73.

11 John L. Austin, *How to Do Things with Words*, The William James lectures 1955 (Cambridge, MA: Harvard University Press, 1962); John R. Searle, *Speech Acts: An Essay in the Philosophy of Language* (London: Cambridge University Press, 1969).

mystical attraction, perhaps because of the way that Derrida has used it.[12] Instead I wish undramatically to use some of the pragmaticians' distinctions in order to use speech acts to shed light upon my idea of the "contract," which the literary opening installs. In particular, I wish to draw attention to some of the elements of Paul Grice's theory of language, in particular his notion of the "cooperative principle," which has only very rarely been related to literary theory.[13] Of course, I thereby implicitly postulate that we must treat literature as language and, hence, as subject to the rules of language.[14] Yet, I also claim that literature differentiates itself from other forms of communication precisely because of its particular pragmatic position.

The central element in Grice's theory is that for any successful communication to take place there must exist an unspoken *agreement* between the speakers. In essence, the speakers must both agree to *cooperate*: their communication must be relevant, with neither too much nor too little information, and it must be true. This is what Grice calls the "cooperative principle" of language. Even if we cannot always live up to every maxim of this principle, we can communicate successfully by indicating that we still pay respect to the principle, for instance by adding the hedge "I guess..." to a statement that we are not absolutely sure about. "I guess Peter is coming" is not false if Peter is not coming because the speaker has cooperatively indicated that the information is not certain. The question is, however, what happens if the cooperative principle is not respected at all? Grice himself points out that a speaker can either *flout* or *violate* the principle. A violation is a rather simple disrespect of the principle, whereas a flouting in certain contexts can render the communication more *creative*. Grice's theory could be summed up as a theory of relevance, but as he himself was aware, it is not all contexts that call for relevance. In fact, it is precisely when things are not "relevant" in the strict communicative sense that they may become creative or even artistic.

These Gricean considerations are highly useful in our literary context. The flouting of the cooperative principle is in fact a common phenome-

12 Jacques Derrida, *Limited Inc*, Collection La Philosophie en effet (Paris: Galilée, 1990); John Searle, "Reiterating the Differences: A Reply to Derrida," *Glyph* I (1977).

13 Paul Grice, "Logic and Conversation," in *Studies in the Way of Words*, ed. Paul Grice (Cambridge, MA: Harvard University Press, 1989). One theorist who has worked with Grice in a literary setting is Teun Adrianus van Dijk, "Pragmatics and Poetics," in *Pragmatics of Language and Literature*, ed. Teun Adrianus van Dijk, North-Holland Studies in Theoretical Poetics 2 (Amsterdam and New York: North-Holland Pub. Co./American Elsevier Pub. Co., 1976).

14 In this respect, I cannot deny being influenced by structuralism, so I may as well admit it openly.

non in fiction. For instance, when literature begins *in medias res* it openly flouts Grice's "maxim of manner," a part of the cooperative principle which dictates an orderly presentation. My suggestion is that literature, like other language, is based on an unspoken agreement, but that some of the terms of this agreement work differently in the case of literature. For instance, it seems not just totally acceptable to flout the cooperative principle from time to time; we as readers actually *expect* a book to flout the cooperative principle. The author is not just supposed to "inform" us through a narrative, but also supposed to surprise us, to challenge us, fascinate us. We therefore begin to understand why "information" and "seduction" at the opening of a narrative almost work against each other: a literary text builds on an implicit, communicative agreement, which it is supposed both to *endorse* and to *challenge*.

Acknowledging that literature, like other language, works through an agreement amounts to acknowledging that it is performative. As mentioned, however, twentieth-century novels more frequently point to this performative quality, which, I have argued, does not make them more performative; like all openings, they are performative by nature. We may, however, use Austin's later distinction between the implicit and the explicit performative to say that although all literary openings are performative, some are *explicitly* performative, whereas most are merely implicitly performative ("implicit" because based on an implicit agreement).

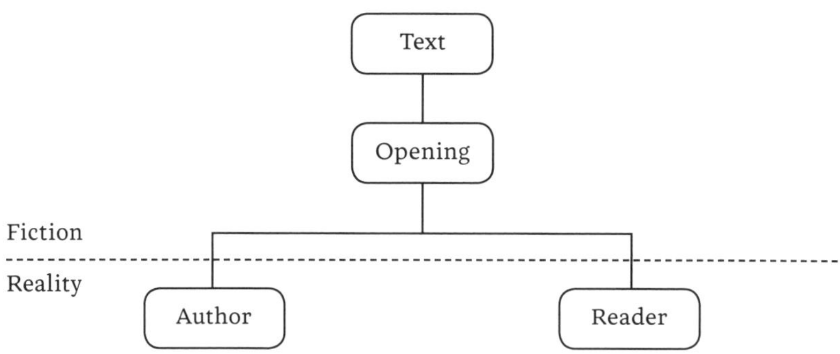

FIGURE 3. The opening as mediator between fiction and reality

That all openings are performative is of course a rather majestic contention. After all, novelistic openings are structurally very different, and one could object, for instance, that some begin with discourse, which gives no immediate point of contact between the narrator and the reader. I maintain, however, that, despite some qualifications, openings are *necessarily* performative, but in order to illustrate this contention further, I find it indispensable to identify the different forms of openings. In the following sections, I therefore establish a taxonomy of openings. On the basis of such a directory, I argue that a novel's performative nature mainly evolves around its *explicit or implicit indications of its own fictionality*. I therefore focus on what I, inspired by Brombert, call "narrative signals." On the basis of this observation I shall also maintain somewhat paradoxically that the *sooner* a narrative indicates its fictional status, the more likely it is to gain the trust and credibility of the reader. That is a consequence of the contractual nature of literature: it is also cooperative to signal a narrative's fictionality.

The Taxonomy of Openings

THE IMPLICIT "INCIPIT" AND THE EXPLICIT "EXPLICIT"

Before establishing a taxonomy of openings, I must explain in more detail how we are to *locate* the opening, a challenge I touched upon in my prologue. Typically there is no *explicit* indication of where a book begins. It is no coincidence that in Latin "incipit" is in fact the antonym of "explicit." The ending, or the "explicit," may be *explicitly* indicated by "The End," "La Fin" or the Latin "explicit est liber." By contrast, the beginning is never indicated by "The Beginning," except in some cases where the author intends an ironic play on beginnings as such.[15] Beginnings may be difficult to understand, yet typically when we open a book, we as readers locate the beginning quite easily. The indication of a literary beginning therefore works at a different level, as an implicit transition into fiction. Yet, since a beginning is a radical phenomenon, our ability to comprehend a beginning must depend on much more than explicit markers: it must depend very strongly on an "agreement," which again depends strongly on a number of cultural codes, such as a conventionality with regard to the structure of books, in the first place, and a conventionality with regard to

15 This is the case in Julio Cortázar's novels, for instance, "This Is the Way it Begins," see Julio Cortázar, *La vuelta al día en ochenta mundos*, La Creación literaria (México: Siglo Veintiuno Editores, 1967).

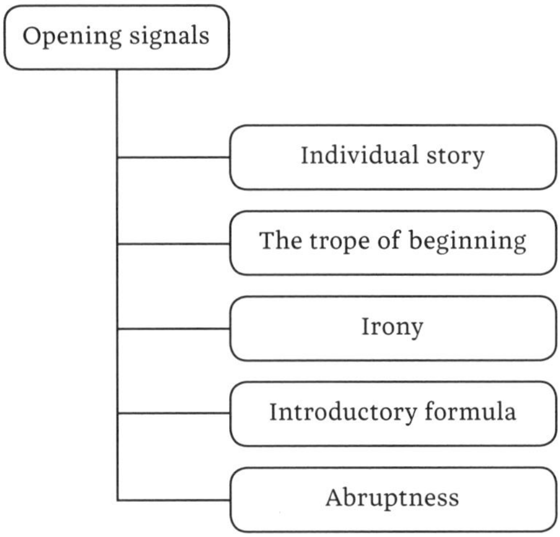

FIGURE 4. Taxonomy of openings

the structure of texts, in the second place. The structure of books, or what is typically referred to as "the paratext," may of course explicitly point to the book's fictional status, for instance by having "A Novel" printed on its front cover. Important as these paratextual markers are for a number of texts, paratext however falls outside the scope of my present study, which is interested in how the text itself orchestrates its own beginning. Furthermore, only some texts rely fundamentally on paratextual markers, whereas all texts will have to rely on a textual indication of beginning (or what Genette would call "architext"). I therefore wish to put paratextual signals aside and instead locate the purely textual means of indicating the beginning of a fictional text, in order to pinpoint the performative nature of all literary openings.

Considering the variety and sheer quantity of novelistic openings—we are talking about no less than all books of fiction ever written—I hope for my reader's clemency with regard to the comprehensiveness of my ambition of setting up a taxonomy of openings. Since I obviously have not read all books ever written, my scheme cannot claim to have taken all books into consideration. My method therefore cannot be deductive, but will have to be inductive. On the basis of all the openings I have worked with, however, I first located about fifteen ways of beginning a text of fiction, which I then further reduced to the following five ways, which I shall discuss in the remainder of this chapter:

1 The insistence on an **individual story** rather than a general one.
2 The use of the **trope of beginning**; the opening uses a natural beginning, say, birth.
3 The use of an indirect signal of **irony**, especially with reference to truthfulness.
4 The use of a familiar **introductory formula**, typically a variation of "once upon a time."
5 The use of **abruptness,** not so much by *in medias res*, but more importantly through subjective, "perspectival" abruptness, realized for instance by the use of demonstratives and "unexplained" pronouns (this point will be explained in much more detail in the second half of the chapter).

Some texts employ two or more of these five techniques; but all fictional texts, I claim, use *at least one* of them.

Exceptions to the Five Signals

When making such a general proposition, I do however need to account first for a number of evident exceptions to these five techniques. Most notably, some openings do not commence with an immediately recognizable narrative component, which could establish the performative parameters of the "contract" of fiction. Some openings, for instance, begin with discourse, with a maxim, with an epistle, with a quotation or even with a preface, which technically may be situated in between paratext and text, for instance the preface to *Dangerous Liaisons* or Fielding's preface to *Tom Jones*. Some examples are:

Discourse:

> "Ah, don't begin to fuss"
>
> REBECCA WEST, *The Return of the Soldier* (1918)

Idiom:

> Ships at a distance have every man's wish on board.
>
> ZORA NEALE HURSTON, *Their Eyes Were Watching God* (1937)

Axiom:

> It is a truth universally acknowledged, that a single man in possession of a good fortune must be in want of a wife.
>
> JANE AUSTEN, *Pride and Prejudice* (1813)

Aphorism:

> Happy families are all alike;
> every unhappy family is unhappy in its own way.
>
> LEO TOLSTOY, *Anna Karenina* (1873–77)

Quotation, in this case (an erroneous) quotation of another beginning:

> "All happy families are more or less dissimilar; all unhappy ones are more or less alike," says a great Russian writer in the beginning of a famous novel.
>
> VLADIMIR NABOKOV, *Ada, or Ardor: A Family Chronicle* (1969)

Some openings even combine discourse and axiom:

> "The act of love is of no importance, since it can be performed indefinitely." All eyes were turned upon the perpetrator of this absurdity.
>
> ALFRED JARRY, *The Supermale* (1902)

Although it is important to emphasize that these exceptions may serve to expose how the narrator adopts phrases from other contexts and may be instrumental in preparing the reader for the remainder of the novel, these examples share the characteristic that the reader appears to be temporarily cut off from interacting directly with a narrator. Nabokov's opening of *Ada, or Ardor* could for instance be the opening of a scholarly book on literary history—that is, of course, if we did not at first notice that Nabokov in fact turns Tolstoy's opening on its head. Austen's opening could perhaps be the opening of a (now obsolete!) book of sociology, although in the literary context the axiom is important in showing how the narrator adopts an axiom and brings this forth to the reader. I claim, however, that the examples are not really exceptions, but that they simply employ an initial confusion, which rarely lasts longer than a line or—at most—a paragraph. In these openings, the pragmatic interaction with the opening is in other words simply postponed a line or two. This postponement, of course not "cooperative" in the Gricean sense, is deliberately designed to create a certain effect. As Jarry's novel cited above goes on to say about its initial utterance: "The surprising sentence had the same effect as a stone dropped in a pond: after a short initial confusion a general interest is created."[16] This is also the effect that such non-narrative opening lines most often help to establish: a short initial confusion, which then generates interest. The maxim, quotation, or dialogue is not irrelevant to the work—it can be very central indeed, but it is "irrelevant" in the sense that it does not determine the narrative structure; only the direct interaction between narrator and reader does. In the above examples, the pragmatic aspect of the opening is therefore simply postponed.[17] This literary "feint" also means that the establishment of the narrative "contract" is slightly postponed.

Demarcation of the Opening

As a consequence, I must also quickly address the question of demarcation of the opening, which I first posed in my prologue. Where does the opening *end*? Since I argue that an opening may employ various techniques of postponing the narrative situation, I cannot otherwise dogmatically claim that the literary opening consists of the first line or the first three lines or is determined by some other rigid rule. Instead I must say more loosely that the opening is whatever suffices to establish the narrative situation. The opening is whatever puts the reader in a position to grasp the contract of fiction. This demarcation could of course be said to be rather vague, but any attempt to set up a rigid rule will simply fail because the variety of books of fiction will in itself break down any such attempt. If, for instance, we insist that the opening consists of the first line of a novel, we would be at a total loss with experimental books, which contain no punctuation, or for example in the case of Marie NDiaye's *Comédie classique* (Classical Comedy) (1987), where the whole novel provocatively is written in one line. A rigid demarcation of the opening simply will not do in any case. I therefore find that the most useful approach is to locate

16 Alfred Jarry, *Le surmâle* (Paris: Bernard Grasset, 1902).

17 I here also argue against Helmut Bonheim's way of classifying openings. Helmut Bonheim, "How Stories Begin: Devices of Exposition in 600 English, American, and Canadian Stories," *The Yearbook of R.E.A.L.* 1 (1982). He claims that there are generally four types of openings: 1. with comment, 2. with description, 3. with report, 4. with speech. The problem is, however, that speech does not determine the narrative situation and therefore will have to be seen in the narrative context. I therefore do not see speech as an independent category in itself.

the opening where the reader is able to establish the narrative situation by accepting the pragmatic contract of fiction.

My demarcation of the opening is, however, open to other difficulties. First of all, I will have to admit that in a sense the contract of fiction is negotiated throughout the novel. My contention is, however, that the further negotiation of the contract is typically still based on the initial contract. As the German novelist Martin Walser claims, the opening adamantly determines how the "game" is played.[18] Rendering the narrative situation more complex does not undermine the initial situation, but is a natural extension of it.

In some rare situations, my demarcation may, however, run into a more serious problem if the initial narrative setting is radically transformed later in the novel. This certainly occurs in modern, experimental novels, but it also occurs in a famous and classic example like Gustave Flaubert's *Madame Bovary* (1856). Flaubert's novel begins with Charles Bovary as the focalizer of the story, but after he has met Emma, the story completely abandons its initial focalizer and instead exclusively adopts the focus of Emma. My own interpretation of this peculiar, narrative abandonment is that it serves to forebode how Charles is later rather casually discarded by Emma. Not even the narrator is faithful to Charles. In this case, the narrative situation at the beginning does not represent the novel as a whole, and from a narratological point of view we need to treat the story as two overlapping stories with two different pragmatic contracts with the reader (who may or may not be entirely conscious about the shift in focalization).

However, the dramatic effect of such narrative shifts also clearly shows that my demarcation is a sensible one. Flaubert's shift of narrative focalizer is a bewildering one, but our bewilderment also shows that the shift is exceptional. By contrast, one is not surprised or puzzled when a few lines of speech stop and a narrator and a narrative situation is introduced. This is due to the fact that speech does not *shift* the narrative situation, but as already argued merely *postpones* the establishment of the narrative situation. I therefore feel justified in maintaining that novels that open with speech, axioms, or other citations must be treated in a broader context in which the narrative situation can be established. Of course, it must not in any way be ruled out that fruitful observations can be made on the basis of, for instance, the historical variations in the frequency with which novels begin with speech. I am merely saying that

18 "The novel is always a game, but the first sentence determines without mercy how to play it." Walser, "Erfahrungen mit ersten Sätzen oder Aller Anfang ist schwer," 162.

speech cannot be analyzed as an opening signal in itself: the study of speech depends on the narrative situation.

Having explained why speech and other utterances are treated as independent classes in my taxonomy, I wish in the following to explain each of the central five signals or techniques sketched above and show how each of them highlights the pragmatic aspect of all openings.

FIRST SIGNAL — INSISTENCE ON AN INDIVIDUAL STORY RATHER THAN A GENERAL ONE

That the story to be told is an individual one is embedded in the concept of literature—seen for instance when Le Clézio begins his novel *The Interrogation,* discussed earlier, with "Once upon a little time, in the dog-days, there was a fellow sitting at an open window." There we plunge into a specific setting, at a specific time and meet a specific individual. Although, in this case, the individual is not specified by name, but simply by an indefinite article, we expect that this introduction is merely suspended a bit. A general story is for instance characteristic in science, which is supposed to generalize in order to obtain working hypotheses. A scientific work could of course begin by saying that "a guy sitting in front of a window tends to catch a cold." But here the tense helps to mark the difference. It is simply part of the contract of fiction that the story must have happened already when we hear it or read it.[19] Of course, not all literary works will begin by insisting that it is an individual story and not a general one. A literary work may in fact attempt to cause initial confusion in the way that, for instance, the first two lines of Nabokov's *Ada, or Ardor* are confusing because a book on literary history *could* have started in the same fashion—and also in the past tense. But that is Nabokov's purpose—the book is also a parody of literary history—and only the third line of the novel establishes the individuality of the story: "That pronouncement has little if any relation to the story to be unfolded now." The indication that the story is an individual one signals that it is a piece of fiction.

It is important to note also that the standard opening "once upon a time there was..." also indicates a story's individuality through the use of the existential component "there was." We therefore have reason to believe that the insistence on an individual story is related to the use of the standard opening and vice versa. I therefore take up this point again

19 I shall conclude on this important presupposition of fiction in the section "Conclusion: Is Literature "Cooperative?"

in my discussion of "once upon a time" and the indefinite, existential component "there was" below (see page 68ff.).

SECOND SIGNAL — THE TROPE OF BEGINNING: THE APPEAL THAT TURNS IRONIC

Instead of using a signal of individuality, for instance through an existential component, the work may engage the reader by explicitly drawing attention to the phenomenon of beginning, outlined in chapter 1. The difficulty of beginning can in this way be alleviated by using the trope of beginning. We remember, for instance, that the word "first" or "primus" is used throughout our literary history to signal primary events in the narration: we saw it in the case of Homer and Hesiod, but it is also the case with Herodotus, Virgil, Propertius, and all the way up to Milton's opening "Of Man's First Disobedience" in *Paradise Lost* (1667). Here the work begins with a beginning so as to justify its own beginning.

In chapter 1, I looked at the ways in which the beginning of a literary work tries to justify its authority and authenticity through a search for natural beginnings. In particular I looked at the ways that literature used cosmological beginnings and natural events like births to set itself in motion and pointed out that the simultaneity between a specific literary opening and an external natural beginning tends not to create the necessity that one would expect, but rather insinuates that any beginning is contingent. In fact, such beginnings often turn ironic, as we saw in the case of several of Dickens's novels and in the case of *Tristram Shandy*.[20] As I now go on to illustrate further, through a number of literary examples, the use of the trope of beginning rather accentuates that a particular beginning is randomly chosen and could be replaced by a number of possible beginnings. Drawing attention to the beginning tends to point to the contingency and dependence of beginnings upon the will of the narrator. The trope of beginning therefore easily introduces another ironic layer to the opening, a layer which, I claim, is at the very core of the work's claim to fictional credulity. When, for instance, a narrator draws attention to the beginning of the tale, it very often becomes a relativization of the narrative perspective: the tale could have begun in several ways, as we see in the following examples:

20 The trope of travel is a way of using a natural beginning, which is not quite as dramatic: "The schoolmaster was leaving the village, and everybody seemed sorry." Thomas Hardy, *Jude the Obscure: An Authoritative Text, Backgrounds and Contexts, Criticism*, 2nd ed., A Norton Critical Edition (New York: W.W. Norton, 1999); Thomas Mann, *Der Zauberberg* (Berlin: S. Fischer, 1924).

> It might be most dramatically effective to begin the tale at the moment when Arnold Baffin rang me up and said, "Bradley, could you come round here, please, I think that I have just killed my wife." A deeper pattern however suggests Francis Marloe as the first speaker, the page or housemaid (these images would appeal to him) who, some half an hour before Arnold's momentous telephone call, initiates the action ... There are indeed many places where I could start.
>
> IRIS MURDOCH, *The Black Prince* (1973)

> In the middle of last summer a small Norwegian coastal town was the scene of some highly unusual events. A stranger appeared in town, a certain Nagel, a remarkable, eccentric charlatan who did a lot of curious things and then disappeared as suddenly as he had come. What's more, the man was visited by a mysterious young lady, who came on heaven knows what business and left after only a few hours, afraid to stay any longer. But this is not the beginning...
>
> The beginning is as follows: When the steamer docked around six o'clock in the evening, there appeared on deck two or three passengers, including a man wearing a lid yellow suit and a wide velvet cap.
>
> KNUT HAMSUN, *Mysteries* (1892)

> Where to begin? A week has passed since I wrote that sentence. ... There! I've done it! I've found a place to begin.
>
> GORE VIDAL, *Kalki* (1978)

In the three openings, attention is drawn to the difficulty of describing the story correctly from the beginning—and this difficulty becomes a theme in itself. It highlights the fragile position of the narrator, whose doubt and insecurity become a circuitous way of augmenting the narration's trustworthiness. The ready acceptance of the narrator's fallibility in fact supports the importance of the tale itself: it is precisely because of its importance that the narrator hesitates.[21] In twentieth-century

21 An example is also Ford Madox Ford, *The Good Soldier; A Tale of Passion* (New York: J. Lane, 1915). One could define this as a narratological "effect of reality" (*effet reel*). This is also the reason why the muse has been important historically. If the opening must begin somewhere into the story (cf. the *fabula/sjuzét* distinction discussed earlier) this could potentially occur anywhere. Only through the guidance of a divine power could the "anywhere" novels, this hesitation very easily becomes a kind of "refusal" to begin; the beginning often becomes a groping with the question of the tale's authority and the role of the narrator in its presentation. It seems to be the case, in fact, that the *more* a novel draws attention to its own mode of beginning, the more it reflects and comments on prior conventions for beginning, as we see in the following examples:

> There was a depression over the Atlantic. It was traveling eastward, toward an area of high pressure over Russia, and still showed no tendency to move northward around it. … In short, to use an expression that describes the facts pretty satisfactorily, even though it is somewhat old-fashioned: it was a fine August day in the year 1913.
>
> ROBERT MUSIL, *The Man without Qualities* (1930–43)

> My reader, my friend, would you, by any chance, expect me to begin this story with: "The pale moon rose on a dark horizon…" or with: "Three young men, one blond, the other brown-haired and the third red-haired, painfully climbed up…" or with… well, no! All these beginnings are vulgar and boring, and since I do not have enough imagination to throw you into my narrative in a somewhat novel way, I prefer not to start at all, but simply inform you that Matteo Cigoli was by all accounts the best, the most gay, the most active and the most witty boy of his village, situated a few leagues from Bologna.
>
> GOBINEAU, *Scaramouche* (1843)

The reflexive emphasis on the beginning often brings with it a certain ironic distance to the novels' own mode of beginning. In Musil's novel, the beginning is shown to depend entirely on the mode of description. Using a different description, in this case a meteorological one, seems almost alienating to the reader, whereas the "old-fashioned" one sounds cliché-ridden. A text's attention on its own beginning *as a way of beginning* is in other words closely related to the third of my five classifications of beginnings, namely the presence of an immediate signal of irony. The attention to the mode of beginning often serves to relativize the authority of the speaking subject, which in fact only underlines the text's status as fiction. The intensity of the beginning's irony and self-consciousness

be eliminated and the "somewhere" justified. I do therefore not see the traditional muse as a power of unmediated inspiration, but rather as a narrative determinant in the dodging of the *ex nihilo*.

is of course subject to historical variation—"modern" or "postmodern" novels may seem more readily to exude self-conscious irony. However, this claim could be qualified by saying rather that the irony of the beginning simply takes different forms in different historical periods. In the modern novel, the irony takes a primarily self-conscious form, but due to its performative nature, all narratives could be said to involve one or another form of irony in its opening, as I shall continue to show in the next section. This opening irony is in fact likely to be a defining characteristic of novelistic narratives and one of the central reasons why the opening is the "literary place *par excellence*."

THIRD SIGNAL — INDIRECT IRONY (AND THE KERNEL OF REALISM)

As shown in chapter 1, as well as in the previous section of this chapter, an opening that explicitly uses the trope of beginning easily gives way to a certain irony. In fact, this irony is in itself an important means of opening a narrative effectively. I now wish to determine more precisely the nature of this irony and its role. Since we may not be surprised to find a certain irony in, say, Julio Cortázar's experimental openings, or even in the calculated ones by Musil, I instead would like to locate ironic components in the genre where one would perhaps least expect to find them: realist and naturalistic novels of the nineteenth century. In fact, these ironic components in the openings of realist and naturalistic novels will also tell us a great deal about the limits of the realist project in literature.

The realist opening characteristically gives a thorough introduction to the setting of the novel. It is quite common to begin with precise temporal and spatial indications and with a detailed description of the physical surroundings—the weather, the landscape, the house, etc.

> On a cold December morning in the year 1612, a young man, whose clothing was somewhat of the thinnest, was walking to and fro before a gateway in the Rue des Grands-Augustins in Paris.
>
> HONORÉ DE BALZAC, *The Unknown Masterpiece* (1831)

> MME. VAUQUER (née de Conflans) is an elderly person, who for the past forty years has kept a lodging-house in the Rue Neuve-Sainte-Geneviève, in the district that lies between the Latin Quarter and the Faubourg Saint-Marcel.
>
> HONORÉ DE BALZAC, *Father Goriot* (1835)

> The clock on the Bourse had just struck eleven when Saccard

> walked into Champeaux's, into the white and gold dining-room, with its two tall windows looking out over the square.
>
> ÉMILE ZOLA, *Money* (1891)

The richness in detail is even more concrete in the case of Zola's openings, where the temporal indication becomes a specific time of the day and the spatial frame is described even at the level of the number of windows in the room. We furthermore notice that both in *Father Goriot* and in *Money*, the characters are introduced directly with their proper name: Madame Vauquer and Saccard. By contrast, in *The Unknown Masterpiece* the protagonist is introduced as "a young man," but the short story makes a point of later disclosing that this young man in fact is the great Nicolas Poussin, a point that could not have been made if the name had been mentioned right away. Although Balzac also opens *Father Goriot* by introducing characters directly with a proper name, Zola is far more radical in his opening. There is no explanation at this point of Saccard's identity, or that of the Champeaux, and we see a heavy predominance of definite articles ("the dining-room," "windows [les fenêtres]," "the square") whereas Balzac's openings are full of indefinite articles ("a person," "a lodging-house," "a morning," "a young man," "a gateway"). This difference between Balzac and Zola is extremely significant to the narrative situation, and I return to this discussion of proper names and indefinite articles in the next section. Zola's opening gives us a sense of an *in medias res* opening, but he rarely uses *in medias res*, which I consider to be a *temporal* device. But the sense of *abruptness* is due precisely to the definitive articles and the unintroduced proper names, which challenges our idea of subjective *perspective*.

The richness of information at the beginning of the novel is precisely what has become the trademark of the realist tradition. The paradox is, however, that these realist details in fact work against the realist principle itself. First of all, too much information flouts Grice's cooperative principle because it becomes difficult to locate the kernel of the communication. This observation lies close to Claude Simon's critique of the nineteenth-century novel expressed in his Nobel speech, in which he deplores the fact that "the descriptions [took] over the novel, completely forgetting the fable that it was meant for."[22] Second, the insistence on

22 Claude Simon, "Discours à Stockholm," Nobel Media AB, www.nobel.se. Also refer to Valéry's "all stories deepen in fables" from the aphorism "In the beginning was the fable." See my discussions of Valéry and the French hesitation towards the novel in chapters 1 and 4.

such details is rather ironically an indication of fictionality because this richness is in no way verifiable by history and other documentary narratives. This second observation lies close to Roland Barthes's critique of the naturalists' use of "effects of reality," *effets réels*, whose only use is to render the narrative more "real," but in fact end up as an implausible technique.[23]

It is therefore no wonder that verisimilitude is hard to obtain in literary texts. In the name of verisimilitude, naturalists end up packing the novel with information to such a degree that it flouts not just the Gricean contract of *relevance*, but also all standards of *verifiability*. Other narratives with a realist impetus have tried to circumvent these difficulties by explicitly asserting the story's truthfulness. It is remarkable, however, that even in such assertions lies a great deal of irony. Think, for instance, of Kurt Vonnegut's anti-war book *Slaughterhouse-Five*:

> All this happened, more or less. The war parts, anyway, are pretty much true. One guy I knew really was shot in Dresden for taking a teapot that wasn't his.
>
> KURT VONNEGUT, *Slaughterhouse-Five* (1969)

The peculiar thing about Vonnegut's opening is that by admitting that all parts of the narrative may not be entirely true, the narrator himself appears more real. Trustworthiness is also a feint, and the literary opening is the place where the text asserts its authority and its truth conditions. The opening is the place where we sense most dramatically the tension between the illusion of reality and the acceptance of that illusion.[24] Generally we can say that narratives cannot get everything right: they will either have to *pretend* to tell the truth about the actual world or *claim* to tell the truth about a fictional universe.[25] Therefore, rather ironically, the assertion of truthfulness at the outset of the story is typically an indication of fictionality.

Recall for instance the opening chapter of *Huckleberry Finn* (1884) where Huck describes *The Adventures of Tom Sawyer* and says "that book was made by Mr. Mark Twain and he told the truth, mainly."[26] Fiction in the realist tradition will attempt to downplay the acceptance of the

23 "Le Bruissement de la langue" in Roland Barthes, *Œuvres complètes*, 5 vols. (Paris: Seuil, 2002).

24 Cf. Victor Brombert's important suggestion in his important article on the opening signals in fiction. Brombert, "Opening Signals in Narrative," 501.

25 Cf. Eco, "Fictional Protocols," 120.

26 Mark Twain, *Adventures of Huckleberry Finn (Tom Sawyer's Comrade)* (New York: C.L. Webster and Company, 1885).

illusion—certainly Zola with his typically covert heterodiegetic narrator would never point directly to issues of the narrator's trustworthiness, but precisely herein lies also the frailty of naturalist fiction. However, Balzac's heterodiegetic, but more overt, narrator does in fact address this question in *Father Goriot*. A few lines into the novel the narrator exclaims: "Ah! once for all, this drama is neither a fiction nor a romance! *All is true*, so true, that everyone can discern the elements of the tragedy in his own house, perhaps in his own heart." Here the narrator in fact tries to undo the novelistic contract, which has already begun, and for instance denies some of the story's individuality. The story is supposedly so true that its elements can be recognized by everyone. Yet, the narrator's exclamation appears so radical that we cannot help thinking that it must be hyperbolic. The sudden reference "All is true" (written in English even in the original French text) furthermore adds an ironic touch. When we then realize that it is a reference to Shakespeare's *Henry VIII*, whose original subtitle was "All is true," we sense that the exclamation should perhaps not be taken literally. That is, *Father Goriot* is as "true" as a literary work can be.

In the earlier section on the trope of beginning, I showed that narrators who display hesitation in choosing between different ways of beginning tend to appear more trustworthy and their narrative appears more important. This technique, however, requires the narrator to be overt, and this is precisely what the realist instinct forbids. We could in fact, rather provocatively, say that the narrator's hesitation is a rather successful "reality effect." The problem is that the situations which a narrative describes are infinitely rich—a description would in principle have to be never-ending. Therefore, there is much insight in Joseph Conrad's summary of the author's role: "All the author appeals to is our credulity, the logic of the situations and the characters can be discussed *ad infinitum*."[27] Conrad reminds us of what his friend and co-writer Ford Madox Ford has already told us: "Life [does] not narrate."[28] Realism is naïve if it pretends that life does narrate, and it is hence caught in a dilemma.

FOURTH SIGNAL — THE INTRODUCTORY FORMULA: "ONCE UPON A TIME"

What I call an "introductory formula" is an opening line that sounds familiar to the reader and creates certain associations and expectations already from the outset. "It was a dark and stormy night" in English

27 Preface to Joseph Conrad, *The Nigger of the 'Narcissus'* (London: The New Review, 1897).

28 Ford, *Critical writings*, 73.

Charles Schulz's *Peanuts*: "It was a dark and stormy night".

literature is one, and "The marquise went out at five o'clock" in French literature is another. Despite often being subjected to ridicule and satirical pastiche, the impact of such sentences is remarkably long-lasting; introductory formulae establish a paradigm which goes far beyond the sentence itself.

"It was a dark and stormy night," which most people now know from Charles Schulz's *Peanuts*, was of course not originally penned by Snoopy. It stems from Edward Bulwer-Lytton—who has sometimes been called one of the nineteenth century's "greatest" bad writers.[29] Bulwer-Lytton's opening of *Paul Clifford* (1830) has been so parodied that San Jose State University now even holds an annual contest that challenges entrants to "compose the opening sentence to the worst of all possible novels."[30] The competition has received such intense attention that it has been covered by international media, and the winning entries have been published by Penguin in several volumes. This interest only proves that the opening sentence certainly holds a sway on authors and readers alike and establishes clear parameters of expectation. In chapter 4 I expound on the nature of such a paradigm of an opening line by looking in close detail at the French variant "La marquise sortit à cinq heures," originally proposed in scoff by Paul Valéry.

If every country has its own opening to scorn, the archetypal opening formula is of course "once upon a time there was..." One may associate this opening with the Brothers Grimm or with Hans Christian Andersen, where the familiar opening assists the child easily to tune into the story and the storytelling itself. It is therefore widely believed that to begin with "once upon a time" is a *convention*. In the following, however, I wish

29 Bulwer-Lytton is commonly described so in the The Bulwer-Lytton Fiction Contest.

30 The Bulwer-Lytton Fiction Contest, see www.bulwer-lytton.com. Edward George Bulwer-Lytton, *Paul Clifford* (New York: Printed by J. & J. Harper, 1830).

to argue that this opening is far more than a convention: it is a universal, cognitive structure.

In English the formula can be detected in writing back to at least 1380 (according to the *OED*), that is, back to the Middle English period. What is more striking is that it exists in all natural languages: "Había una vez" (Spanish), "Il était une fois" (French), "Hajitek ma jitek" (Algerian Arabic), "Mukashi mukashi" (Japanese), "Der var engang" (Danish). There are of course variations between the precise wording in the different languages, but the structure remains essentially the same. English requires temporal phrases to stand first in a sentence, so the formula begins "once upon a time," but in many other Indo-European languages, for instance in the Romance and Germanic languages, the first two words make up an *existential* structure through a personal pronoun and "to be" in past tense: "Il était une fois," "Había una vez," "Es war einmal," "Der var engang." In several Slavic languages the universal formula begins with an existential phrase, only to negate it immediately afterwards: "there was, there was not," which helps underscore the fictional status. In any case, the formula is omnipresent, both temporally and geographically: it is part of all languages and always has been.

Moreover, not only children's stories, but nearly all oral narratives, use this opening formula across cultures and languages. It may therefore be most correct to argue that the formula is *universal*, perhaps even a complex extension of our "universal grammar" in the Chomskian sense. For one thing, linguists have recently suggested that the opening formula is not just *conventional*, but *inherent* in children's own way of creating narratives.[31] Story "conventions" such as opening formulae occur more often among school pupils than preschoolers, which could suggest that it is an acquired convention. However, studies surprisingly suggest that children with weak text comprehension skills demonstrated comparable use of story "conventions" as other children, although the narratives they produce are weak both in terms of structural coherence and local cohesion, indicating that knowledge of story structure does not depend on reading comprehension skills. The idea of opening a story with a formula seems not to depend on our acquisition of general reading skills; rather than being a convention we acquire, it seems to be a structure already inherent in us from a certain age.

It is also this familiarity—or even universality—that allows the ar-

31 Kate Cain, "Text Comprehension and its Relation to Coherence and Cohesion in Children's Fictional Narratives," *British Journal of Developmental Psychology* 21 (2003).

chetype of an opening to serve as a *prototype* for a number of variations, when the narrative turns from the oral to the written domain. In his reflections on opening lines, the German author Martin Walser claims that the author is *less responsible* for the first line, no doubt because of the weight of archetypes or conventions.[32] Yet, his comment is misleading in another sense because the weight of our universal understanding of openings is precisely what allows the author to control the reader's expectations. The slightest deviation from the formula makes it easy for the author to adjust or stir the reader's expectations; we are often more surprised by deviations from something familiar than by something entirely unfamiliar. This circumstance can be employed by the author to a certain effect, often inducing some level of irony. In John Barth's "Frame Tale" from *Lost in the Funhouse*, the opening mode mocks the sway of the familiar opening by losing itself in the purely ritual situation:

> Once upon a time there was a story that began once upon a time...
> JOHN BARTH, *Frame Tale* (1969)

Barth's self-falsifying, "postmodern" Möbius-strip does not, however, work without previously established readerly expectations. If there were nothing to flout, it would not be interesting to try to flout it.[33]

In my view, the central element of the archetypal opening "Once upon a time..." is, however, not the temporal indication, but the existential construction: "Once upon a time, *there was*." It is noteworthy for instance that this existential component begins the formula in most other languages than English where the temporal phrase comes first—in French, for instance: "il était une fois." After all, all narratives, I believe, presuppose the precedence of the events to the time of the storytelling—this is simply part of the narrative "contract." Michael Frayn's opening of *A Very Private Life* (1969) could indeed be read as a *reductio ad absurdum* of the belief that precedence is not a defining condition of narrative:[34]

> Once upon a time there will be a little girl called Uncumber.
> MICHAEL FRAYN, *A Very Private Life* (1969)

32 "The author is less responsible for the first line than for any other subsequent line." Walser, "Erfahrungen mit ersten Sätzen oder Aller Anfang ist schwer," 155.

33 This is again a reference to the Gricean cooperative principle. In such openings there is a clear tension between authority and conventionality. The beginning asserts its own authority by evoking conventionality.

34 This reflection and example is due to H. Porter Abbott, "The Future of All Future Narratives," in *A Companion to Narrative Theory*, ed. James Phelan and Peter J. Rabinowitz (London: Blackwell Publishing, 2005).

The passive, existential construction—"there was"—is neutral in terms of narrator and therefore more central to the opening mode than the temporal indication because the existential construction allows the positing of a character or a place without evoking problems about the initial perspective. The characters or places are introduced, as it were, *ex nihilo*, as an almost cosmologically given, as discussed in chapter 1. The formula indicates a fictional universe, with an existential phrase introducing the reader to its ontology. The literary opening is almost always proleptic in the sense that it introduces characters and situations which will only later become well-rounded. Yet, contrary to cosmology, a book does not pretend that the universe it describes is created. Rather, the fictional universe is most effectively established when the universe appears to be entirely created and simply requires the reader to accept its textuality.

Many openings imitate more or less deliberately this archetypal existential construction, for instance this one by Diderot:

> Here were two men, who might be called the Pylades and Orestes of Bourbon
>
> DIDEROT, *The Two Friends of Bourbon* (1770)

Diderot's opening differs from the archetypal phrase by using "here" ("ici"), introducing a narratorial and temporal presence, which the existential phrase otherwise neglects.

Another example is Le Clézio's opening, which I discussed earlier:

> Once upon a little time, in the dog-days, there was a fellow sitting at an open window.
>
> LE CLÉZIO, *The Interrogation* (1963)

Here "a time" is transformed into "a little time," a surprising synthesis between two familiar expressions; the archetypal opening "Once upon a time" is combined with an infantile dedramatization of an event. This cosmological structure of the archetypal opening line may in fact echo in all openings, in one way or another, but as I shall show in my discussion of "perspectival abruptness" below, there is a large historical shift from the use of existential openings towards openings that employ proverbs that are abrupt in terms of perspective.

If these introductory formulae often introduce layers of irony to the tale, it is because the reference to a familiar component being transformed is in fact one of the principal ways in which a narrative can signal its fictionality to the reader. As already mentioned, we can generally say that all fictions will either *pretend* to tell the truth about the actual world or *claim* to tell the truth about a fictional universe.[35] These signals are strong indications that fictional narratives are conceptually more complex than so-called natural narratives—which we could call "documentary narratives"—typically history and personal journals.[36]

The familiarity of the introductory formula allows the reader to recognize the literary situation and the expectations to his or her interaction with the work. The formula is in this sense a device that permits the transition from one phase to another—as a two-headed "god" of beginnings—such as Janus, mentioned in my prologue—who allows the reader to slip from the extratextual world into the fictional world.

FIFTH SIGNAL — A USE OF PERSPECTIVAL ABRUPTNESS

All these four techniques (individuality, trope of beginning, irony, formula) point to the necessity for an opening to exhibit or establish the text's status as fiction. Opening signals serve to direct the reader's expectations. These various techniques lead to our final technique, the use of what I call perspectival abruptness. This technique requires a great deal of discussion due to both its complexity and importance. In many ways, this discussion is the most critical aspect of the opening because it also explains the significance of the other techniques, even the use of a recognizable introductory formula like "once upon a time." Moreover, I shall devote a lot of attention to the signals of perspectival abruptness because historical shifts in literature can be read very directly in the shifts in the use of these signals. In other words, with this entry into openings, we can obtain results pertaining to the general historical direction of literature. In order to clarify this, I shall begin by differentiating between an opening's temporal abruptness (traditionally called *in medias res*) and its perspectival abruptness.

35 Eco, "Fictional Protocols." Note also Nuttall's comment: "Literary beginnings group themselves with surprising clarity, either devoutly natural … or as proudly artificial," in Nuttall, *Openings*, 204.

36 I discuss these further below.

When Is an Opening "Abrupt"?: Understanding *in medias res* Correctly

IN MEDIAS RES VS. AB OVO

In chapter 1, I showed that the question whether a work begins "abruptly" or "orderly" has always been central to the discussion of literature and pointed out, for instance, that literary authorities throughout history—such as Horace, Ronsard, and Dante—have defended the principle of beginning *in medias res*. The question I now wish to ask is, however, whether an opening *in medias res* really is to be considered an "abrupt" opening, or whether, on the contrary, an opening *in medias res* rather supports the narrative's orderliness by providing symmetry and invoking an initial interest. This is an important question because we must understand the notion of *in medias res* correctly if we wish also to understand the abruptness of the modern novel. In order to resolve this question, I shall begin by considering the level of information provided by a narrative opening.

In classical rhetoric, it is common to distinguish between *rheme* and *theme*.[37] "Theme" applies to the information already known to the listener, while "rheme" applies to the information that is new to the listener.[38] It is an important rule for a speaker always to combine rheme and theme in such a way that the listener is provided new information only if it is based upon information that is already familiar.

The distinction between rheme and theme is useful for highlighting the historical shifts in the level of information provided at the beginning of the narration. The Greek and Latin epics may begin *in medias res*—as I discussed earlier—but they rely on the information that the readers already have of the historical or mythical events. Of course the *Iliad* does not have to begin with the twin eggs (cf. *ab ovo*) because the listeners are already familiar with the genealogy of the Greek heroes and gods as well as with the events that led to the Trojan War. In terms of information,

37 The distinction is also used in modern linguistics, where "theme" applies to the subject matter of the clause and "rheme" to the information that develops the "theme." Cf. Michael Cummings, "The Role of Theme and Rheme in Contrasting Methods of Organization in Texts," in *The Dynamics of Language Use: Functional and Contrastive Perspectives*, ed. Christopher Butler, Maria A. Gomez-Gonzalez, and Susana Ma. Doval Suarez, *Pragmatics & Beyond* (Amsterdam and Philadelphia: J. Benjamins Pub., 2005).

38 This distinction corresponds quite well to my initial distinction between a narrative's "informative" and "seductive" principles.

the opening *in medias res* did not signify abruptness, but on the contrary poetic harmony.[39]

The novel, however, from *Don Quixote* up until today, deals precisely with characters and situations that are not already familiar to the readers. It is therefore only natural that this relatively new genre will have to find its own correct balance between rheme and theme. Since the story is not familiar to the reader prior to the exposition, the beginning will have to guide the reader gently into the plot and will tend to introduce itself to the reader, for instance in terms of a teller-character.[40] In other words, the novel introduces an entirely unknown narrative and therefore it will have to confront the *ab ovo*, either by reverting to it or more radically by simply ignoring it.

The discrepancy between *ab ovo* and *in medias res* is significant precisely because, quoting Ford Madox Ford again, "life [does] not narrate."[41] When we hear a story, whether "real" or fictional, we always hear it through someone—and that narrator faces a number of decisions when presenting the events. The narrator is constantly mediating between the *story* (the "what?") and the *presentation* (the "how?"), or what the Russian formalists have defined as *fabula* and *sjuzét*. The narrator may choose to present the story A→B→C with a straightforward A→B→C (*ab ovo*) but may also opt for some flashback such as A→C→B or may altogether adopt the Horacian principle and open *in medias res* with B→C, which in practice often combines with some form of flashback, for instance B→A→C. The presentation may not open at the beginning; yet the fact that it does not may not undermine the idea of a beginning. By paraphrasing the filmmaker Jean-Luc Godard, we could say that every text has to have a beginning, middle, and end, but not necessarily in that order.[42] In chapter 1, I distinguished between the opening and the beginning of a text. What we see now is that the "opening" belongs to the level of the presentation, while the "beginning" belongs to the level of the story.

The opening may be the beginning (*ab ovo*), but it is not difficult to see

39 This idea is supported by Ronsard who allows only one exception to his general advice of opening midway: lyrical odes may begin "abruptly." Ronsard, "From a Brief on the Art of French Poetry." This suggests that the principle of the midway opening signifies poetic harmony, not abruptness.

40 This arrangement of rheme and theme is susceptible to historical fluctuations, and it is noteworthy that a number of linguists have pointed to significant formal differences between nineteenth- and twentieth-century literature, which may help us make our historical observations about modernism more concrete (see chapter 3).

41 Madox Ford, *Critical Writings*, 73.

42 "Every film has to have a beginning, middle, and end, but not necessarily in that order." "Godard only knows...," *The Observer*, 26 November 2000.

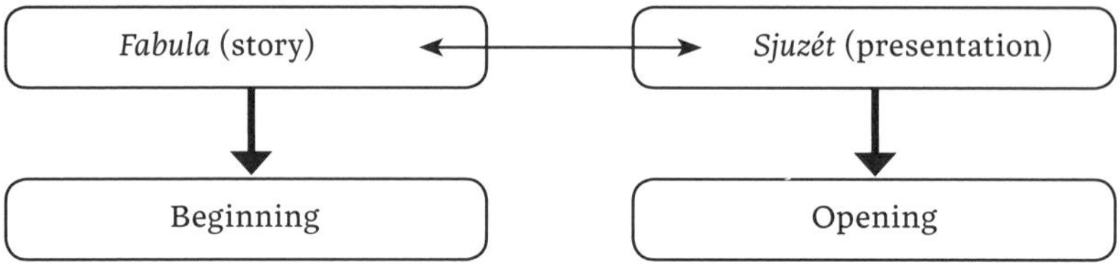

FIGURE 5. Opening and beginning belong to different levels of description

why it may not be. In fact, it becomes quite evident how the presentation's opening in practice rarely pretends to be the story's beginning. The story is "the continuum of events presupposing the total set of all conceivable details, that is, those that can be projected by the normal laws of the physical universe," as Seymour Chatman puts it.[43] The presentation need not mention all the events that lay chronologically before the opening of the presented "plot," for instance the birth of the characters, yet the *story* must take account even of these events. Even when the narration does not mention the characters' births, the presentation will rest on a presupposition, for instance, that they were all born. Literary art is hence an art of presuppositions: the ability to read fiction rests on the ability to make what Chatman has called "a narrative projection," which allows the reader on the basis of these presuppositions to fill in the narration's unavoidable gaps.

The problem lies in the beginning: how does the reader move from his or her reality into the field of fictionality with its necessity of "filling in the gaps"? The truth is that our perception of reality also relies on a multitude of presuppositions that we do not constantly verify. Yet the reader will have to accept the mode of transmission of the story, and the narrative's beginning becomes so crucial because the first words of narrative will mould the reader's imaginative presuppositions and prepare it for a certain mode of transmission.

This marks an important difference between the historical and the fictional mode. As the philosopher of history Arthur Danto makes clear, sentences that include beginnings cannot help being narrative sentences.[44] Hence, in history, the central structure is also a narrative, but a narrative of a rather orthodox nature. It is noteworthy, for instance,

43 Seymour Chatman, "Towards a Theory of Narrative," *New Literary History* 11 (1975): 303.

44 "Each of these terms, to be true of an event E-1, logically requires the occurrence of an event temporally later than E-1, and sentences making use of such terms in the obvious way will then be narrative sentences." Danto, *Analytical Philosophy of History*, 157.

that Claudius, an Roman emperor and historian, feels an urge to break with Homer's structure and rewrite the entire *Iliad ab ovo*. This, I believe, can be explained by history's *deductive* nature. A basic narrative, with a beginning, middle, and end, logically resembles a basic deduction:[45]

F(a)
y
∴ G(a)

"a" is in the state of "F," then "y" happens, causing "a" to be a state of "G." The explanandum, that is, what needs to be explained by a historical account, automatically defines the beginning as the state "F" before "a" changed into its present state, "G." Due to the powerful analogy between the narrative structure and the deductive argument and the overall importance of the explanandum in history, it is characteristic of historical accounts that what they select as the beginning of a narrative is already determined by the end.[46]

Therefore, a literary narrative can allow itself to be temporally "abrupt" in a way that historical accounts cannot. As Edmund Spenser notes in relation to the *Faerie Queene*: "Because the beginning of the whole work seemeth abrupte and as depending on other antecedents, it need that ye know ... [that] the Methode of a Poet historical is not such, as of an Historiographer."[47] A beginning will always rely on other antecedents, but in the case of a historical account, the beginning is determined by the end and this makes it less problematic to exclude a consideration of the antecedents of that beginning. In a literary context, however, where there is no deductive structure to respect, the beginning is not necessarily determined by the end. The beginning is therefore naturally abrupt in the sense that the antecedents seem always to come into consideration. For this reason, it becomes more natural and more harmonic to begin *in medias res*: to begin *ab ovo* becomes almost impossible since it involves a sort of infinite regress where one cannot ever exclude the consideration of further antecedents.

A novel is therefore caught between, on the one hand, the necessity to confront the antecedents through *ab ovo* and, on the other hand, the danger of slipping into an infinite regress when confronting those antecedents. In my view, this is the reason why literature is so enormously

45 Ibid., 251.
46 Ibid., 248.
47 "A Letter of the Authors," in *Edmund Spenser, The Faerie Queene*, ed. Thomas P. Roche and C. Patrick O'Donnell, The English Poets (New Haven, CT: Yale University Press, 1981).

focused on *in medias res*: it can be employed as a technique that forcibly ignores the antecedents and jumps right into the action.

Anthony Trollope is one novelist who dissects and reflects upon precisely this deceptive aspect of *in medias res*. He openly scorns the reader for wanting to jump "at once into the middle," when in fact it is not natural: "It is as though one were asked to eat boiled mutton after woodcocks, caviare, or macaroni cheese. I hold that it is better to have the boiled mutton first, if boiled mutton there must be..."[48]

With humorous reluctance, Trollope (or, rather, his implicit writer) accepts the reader's inclination: "I have always found ... that by rushing '*in medias res*' I was simply presenting the cart before the horse. But as readers like the cart the best, I will do it once again,—trying it only for a branch of my story,—and will endeavour to let as little as possible of the horse be seen afterwards."[49]

My claim is here that literary narratives are more powerful and credible precisely if "as little as possible of the horse is seen afterwards." A focus on the "cart" will eliminate the danger of the infinite regress of antecedents that I mentioned above. This is the reason why literary openings are often proleptic, thereby introducing characters and situations which only later become well-rounded. Contrary to the cosmologies that I discussed in chapter 1, a book should not pretend that the universe it describes is created. A natural beginning is actually, I argued, not the most reliable one. Rather, the fictional universe is most effectively established when the universe appears to be entirely created and simply requires the reader to accept its textuality. For this reason, I claim that prolepsis—and *in medias res*—makes it easier for the reader to embrace the fictionality. And this readerly acceptance of fictionality is the very key to the essence of fiction.

In other words, I have tried to explain how *in medias res* serves not just a purpose of "a bill of fare to the feast" or suspense in the name of literary "entertainment": it is logically easier for a narrative to be credible when it begins *in medias res*. Strictly speaking, in terms of communication, the abruptness of *in medias res* goes against the cooperative principle that Grice sets up (cf. page 1). Compared to other texts, literary narratives are therefore unique because they tend to object to their own linearity.[50]

48 Anthony Trollope, *Is He Popenjoy?* (New York: Elibron Classics, 2005 [1879]), 2.

49 Anthony Trollope, *The Duke's Children*, The Centenary Edition of Anthony Trollope's Palliser Novels (Oxford and New York: Oxford University Press, 1983 [1880]), 70.

50 Cf. Hillis Miller and his thoughts on the *refus du commencement* in J. Hillis Miller, *Ariadne's Thread: Story Lines* (New Haven and London: Yale University Press, 1992).

Retardatory patterns are very common, and a literary text may even be conceived of as a dynamic system of gaps, in the way that Wolfgang Iser and the hermeneutically inspired reader-response school do.

Perspectival Abruptness: The "Painful" Beginning

It is important to realize, however, that *in medias res* marks only one kind of opening abruptness. Strictly speaking, *in medias res* means no more than a certain chronological deformation at the beginning.[51] There is another way of rushing into the story, I claim, which has often been confused with *in medias res*: an abruptness which I call "perspectival," as opposed to the "temporal" abruptness of *in medias res*. This implies that abruptness is not just a question of chronology. An opening, which is temporally abrupt (*in medias res*), may be orderly in terms of perspective, and vice versa.

	Perspectivally abrupt	Perspectivally orderly
Temporally abrupt (*in medias res*)	Doubly abrupt	Abrupt in one aspect
Temporally orderly (*ab ovo*)	Abrupt in one aspect	Orderly

FIGURE 6. Abruptness is not just a question of chronology

For instance, an opening *in medias res* may be orderly in terms of perspective if, from the outset, it provides the reader with the narrative references and characterizations necessary for the reader to order the information at the opening. By contrast, an opening *in medias res* may be doubly abrupt if its narrative suspends the references and characterizations, thereby leaving the reader to construct both the chronology and the narrative perspective.[52]

51 Cf. Meir Sternberg, *Expositional Modes and Temporal Ordering in Fiction* (Baltimore, MD: Johns Hopkins University Press, 1978).

52 Cf. Gilles Philippe, "Les Démonstratifs et le statut énonciatif des textes de fiction.

The perspective at the beginning determines whether the beginning is easy for the reader to enter: will the reader move smoothly into the story or be held at a distance? In Ernest Hemingway's short story "The Snows of Kilimanjaro," the protagonist, an author, says of his opening that "the marvelous thing is that it's painless ... That's how you know when it starts."[53] But the question is precisely to what extent an opening really is "painless"? Let us consider, for instance, Hemingway's own opening to *The Old Man and the Sea* (1952):

> He was an old man who fished alone in a skiff in the Gulf Stream and he had gone eighty-four days now without taking a fish.
>
> ERNEST HEMINGWAY, *The Old Man and the Sea* (1952)

Although this sentence chronologically opens at the beginning, the reader nevertheless has a strong sense of abruptness. This is due to what I call perspectival abruptness. In this case, the pronoun "he" causes considerable confusion because the reader has not in any way been introduced to the protagonist.

The reason why the use of pronouns at the beginning is particularly noteworthy is that pronouns act as what linguists call "sequence signals."[54] This means that the use of pronouns will have to rely on something preceding them. It is a common literary technique to begin with the character, but in a literary opening, however, nothing precedes a pronoun, unless of course paratextual elements such as a title have helped introduce the main character, as in the case of the novels *Tristram Shandy* or *Germinie Lacerteux*. A personal pronoun that has not received a reference is perspectivally abrupt and must therefore immediately appeal to the reader's imaginative presuppositions. Perspectivally abrupt pronouns thus create a particular effect at the opening; the reader is not introduced to the character and entrance into the story will consequently have to pass through other routes, such as initial astonishment, which may either distance the reader or stimulate a curiosity that will involve the reader in the story. The higher level of anonymity involved in the use of a perspectivally abrupt pronoun may furthermore change the

L'exemple des ouvertures de roman," *Langue Française* 120 (1998). In this article Philippe points out that *in medias res* paradoxically lets us wait to obtain the reference or characterization.

53 Ernest Hemingway, *The Complete Short Stories of Ernest Hemingway* (New York: Simon & Schuster, 1987), 39.

54 Cf. Joseph M. Backus, "'He came into her line of vision walking backward': Nonsequential Sequence-Signals in Short Story Openings," *Language Learning* XV, no. 1/2 (1965).

reader's perception of the story's verisimilitude: characters may simply stay anonymous if we have no one to introduce them to us.

In this way, openings that contain perspectivally abrupt pronouns tend to be more "painful" for the reader (cf. Hemingway's mention of the painless beginning in "The Snows of Kilimanjaro"). This "pain," or initial disorientation, at the opening is precisely what helps pique the reader's curiosity—unless, of course, the "pain" is so intense that it ends up by throwing the reader off. Just as in the case of the temporal abruptness of *in medias res*, the perspectival abruptness gives the reader "a sense of immediacy or involvement."[55]

In this regard, we are back to the central element of the Horacian principle: it may be more "painless" to begin with a full presentation of the character. However, central to the generation of literary interest is the stragedy of withholding a part of the story, which will force the reader to rely either on prior knowledge or on a willingness to imagine the narrative situation through fictional presuppositions.

This shared feature of temporal and perspectival abruptness may be the reason why scholars have so far not distinguished clearly between temporal and perspectival abruptness, as I recommend we do. Joseph M. Backus does not define *in medias res* as a merely temporal phenomenon, yet he does not seem to recognize that abruptness is not just a consequence of *in medias res*, but a question of the position of subjectivity.[56] For instance, in a perspectivally abrupt opening, an unintroduced pronoun lacks that contextual information which Gricean conventions of conversation would otherwise require. Such an opening lacks precisely what pragmaticians call "deictic center," or even more appropriately *origo*. The kind of opening which becomes common with modernism openly disrespects *origo*. By letting our thoughts return to the distinction between beginning and origin from the previous chapter, we can conclude that modern openings tends to escape origin—and it does so by avoiding *origo*.

This difference in the position of subjectivity can be illustrated by the difference in narratological perspective between what the Austrian narratologist Franz Stanzel calls a "teller-character" and a "reflector-character."[57] The teller-character usually announces his or her presence in the opening sentences of the narrative and conveys to the reader the

55 This is Backus's description of *in medias res*, ibid., 69. Backus, however, fails to distinguish perspectival abruptness from *in media res*. See my discussion below.

56 Ibid. Gilles Philippe has seen this problem quite clearly in his short, technical article "Les Démonstratifs et le statut énonciatif des textes de fiction."

57 Stanzel, *A Theory of Narrative*, 146.

preliminary information necessary for the understanding of the story, that is to say, the teller-character deliberately leads the reader to the threshold of the story. The teller-character is in other words very conscious of the narrative setup that can lead the reader into the story. The reflector-character, on the contrary, is not conscious of the narrative situation; the story is not arranged by the character, but merely *reflected*. This reflection is more difficult for the reader to follow; the narrator does not assist the reader across the threshold of fiction and the literary opening will appear more abrupt or clipped. Readers are therefore left to establish the order of exposition themselves and rely on their own presuppositions.

Meanwhile, linguists as well as anthropologists have successfully isolated two perspectives: the emic and the etic. The etic is what is defined externally and extralinguistically whereas the emic is what is defined internally and structurally.[58] This well-established distinction indicates that Stanzel's division into teller-character and reflector-character is a viable one also in a narrative context: the perspective of the teller-character is "etic," involving narrative preliminaries, an explicit introduction, and an exposition that is oriented towards the reader. The reflector-character, on the other hand, is "emic," resulting in an abrupt or clipped opening that tends to rest on the reader's presuppositions and in which the reader will have to deduce the exposition.[59]

The considerations will spell out the central schism between perspectivally abrupt and perspectivally orderly expositions in more detail:

From this schism it also becomes apparent that the traditional distinction between heterodiegetic and homodiegetic narrations with which I began the chapter is not sufficient either. Two heterodiegetic narrations can be fundamentally different if one is based on a teller-character and the other is based on a reflector-character.

In order to illustrate this fundamental difference between two kinds of openings further—the externally based narrative relying on a teller-character and the internally based narrative relying on a reflector-char-

58 See for instance Roland Harweg, *Pronomina und Textkonstitution* (Munich: Wilhelm Fink Verlag, 1968).

59 Vance Smith has pointed out that medieval texts manage to formulate a difference between internal and external beginnings, which elucidates the schism between emic and etic. For more details, see Smith, *The Book of the Incipit*, 220. This distinction has since been neglected and only recently renewed by the modern literary theorist Pierre Macherey's thoughts on literary production, cf. Pierre Macherey, *Pour une théorie de la production littéraire*, Théorie 4 (Paris: F. Maspero, 1966). See also Harweg, *Pronomina und Textkonstitution*. Gérard Genette also evokes the difference between the emic and etic in chapter 11 of his *Nouveau discours du récit*.

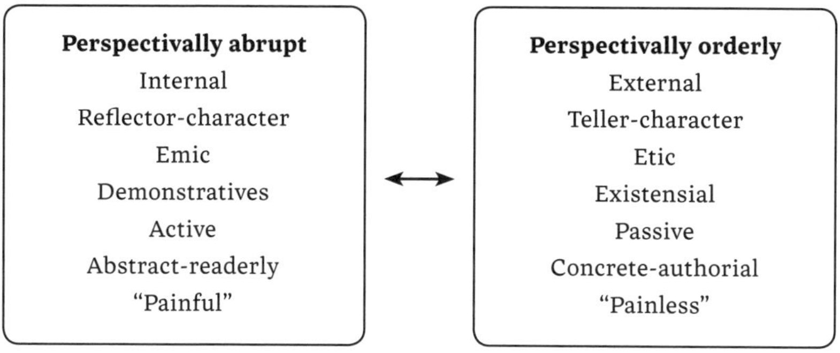

FIGURE 7. The central schism in perspectives

acter—I will now focus on the use of two personal pronouns at the beginning of novels; the first-person pronoun "I" and the third-person pronoun "he." The two pronouns do of course naturally create two very different presentations: one will be a first-person narrative, the other a third-person narrative. But there is a difference in information attached to the pronouns: does the reader have enough information to identify the character—or is the effect that of deliberate confusion? Moreover, to what extent could we trace a historical shift in the information provided at the beginning?

For these questions we can refer to work done by the German linguist Georg Bossong, who has statistically demonstrated a historical shift from what he calls "canonical" to "acanonical" openings. Canonical openings use an existential claim, which serves to introduce a place or character—for instance, "there was a man," etc. (canonical openings therefore implicitly evoke "once upon a time" because of its existential claim). Acanonical openings, on the other hand, rely on a subject that is implicitly presupposed, for instance Hans Henny Jahnn's *Perrudja* which opens "Perrudja ate his evening meal." Jahnn's title, *Perrudja,* does of course help to introduce the scene, but otherwise the scene is entirely unknown to the reader, who has no temporal or spatial guidance; the only thing the reader knows is that Perrudja is probably the name of the story's protagonist. Bossong points out that the use of proper names is far more common in the nineteenth century than for instance in the fifteenth or sixteenth centuries. This shift is in other words a change in the verb/subject priority; with the canonical opening the verb is used to introduce the subject, whereas the acanonical opening will use a proper name that precedes the verb. In the nineteenth century, the emphasis is in other words on the subject whose proper name is introduced without much ado. In fact it is striking how many novels of the nineteenth century carry a proper name in its title—think of *Germinie Lacerteux* by the Goncourts and the novels by Balzac.

Although emerging in the nineteenth century, the opening with a proper name (the proprial opening) also remains popular amongst naturalists and the twentieth-century avant-garde. A quick, indicative list of authors using the proprial opening includes Trollope, George Eliot, Conrad, Henry James, Theodore Dreiser, Jahnn, Joyce, Kafka, Achebe, and Woolf.

The attraction of the proprial opening is evident if we remember John Stuart Mill's definition of a proper name: A proper name shows us "what thing it is that we are talking about, but [does not tell] anything about it."[60] In other words, proper names are in Mill's view not connotative, but denotative.[61] The proper name therefore lives perfectly up to the two principles of literary openings sketched at the beginning of this chapter: the informative and the seductive principles. The proper name both *informs us*, by *showing* someone, and *withholds information*, by *not telling us* anything about the person in question.[62]

Twentieth-century literature continues this movement away from the existential claims and makes the subject even more implicitly presupposed. It is a move from the external to the internal; the focalization, as the narratologists call it, becomes internal.[63] The first-person narrative may be less common in the twentieth century, but there is nevertheless a considerable innovation in the genre due to this perspectivally abrupt use of the first-person pronoun, which leaves the reader without a proper introduction to the narrator. This also emphasizes the twentieth-century concern with the distinction between author and persona.[64]

60 John Stuart Mill, *System of Logic; Ratiocinative and Inductive* (New York: Elibron Classics, 2005), 1. ii. 5.

61 In novels, certain proper names do, however, often become deliberately connotative, for instance in the novels of Dickens and in Flaubert's *Madame Bovary*.

62 Given their pseudo-informative nature, proper names have within analytic philosophy been called "rigid designators." In *Naming and Necessity*, Kripke has explained that a proper name derives its (denotative) meaning from a series of actions which can be causally traced back to an initial "baptism." Saul A. Kripke, *Naming and Necessity* (Cambridge, MA: Harvard University Press, 1980). In the case of fiction, the question as to who has made this "baptism" remains even more complex. From the point of view of the reader, the baptism seems implausible.

63 Genette mentions a change in external to internal focalization in the nineteenth century. "It is common in literary texts from before the twentieth century that the narrative is presented as the transcription of an oral narrative that the narrator heard." Gérard Genette, "Discours du récit," in *Figures III* (Paris: Seuil, 1972), 207–8.

64 It is, for instance, important to contrast openings of first-person narratives like

Type:	Existential opening	Proper name (proprial opening)	Pronominal opening
Period:	Fifteenth–sixteenth century	Nineteenth century	Twentieth century
Example:	"There was..."	"Madame Vauquer..." (Balzac)	"He was an old man who..." (Hemingway)

FIGURE 8. Historical transition in openings

In the case of third-person narratives, the move to the perspectivally abrupt introduction of a subject appears even more radical. When a pronoun like "he" or "she" is used in the opening without further introduction, it creates a very special effect on the reader, as in the following examples:

> She waited, Kate Croy, for her father to come in, but he kept her unconsciously, and there were moments at which she showed herself, in the glass over the mantel, a face positively pale with the irritation that had brought her to the point of going away without the sight of him.
>
> HENRY JAMES, *The Wings of the Dove* (1902)

> As a junior of exceptional promise, he had been sent to Egypt for a year in order to improve his Arabic and found himself attached to the High Commission as a sort of scribe to await his first diplomatic posting.
>
> LAWRENCE DURRELL, *Mountolive* (1958)

Melville's "Call me Ishmael" with Frisch's "I'm not Stiller" and Proust, "For a long time I used to go to bed early." Note also Backus's reflection: "While twentieth-century writers use the 'I' less often than earlier ones, they tend to be more concerned with the distinction between author and persona." Backus, "'He came into her line of vision walking backward'," 73. The shift to proper names and then to non-sequence indicates a surge in individuality followed by a crisis in subjectivity as I have previously discussed in my two articles: Niels Buch-Jepsen, "What Happened to the Author? Modernist Impersonality and Authorial Selfhood," in *From Homer to Hypertext: Studies in Narrative, Literature and Media*, ed. Hans Balling and Anders Klinkby Madsen (Odense: University Press of Southern Denmark, 2002); Niels Buch-Jepsen, "Le Nom propre et le propre auteur—qu'est-ce qu'une fonction-auteur?," in *Une histoire de la fonction-auteur est-elle possible?*, ed. Nicole Jacques-Lefévre (Saint-Etienne: Publications de l'Université de Saint-Etienne, 2001). If the story begins with a first-person pronoun that introduced a third-person pronoun in a perspectivally abrupt fashion then the reader's feeling is that the speaker is withholding information.

> He was an old man who fished alone in a skiff in the Gulf Stream and he had gone eighty-four days now without taking a fish.
>
> HEMINGWAY, *The Old Man and the Sea* (1958)

This mode of opening is more radical than one may initially imagine. Let us compare the openings of one of Thomas Mann's early novels, *The Magic Mountain* (1924), and one of his later ones, *The Tables of the Law* (1943):

> An ordinary young man was on his way from his hometown of Hamburg to Davos-Platz in the canton of Graubünden. It was the height of summer, and he planned to stay for three weeks.
>
> THOMAS MANN, *The Magic Mountain* (1924)

> His birth was irregular, and so he passionately loved regularity, the inviolable, commandment and taboo.
>
> THOMAS MANN, *The Tables of the Law* (1943)

The first opening is not an existential phrase, but the indefinite subject makes the sentence function almost as if it were: logicians would render Mann's sentence as an existential claim followed by a description: "there is a young man and that young man traveled etc." Notice that the subsequent naming of that subject becomes very easy: 1) there is a man, 2) that man traveled etc., 3) that man was called x. The naming becomes easy because the existential claim at the beginning makes the reader aware of the teller-character who first "invents" the character by claiming his existence and therefore subsequently naming him.

In Mann's second opening things are more complicated: "His" is perspectivally abrupt and without an existential claim we almost feel an inclination to ask "who?," especially since we are told about his very birth. We get the impression that the narrator is either deliberately withholding information or is building on information that readers are supposed already to know. Even in this opening that mentions a birth, there is no existential claim; the existence of the main character is taken for granted even before the novel begins. We notice that the lack of existential claims also makes the naming far more awkward; why would it ever be necessary to introduce the name if the narrator presupposes (if misinformed about the reader's knowledge) or wants to presuppose (that is, if the narrator is "unreliable" as the literary term goes) that the reader knows the character? "His birth was chaotic. His name was x" is awkward whereas "there was a man whose birth was chaotic. His name was x" is acceptable. The opening of *The Tables of the Law* is therefore particularly frustrating; Mann uses the mention of a birth as the natural beginning of a story and it begins with an immediate awkwardness that prevents even the naming of the character whose birth is referred to.

To note the use of these perspectivally abrupt pronouns at the opening of a novel becomes illuminating in relation to literary history. Perspectivally abrupt pronouns in the first lines were very rare before 1880, but were then increasingly used by two very different kinds of authors. The naturalists occasionally use the perspectivally abrupt pronouns, possibly as an indication that "life" does not introduce the characters. Presumably the desired effect would not primarily be to stimulate the reader's curiosity, but to enhance a feeling of verisimilitude; there is no special indication of a beginning. However, the pioneer in the use of perspectival abruptness is Henry James. His motivations would presumably be altogether different from that of the naturalists. Perspectival abruptness would to him rather serve as a psychological realism that could seize the reader. In both cases, however, the "painful" opening tends to serve in the name of realism, and this is important to remember when we notice in which historical period the use of the pronominal openings culminates. Backus concludes on the basis of statistical material that apart from Henry James and some little-known authors, the majority of authors using this opening strategy emerged around 1925, culminating around 1945. Backus singles out in particular Ernest Hemingway, whose openings we have already discussed, as the master and culmination of the pronominal opening. Moreover, the pronominal opening is more common when part of a first-person narrative such as Conrad's *Chance*:

> I believe he had seen us out of the window coming off to dine in the dignity of a fourteen-ton yawl belonging to Marlow my host and skipper.
>
> JOSEPH CONRAD, *Chance* (1913)

The central distinction when it comes to the perspectivally abrupt is that enunciative continuation is not just referential continuation.

Thus, the twentieth-century novel tends to move away from the use of the proper name in its opening, which, despite various exceptions, generally characterized the nineteenth-century novels. Instead it moves towards a wider use of a personal pronoun at the beginning. When at the same time we think of the twentieth-century French literary avant-garde's vision of establishing an art entirely without proper names,[65] we may

65 Barthes talks of a "novel without proper names" and Valéry of a "literary history be able to explain the disappearance of proper names at the beginning of novels as no less than a concrete symptom of the crisis of humanist subjectivity that dominated twentieth-century intellectual life.[66] With a personal pronoun, focus shifts from the individuality and social position of the character to the function of the persona in the overall construction.

What is more, the use of the perspectivally abrupt pronoun, especially in third-person, draws further attention to the novel's fictionality. We can fairly easily accept an opening that contains a proper name like "Mr. Hansen got up from the table" or even one containing a perspectivally abrupt first-person pronoun: "I got up from the table." The perspectivally abrupt third-person pronoun seems rather different: "He got up from the table." A novel may of course begin like that, but there is a fundamental difference. The first two constructions make it possible for the reader to locate a teller-character who could begin a report or a journal; in fact, these two openings could be non-fictional as well as fictional, and this analogy with the non-fictional makes the opening less conspicuous. I could for that matter begin an insurance claim with "I got up from the table," just as the insurance company could begin their report with "Mr. Smith got up from the table." But what about "He got up from the table"? Opening a text with a perspectivally abrupt third-person pronoun does simply not seem possible in a non-fictional text; the reader cannot locate a teller-character who presents the story. Left with only a reflector-character, no analogy to non-fictional texts can be found and the opening will appear abrupt.

This leads to a somewhat surprising conclusion. Far from being confined to fictional texts, a teller-character can be central even to non-fictional texts; in fact, the naturalness of an opening with a teller-character stems precisely from the possibility that the text could be non-fictional. As a result, we must conclude that the teller-character may be more natural, but less literary, whereas the reflector-character is less natural, but more literary: texts dominated by a reflector-character can only be fictional.

When the twentieth-century novel tends to employ a perspectivally abrupt opening, it is therefore not just a question of reformulating subjectivism, but of drawing further attention to the novel's own literariness. The pronominal opening is abrupt because the reader is left with no

without proper names." Roland Barthes, *Roland Barthes par Roland Barthes* (Paris: Seuil, 1975), 110. For a discussion of Valéry on this stand, see chapter 4.

66 See note 64 on page 84 with references to my two articles on subjectivism in the twentieth century. This issue will be discusssed in more detail in the next chapter.

mediator between his own world and the world of the text in front of him; something is immediately presupposed and the reader will have to activate his or her narrative imagination in a more radical fashion.

Although the narrative incipit prior to the twentieth century in this way could be said to be more "natural," we notice that its naturalness most often stems from the presence of a teller-character who presents the story through either an existential claim ("There was a man ...") or, as was later the tendency, through a proper name such as Zola's typical openings, for instance:

> Claude passed by the town hall
> ZOLA, *The Work* (1885)

By introducing the character in this way, this type of opening will therefore be different from the body of the text as the teller-character initiates the story for the reader, and we could therefore say that eighteenth- and nineteenth-century openings despite their "naturalness" in fact formally stand out from the rest of the text.[67] Although we may tend to think of twentieth-century openings as more "radical," formally they differentiate themselves *less* from the rest of the text. Twentieth-century openings increasingly open with, as we have seen, perspectivally abrupt pronouns or with direct discourse (as Rebecca West, *The Return of the Soldier*, mentioned earlier) and the reader will therefore be less able to tell formally whether the extract with which the novel opens is in fact an opening. In a sense, it is not that the twentieth-century opening is abrupt in itself; rather, the reader will *experience* it as abrupt precisely because it does not stand out from the rest of the text.

The paradoxical observation is that the more an opening looks like the rest of the text, the more likely it will stand out from other openings; such an opening will naturally rely less on certain conventional modes of opening, allowing more room for differentiation. If the modern author could be said to be more "anxious" about the opening it may be due to precisely this higher possibility of differentiation. German author Hans Henny Jahnn's concern with the opening sentence does, in any case, seem typical: "I had definitely rewritten the first sentence of *Perrudja* at least

67 It therefore seems incorrect when Aldo Nemesio argues that the narrative incipit in eighteenth- and nineteenth-century novels does not present specific characteristics capable of differentiating it from the body of the text. Aldo Nemesio, "La definizione dell'Incipit," *Annali d'Italianistica* 18 (2000). Nemesio's conclusion that the focus of research for that reason should not be the text itself but the reader's response to reading the initial words therefore also seems flawed.

50 times and endlessly turned it back and forth, until it simply went: 'Perrudja ate his evening meal'."[68] As fewer conventions guide the opening of the novel, they relate to each other in different ways than before. In the presence of certain formulaic modes of opening, any particular opening will relate not so much to other texts as to certain generic conventions of opening. When these formulaic modes of opening lose their importance, the opening will relate less to the conventions and more to specific existing texts which the opening positions itself against. This difference is central to our conception of intertextuality, which will be discussed in chapter 3 and illustrated in chapter 4.

The striking thing about open beginnings is that they tend to generate open endings, in the sense that they contain little resolution. Stanzel has shown that structurally speaking a narrative opening with a reflector-character will generally lead to an open ending.[69] When no particular direction is adopted from the outset, the modalities of a possible resolution are not clearly defined. It is in other words the beginning that sets out the criteria for the possible later *dénouement*. If a beginning fails to set these criteria, it is not clear that they will ever be set out. This observation may explain the importance that Aristotle attaches to finding the correct starting point because the middle and end will simply follow from the beginning.[70] When modern writers deliberately try to evade the generic conventions of the novelistic opening, they do so with the conviction that this will change the novel's overall rhetorical structure; thus a writer like Claude Simon therefore willingly accepts his critics' claim that his novels have "neither a beginning nor an end."[71] Consequently the sense of plot tends to break down in certain novels; in turn, a stronger reliance on the consciousness of the reader will secure a higher degree of fictionality, which will preserve the work's narrative quality.[72] Again, fictionality can be seen as the defining quality of the twentieth-century novel and we can repeat what Quentin Anderson has famously said about Henry James, who was, we will remember, one of the first to use perspectivally abrupt pronouns at the novel's opening: "The reader's initial assumptions are quite as much the matter of his story as the situation itself."[73]

68 Walter Muschg, *Gespräche mit Hans Henny Jahnn* (Frankfurt am Main: Europäische Verlagsanstalt, 1967), 123.

69 Stanzel, *A Theory of Narrative*, 163.

70 Aristotle, *Poetics*, 96.

71 Simon, "Discours à Stockholm."

72 This is a point also made by Monika Fludernik in her *Towards a 'Natural' Narratology* (London: Routledge, 1996). Contrast also with Brooks, *Reading for the Plot*.

73 Henry James, *Selected Short Stories; Edited with an Introd. by Quentin Anderson*, Rine-

Towards the Conclusion: The Opening as the Key to the Work

Perspectival abruptness makes the opening more like the rest of the text; and it thereby appears more "arbitrary"—more "open." And when an opening looks more like the rest of the text, it may look more distinct from other openings, thus losing some of its conventional affinity with other openings. In making the opening more "open" by using perspectival abruptness, the opening also tends to become more inscrutable and more individual.

The opening therefore becomes doubly important when modern novels employ perspectival abruptness. First, the opening becomes more distinct in itself by being progressively unleashed from the conventions of openings and, second, it increasingly becomes a key to the whole work as such. The opening determines the parameters of reading, and the opening page becomes a key to the work that will unfold in the light of it. This is what authors have increasingly become aware of since Theodor Fontane noted in 1880, at the brink of the naturalistic period, that "the first chapter is always what is most important and in the first chapter it is the first page. ... The right structure [Aufbau] always puts the germ of the whole in the first page."[74] Just like in Fontane's novels, even those clinging on to conventions know that the conventions have broken down.

This tendency is further enforced in the twentieth century. A central theorist like Serge Doubrovsky refers to the first sentence of Proust's *In Search of Lost Time* as a "generator" of the work through the interplay between the novel's two first persons (what in semiotics is called "referent" and "reference").[75] The German novelist Martin Walser has written an entire essay about the first sentence in which he stresses its pivotal importance to the work: "The entire novel is nothing but a development from the [first] sentence. In this sense, the novel does not progress. It consists of variations of the opening."[76] The parameters of the novel, Walser claims, are determined by the opening: "The novel is always a game, but the first sentence adamantly determines how the game is to be played."[77]

hart Editions, 31 (New York: Rinehart, 1950).

74 Fontane cited in Gunter H. Hertling, *Theodor Fontanes Irrungen, Wirrungen, Die 'Erste Seite' als Schlüssel zum Werk* (Frankfurt am Main: Peter Lang, 1985), 7.

75 Serge Doubrovsky, *La Place de la madeleine. Ecriture et fantasme chez Proust* (Paris: Mercure de France, 1974).

76 Walser, "Erfahrungen mit ersten Sätzen oder Aller Anfang ist schwer," 159.

77 Ibid., 162.

The tendency is that each text determines its own parameters instead of resting on already existing conventions. For this reason the next chapter looks more closely at conventions vs. intertextuality.

Moreover, the fact that the beginning is increasingly a "key" to the work is further supported by beginnings tending to lead to open endings, as discussed earlier. As Aragon puts it: "A path does not necessarily have an end; it could fade away, it fades away. It necessarily has a beginning."[78] With this in mind, it appears that beginnings have historically become increasingly more important, and grown more important than endings. In turning Kermode's title on its head, I propose that rather than "a sense of an ending" we need "a sense of a beginning." I shall expand upon my position in relation to Kermode in the next chapter on intertextuality and historization.

Conclusion: Is Literature "Cooperative"?

At the beginning of this chapter, I evoked Grice's cooperative principle, which posits that in normal communication our interaction is based on a mutual agreement that the interlocutors are cooperating. As Grice himself was aware, this principle does not hold in literature, but nevertheless the principle is illustrative of many of the mechanisms that take place in literature. Literature is also cooperative, but in a different sense because it serves a different purpose. For one thing, literary communication is not measured according to relevance in the same way as ordinary communication. In fact, it will often blatantly flout the cooperative principle of normal communication. On the basis of the discussion in this chapter, it therefore appears that there is a higher-level "literary cooperative principle" with its own maxims, which I have established via my investigation into the taxonomy of openings:

1. It is cooperative to signal a narrative's fictionality. The sooner this is done, the sooner a narrative can be allowed to flout the general cooperative principle of communication.
2. An opening is as informative "as necessary," but not "too informative"
3. Narrative events precede us

78 Aragon, *Les Incipit*, 90.

4 Abruptness is to be expected in narrative
5 Narrative is based on postulated existence (cf. Kate Cain)
6 There is a narrator
7 The story is individual
8 Beginning is artificial (includes irony)
9 Narration is aware that truth condition is somewhat different (realism)
10 The verisimilitude of narratives depends on the narrator's credibility, not reality effects
11 Truth is not referential, but relational and conventional

We must not understand "truth" in literature as a property of the single literary sentence. In the case of natural languages, the analytic philosopher David Lewis has shown that "truth" is not a property of sentences, but rather consists of relations between sentences and language as a whole.[79] The use of language therefore rests on conventions of truthfulness and trust amongst members of the population. This is relevant to our understanding of literature as well. We can treat literature as a language in itself with its own conventions based on "trust." We must therefore not look for referentiality of literary sentences because this will lead us to think that there is no such thing as truth in literature.[80]

79 David K. Lewis, *Convention: A Philosophical Study* (Cambridge, MA: Harvard University Press, 1969).

80 Which may lead some to end up in notions of pure textuality, as poststructuralism has sometimes been accused of expounding.

CHAPTER 3

Beginnings and Modernity: A History of Openings

Sure, I tell myself, it'll all be over soon
CÉLINE, the opening of *North*

Opening vs. Endings

In the prologue, I outlined the tendency in Anglo-American literary criticism to focus on endings rather than openings. In this chapter I relate this tendency specifically to considerations of literary modernism and its definition. As I endeavor to show, modernism can be characterized by its tendency to define itself by means of averting from "static" notions like origins and traditions in favor of "dynamic" notions like beginnings and originality. Moreover, in this chapter on modernism I wish to illustrate that one's conception of beginnings in many ways defines one's general literary outlook as well as one's conception of literary history. While doing so, I wish to retain a skeptical attitude towards what I call the "clichés of modernism." That is to say, I would like to isolate the genuine *formal* traits of modernism from the flourishing, preconceived, and "ideological" ideas of what modernism is or is not. In order to do so, I point out that the methodology of literary criticism in its very outlook is largely influenced by literature itself; a certain kind of criticism can also in itself be called "modernist." And if we look at literature through the lens of a modernist criticism, all literary texts will tend to look modernist—just as the lens of postmodernist criticism will tend to render all literary texts postmodernist.

I begin by discussing the notion of death and the influence that this notion has had both on beginnings and on critics who have dealt with the central schism between openings and endings. In particular, I discuss two seminal works: Peter Brooks's *Reading for the Plot* and Frank Kermode's *The Sense of an Ending*. As can be seen simply from the title of my book, "The Sense of a Beginning," Kermode's book has been a particularly central text in my study. Since I deliberately turn Kermode's central phrase on its head by claiming that the opening is (the) key to the work, it would only be natural to position this book in relation to Kermode's thoughts—and I do this by looking at the characteristics of modernism in terms of openings. In particular I involve the structuralist thinking of Roland Barthes and Julia Kristeva and the poetics of Aragon and Martin Walser as well as use literary examples from Conrad and other writers. On the basis of these observations I reach a notion of "modernist criticism," with which I turn to another seminal book, Edward Said's *Beginnings*. Since Said's book does not provide an insight into concrete literary openings, I focus instead on the notions that Said's book expresses at the critical level. Inevitably the chapter touches on the notions of intertextuality and influence, which inspired the structuralist thinking on which Said's book rests.

Death and the Desire for Finality

If, as my previous chapters have shown, *beginnings* are either ironically natural ("I am born," etc.) or wholly artificial ("The marquise went out at five o'clock"), *endings* may, at least at first, seem to possess a different solidity. It is characteristic that the critics and novelists who have been preoccupied with endings point to death as a human condition that creates a narrative desire for finality. For instance, Joseph Conrad, in his famous essay on Henry James, writes:

> [Conventional novelistic] solutions are legitimate inasmuch as they satisfy the desire for finality, for which our hearts yearn, with a longing greater than the longing for the loaves and the fishes of this earth. Perhaps the only true desire of mankind, coming thus to light in its hours of leisure, is to be set at rest.[1]

1 Joseph Conrad, "Henry James: An Appreciation," in *Notes on Life and Letters* (London: Dent, 1924 [1905]), 18–19.

In this passage, Conrad insinuates that a novel's ending not just mimics death, but reflects a universal longing for death both in the conception and reception of the literary work. The literary reflection of death is in other words not just formal or structural, but appears to be subordinated to non-literary patterns in the writer or reader. If so, our conception of a novelistic ending would be double: while reading, we long for the ending in order to be set at rest. Yet, it is important that this desire for finality is present *from the outset* and directs our reading. In fact, the story's finality satisfies a desire that even precedes the story itself, a desire that only came to be directed by the story.

I believe that this is the observation that has led a number of prominent literary scholars to proclaim that the story always points towards its own ending, its own death—that the entire story depends on its ending. The classic formulation of this view is Walter Benjamin's famous words from "The Storyteller": "Death is the sanction of everything the storyteller can tell. He has borrowed his authority from death."[2] In his *Reading for the Plot,* Peter Brooks uses Benjamin when exclaiming that "the telling is always *in terms* of the impending end."[3] According to this view, finality is what lends authority to the story. The ending is therefore at all times present in our interaction with the text:

> We read the incidents of narration as "promises and annunciations" of final coherence, that metaphor that may be reached through the chain of metonymies: across the bulk of the as yet unread middle pages, the end calls to the beginning, transforms and enhances it.[4]

The ending is therefore precisely what establishes the semantic situation of the reading: "The revelation of meaning ... occurs when the narrative sentence reaches full predication."[5] Brooks's method of reading could therefore be characterized by what he calls "anticipation of retrospection,"[6] a method which bears a striking resemblance to Kermode's, as will be described below. Both Brooks and Kermode describe our reading as a recursive method by which the end is constantly projected when reading. The very beginning points to the ending.

2 Walter Benjamin, "The Storyteller," in *Theory of the Movel: A Historical Approach*, ed. Michael McKeon (Baltimore, MD: Johns Hopkins University Press, 2000), 84.

3 Brooks, *Reading for the Plot,* 52.

4 Ibid., 93–94.

5 Ibid., 20.

6 Ibid., 23.

I hold that in many ways Brooks's and Kermode's perspectives are not as innovative as they may seem, since they are in fact on a par with Aristotle's classic notion of dramatic harmony. According to Aristotle, the ending makes "possible a satisfying consonance with the origins and with the middle," thereby giving "meaning to lives and to poems."[7] Brooks's and Kermode's recursive method differs from Aristotle, however, by seeing the ending as a projection, whose semantic effectiveness may not stem from the text alone. According to Kermode, we as readers create "our own sense of an ending" by making "considerable imaginative investments in coherent patterns."[8] As the critic Yellowlees Douglas puts it: "Like Brooks's 'anticipation of retrospection', Kermode's act of reading is endlessly recursive, continually building a structure that presupposes an ending that in turn modifies the building of the structure."[9] This means that the actual ending of a text may in fact end up annulling the reader's predictions of the outcome.

Faced with this insight, it may be beneficial to analyze the reader's prejudiced expectations more systematically. This has been done for instance by the theorist Richard Ohmann, who tried to erect the prejudiced expectations of the ordinary reader into rules based on analytical philosopher J. L. Austin's ideas of illocutionary acts.[10] Yet, it is important to realize that this potential annulment of narrative predictions in no way constitutes a breach of the narrative model. On the contrary, according to Kermode it is a fundamental condition of literature that predictions and expectations can be invalidated—very much in the way that my previous chapter described the mechanisms of the "cooperative principle" in literature and how literature often failed to "cooperate." On this point I concur with Kermode, but I hope that my introduction of the cooperative principle into the literary debate would further illustrate that a lack of closure is in reality not a breach of the literary "contract."

However, my position on literary texts differs from that of Kermode and Brooks as I object to their recursive method in three ways:

1. It appears plausible that for a great number of novels, we can rely on our projection of the ending. Yet, Kermode and Brooks do not take into

7 Aristotle quoted in Jane Yellowlees Douglas, *The End of Books—Or Books without End? Reading Interactive Narratives* (Ann Arbor: University of Michigan Press, 2000), 91.

8 Kermode quoted in Douglas, *The End of Books*, 92.

9 Ibid.

10 Richard Ohmann, "Speech, Action, and Style," in *Literary Style: A Symposium*, ed. Seymour Chatman (New York: Oxford University Press, 1971).

consideration that open beginnings tend to create open endings, which become inconceivable to project. There would therefore clearly be works whose openings serve as the key itself. If beginnings cannot be considered as a universal exegetic tool, why should endings?

2. Is the recursive method universal—or is it tied to particular texts and periods, say, modern texts? Kermode is not quite clear on this point, but in different passages, he seems to insinuate that his method is specially applicable to modern, more "self-reflexive" works:

> Readings of such books are necessarily recursive. The best reader in the world cannot get much out of the beginning of *The Good Soldier*, or of *The Sound and the Fury*, unless he goes back to it and codes it in accordance with later discoveries. So good reading, even first reading, is recursive and can be required to be so in a high degree. The more self-reflexive the text, the more recursion is necessary and the harder it is to code information unequivocally.[11]

By making such claims about twentieth-century literary works, Kermode is aligned with a number of theorists who see recursion as emblematic for modernism. James Joyce's oeuvre, arguably modernism's climax, is for instance described in this way by the theorist Joseph Frank: "Joyce cannot be read—he can only be reread" and Frédérique Chevillot conceives in a similar fashion a number of modernist works in his book *Réouverture du texte* ("The Text's Reopening").[12]

Although modernist novels tend to make the beginnings opaque, an entry into the text is not necessarily made possible by making a projection of the ending. It could be that this "refusal of the beginning" ("refus du commencement") instead deserves analysis and attention in order to unravel the literary work.

3. We should not underestimate the concepts that we have inherited. While Brooks's and Kermode's perspective appears persuasive, it is important to realize that it underestimates the weight of linguistic and

11 Frank Kermode, "Novels: Recognition and Deception," *Critical Inquiry* 1 (September 1974): 119.

12 Joseph Frank, "Spatial Form in Modern Literature," in *The Widening Gyre: Crisis and Mastery in Modern Literature* (New Brunswick, NJ: Rutgers University Press, 1963); Frédérique Chevillot, *La Réouverture du texte. Balzac, Beckett, Robbe-Grillet, Roussel, Aragon, Calvino, Bénabou, Hébert* (Saratoga, CA: Anma Libri, 1993).

textual conventions as well as that of intertextuality; it ignores the idea that our reading is shaped and determined by concepts which we inherit. As Stanley Fish explains: "Meanings come already calculated ... not because of norms embedded in language but because language is always perceived, from the very first, within a structure of norms ... a structure, however, [that] is not abstract and independent but social."[13]

We are thus back to the central schism between Anglo-American and "Continental" thinking as we encounter it first and foremost in the discipline of epistemology: schematically speaking, the Continental tradition of philosophy emphasizes the existence of categories that are prior to our experience, created via socialization or existing innately, whereas the Anglo-American tradition emphasizes our dependence on the *a posteriori* interaction with the world. Similarly, Kermode and Brooks rely on the conception that the reader interacts *a posteriori* with the literary text, being driven forward through the text by his or her own independent decipherment and analysis.

It is therefore notable that Brooks at one point refers to a quintessentially Continental critic like Roland Barthes. Brooks quotes Barthes in the context of "the passion of meaning," which Barthes defines as "the active quest of the reader for those shaping ends that, terminating the dynamic process of reading, promise to bestow meaning and significance on the beginning and middle."[14] It is precisely characteristic of Barthes that, despite the complexity in his method, he deliberately limits precisely the recursiveness which Brooks and Kermode promote. As will further emerge from my discussion below, Barthes's reading progresses surprisingly simplistically from left to right: his ambition is altogether a different one.

To shed more light on my debate with the recursive method, it becomes almost indispensable to focus on modernism and its relation to beginnings and endings. Do the central elements in modernism point more towards endings or do they point towards beginnings, and in general to which degree is a particular period tied to a particular way of conceiving beginnings and endings?

In this interrogation of the schism between opening and ending, and implicitly between Anglo-American and Continental ideology, the concept of *intention* plays, I believe, a pivotal role. By emphasizing its

13 Stanley Fish, *Is there a Text in this Class?* (Cambridge, MA: Harvard University Press, 1982), 318.

14 Roland Barthes, "Introduction à l'analyse structurale des récits," quoted in Brooks, *Reading for the Plot*, 19.

original etymology, intention could be read precisely as a tension between beginning and end. As Vance Smith puts it: "Thinking about beginnings means thinking about what they intend, toward what ending they tend, and also means thinking about the tension that unites them."[15] This is precisely the intentional framework in which Kermode and Brooks operate, and also Edward Said in his book *Beginnings*, which in fact ends up dealing more with *intentions* than beginnings. He writes: "The continuity of the work is ensured by the conceptual act of beginning."[16] Beginnings and endings thereby become inseparable: "Formally, the mind wants to conceive a point in either time or space that marks the beginning of all things (or at least of a limited set of central things), but like Oedipus the mind risks discovering, at that point, where all things will end as well."[17] In this formal interest there is a profound need for establishing unity—which leads to the idea that a beginning must *imply* the end, in the way that is so central to Aristotle in his *Poetics* (hence another point shared by Kermode and Aristotle). It is this unity that is so important, for instance, in medieval works, which show how the beginning entails the end by literally *imitating* the relation between beginning and end. As Smith concludes in his important work on medieval literature: "Some university sermons conclude by restating the opening *thema*, and at least fifteen Middle English poems use their opening lines as their concluding lines."[18]

Modernist writing, on the other hand, reveals that this unity cannot be found in the first place. As I go on to explore in the next section, modernist texts do not ask for that unity between beginning and end; instead the work proceeds from the beginning in an unforeseeable and unpredictable fashion: "One may as well begin with Helen's letters to her sister," as the first line in *Howards End* reads.[19] Lacking a sense of cohesion between beginning and end in order to establish its origin, modernist writing could thus be said to be exposed to a rising pressure on the beginning

15 Smith, *The Book of the Incipit*, 47.

16 Said, *Beginnings*, 48.

17 Ibid., 41.

18 Smith, *The Book of the Incipit*, 48.

19 E.M. Forster, *Howards End* (New York: Penguin Books, 2000). See also my discussion of Aragon and Walser. Harry Shaw has pointed out to me that the opening of *Howards End* could also be interpreted not as "open," but on the contrary as an indication that, no matter where one starts, the narrator knows that the story will lead to a particular endpoint, and that this route is determined by the narrator. This interpretation would radically change the perception of openness of the novel, but would emphasize another narrative tendency in the modernist period: that the relation between narrator and reader is more disrespectful.

that becomes increasingly detached and artificial as device. A real beginning would lead so strongly to an end that a beginning appears almost impossible: "If the book could for a first time really begin, it would … long since have ended," as Maurice Blanchot overdramatically expresses it.[20] Blanchot's claim looks like a cliché, but let us turn to modernism for further exploration of the degree to which it addresses the recursive method in particular.

Modernism and its Urge for Self-Definition

> "Nothing in short. Absolutely nothing"
> AZORÍN, the opening of *The Writer* (1942)

Azorín's novel opens with the author's angst of nothingness; the blank page here stands as a metaphysical syndrome, which in its incapacity to open creative avenues instead opens up a different metafictional space. The second sigh—"absolutely nothing"—further radicalizes this nothingness, yet the frustration is also what sets the novel in motion. The dwelling on nothingness, so familiar since at least Mallarmé, becomes a reference amongst a certain generation of authors whose conception of the artwork is nourished by the simultaneous excitement and anxiety of building on nothing. This conscious complication of the creative process has in fact been singled out as a central, definitional pillar of modernism. Stephen Heath, for instance, points out that although premodernist writers like Balzac also experienced a "problem of writing," "the writing *itself* [did] not in any way represent a problem."[21] The awareness of nothingness interferes with the possibility of commencing the text since, in the absence of metaphysical authority, the text simultaneously loses its own claim to authority.

Modernism may consist in the realization that something else *must* precede the beginning, but also in the inability to see what could possibly precede the beginning. It consequently drifts towards the struggle with, and fascination for, the *ex nihilo*. There is a nothing before the beginning and a fixation on the writing that follows that nothingness,

20 Blanchot quoted by Smith, *The Book of the Incipit*, 113.

21 Stephen Heath, "The Practice of Writing," in *The Nouveau Roman: A Study in the Practice of Writing* (Philadelphia, PA: Elek, 1972), 15–42.

as epitomized by Azorín's *The Writer*. Mallarmé's *néant* (nothingness) is one of the most famous examples of this tendency. The *néant* is naturally a threat to Mallarmé and implicates that any beginning is better than no beginning—that the *act* of beginning becomes more important than the actual constituents of that beginning. One could say that the panic of nothingness can be overcome by opening up for the fiend of chance (cf. "Un coup de dés n'abolira jamais le hasard" ("A dice throw will never abolish chance")). But this is also a liberation, albeit a problematic one: the "modern condition," in short.

The self-questioning mode of beginning is therefore characteristically "modern": when authoritative beginnings cease, literature becomes "modern." Various scholars confirm this fundamental change in the level of authority from the nineteenth to the twentieth century. Narratologists like Gérard Genette point to a shift throughout the nineteenth century from external to internal focalization, which lowers the level of authority.[22] In the previous chapter we saw that linguists like Georg Bossong point to a simultaneous movement from so-called canonical to acanonical openings, that is to say, openings containing existential indicators ("there was a man") lose ground to openings in which the subject is not stipulated, but implicitly presupposed, such as the opening of Joseph Conrad's *Lord Jim*:

> He was an inch, perhaps two, under six feet, powerfully built, and he advanced straight at you with a slight stoop of the shoulders, head forward, and a fixed from-under stare which made you think of a charging bull.
>
> JOSEPH CONRAD, *Lord Jim* (1900)

This internal focalization and the implicitly introduced subject effect a lower level of authority and make it more implausible for the narrator to perceive the story in its entirety.

If modernism is the period with which we associate the "unreliable narrator"—just think of Faulkner's *The Sound and the Fury*, Scott Fitzgerald's *The Great Gatsby*, Henry James's *The Turn of the Screw*, Ford Madox Ford's *The Good Soldier*, and Vladimir Nabokov's *Lolita*—it is not so much, I claim, because the narrator with modernism *becomes* unreliable, but because an internally focalized narration *always* tends to be unreliable. In this more widely used mode of narration, a perfectly reliable narrator will appear suspiciously unrealistic—and an "unreliable" narrator will paradoxically appear more trustworthy. It can therefore be claimed that

22 Genette, "Discours du récit," 207–8. Also quoted in note 63 on page 84.

modernism does not *per se* promote narrative unreliability, but rather tends to adopt a mode of narration that simply cannot escape the "unreliable" in its conception of verisimilitude. When the entire story escapes the narrator, its point of departure becomes more revealing since it clarifies the signals that the reader can subsequently look for and challenge.[23] Similarly, Marcel Proust's narrator does not pretend to perceive the entire *Recherche*; on the contrary, the opening of the novel reveals a dynamic between the narrator's two first persons—a dynamic between "référent" (referent) and "référé" (reference)—without which the work could not even have been generated:[24]

> For a long time I used to go to bed early.
>
> MARCEL PROUST, *In Search of Lost Time* (1913)

This modernist awakening from nothingness is pursued by Marcel Proust, whose never-ending novel opens with the narrator's constitution of a random self after the nothingness of a sleep, the very image that became so powerful to Georges Poulet and the very high-modernist Geneva school of criticism.[25] Paul Valéry clearly perceives the prospect that lies in the opening: "Upon awakening there is a time of birth, a birth of all things before anything takes place,"[26] and this prospect is what is carried forward in the French critical tradition.

The awareness of nothingness and its lack of external authority, which radicalizes the need to begin, unsurprisingly provokes a stronger sense of individualization of the artistic process and a firmer belief in the autonomy of the artist (a tendency which is not consistent when it comes to the discussion of the avant-garde, which reacts against the autonomy of the work, cf. below page 120). Indeed this has been pointed out as one of the main characteristics of modernism to such an extent that it has become something of a critical cliché that a modernist work is to be found in a traditionless space, where influence is claimed to be both undesirable and impossible. Part of the reason for this depiction is that modernist literature tends to interrogate conventions such as the traditional identification of reader and writer. The increasingly provocative

23 Nuttall, *Openings*, 194. See also del Lungo's scheme in del Lungo, *L'Incipit romanesque*, 154–55.

24 See Doubrovsky, *La Place de la madeleine*, 101. Harry Shaw has pointed out to me that Genette seems to think of Marcel as having perceived the entirety of the novel, see Genette, "Discours du récit."

25 Poulet, *Le Point de départ*. For more discussion, see my encyclopedia entry, Buch-Jepsen, "Georges Poulet."

26 Paul Valéry, *Tel quel*, 121, quoted in Poulet, *Le Point de départ*, 13.

mode of writing results from this loosening identification, as Siegfried Jüttner posits: "The authors feel free of personal ties to the reader, whom they do not know, and reject the relation to traditional norms."[27] When the connection between the writer and the reader loosens, the writer will not feel compelled to appeal to their shared sense of literary norms: tradition easily becomes the target, and provocation the artistic means.

This reaction may simply be, as the modernist critic *par excellence* Walter Benjamin cynically claims, the "recurrence of the ever-same in the guise of the ever-new."[28] Even so, it is important to consider why this particular conception of the break with tradition becomes so pervasive in precisely this period—and precisely a reflection on openings serves to illustrate this quite well. In his seminal text on the opening line as the generative principle of novels, Aragon explains: "I considered the nineteenthth century to be the century that broke away from tradition."[29] Aragon points to Arthur de Gobineau's *Scaramouche* from 1843, which opens by suggesting different clichéd openings in order only to express to the reader an exasperation with the vulgarity of the beginning: "Well, no! All these beginnings are vulgar and boring, and since I do not have enough imagination to throw you into my narrative in a somewhat new way, I prefer not to start at all." In this refusal to begin, Aragon locates the new attitude to literary convention:

> Thus, the young Gobineau manifests the anxiety which necessarily seizes the writer in front of the conventional character who seems necessarily to take the primer, the opening of all writing, any sentence that seems to initiate the mental ceremony—be it a tale or novel—which will make up the undertaken narrative.[30]

This initial frustration with a conventional opening is partly a product of a shift in the function of literature from what I call recital to *récit* (narrative). In the nineteenth century, the novel gradually came to dominate the literary scene, both commercially and creatively, which, as the novelistic opening became increasingly institutionalized, threatened the work with banality. To a twentieth-century observer, the nineteenth-century openings are easily recognizable and classifiable according to the individual

27 Siegfried Jüttner, "Der beschimpfte Leser. Zur Analyse der literarischen Provokation," *Romanische Forschungen* 86 (1974): 95.

28 Quoted in David Frisby, *Fragments of Modernity: Theories of Modernity in the Work of Simmel, Kracauer and Benjamin* (Cambridge: Polity Press in association with Basil Blackwell, Oxford, 1985), 36.

29 Aragon, *Les Incipit*, 37.

30 Ibid., 75.

author. Aragon thus notices the individualized uniformity of openings: "Under the apparent diversity of the openings of the Romantic novel, I began to rediscover a simple uniformity, that of the man, the author. There was the style of Balzac, that of Hugo, that of Flaubert. And so forth."[31]

This predictable scheme becomes increasingly objectionable as the opening appears to both restrain and challenge the post-realist author's creative possibilities. Openings have thus generally become more "striking" because they have become more crucial for the "positioning" of the work as such. Like the preface in the seventeenth and eighteenth centuries defined the work's rhetorical status by explicating its reality mode and its moral intent, much of the modern work's rhetorical and polemic status is to be read through its mode of opening. The rhetorical dynamics of the opening is, however, of an entirely different kind than that of prefaces; openings clearly belong to what Genette defines as the "architext" whereas prefaces belong to the "paratext."[32] Simply put, this means that the opening is part of what we normally consider to be "the text." Stripped of most of its paratext, the modernist text thus increasingly needs its opening to position itself more consciously against other texts.

Intertextuality and the Critical Challenge of Modernism

What I hope to have shown at this point is the existence of an inherent conflict in our common impression of modernism. As mentioned, the modernist vein is perceived to rebut the pre-existent and confess to the absoluteness of creation and the autonomy of the artistic work. Yet, when the text loses its external authority and its sense of originating from a specific tradition, it becomes easier to see its interrelations with a multitude of other cultural manifestations. When specific sources of influence are eliminated, the entire span of connections seems wider, which in turn reduces the potential autonomy of the work. When the originating source is eliminated, every text is, as Stephen Heath puts it,

31 Ibid., 37. Refer also to Barthes's critique of the author function, which breaks down simultaneously. Barthes, "La mort de l'auteur."

32 Gerard Genette, *Introduction à l'architexte*, Poétique (Paris: Seuil, 1979).

> always (an)other text(s) that it remakes, comments, displaces, prolongs, reassumes. A text opens in and from that complex formation of modes of articulation that gives, as it were, the theatre of its activity, a series of settings always already there as its very possibility; as the setting of language is always there, without origin and elsewhere to any individual moment of discourse, always received 'such as it is'.[33]

The loss of origin is in a sense supplanted by a sense of belonging to a larger literary community; the synchronic replaces the diachronic (as is the case also for Ferdinand de Saussure and the linguistic theories that support the literary critic). This phenomenon has later been coined "intertextuality" and has become one of the central concepts associated with modernism. Julia Kristeva thus affirms that "beginning with this break—not only literary but also social, political, and philosophical in nature—the problem of intertextuality (intertextual dialogue) appears as such."[34] What critics previously saw as "influence" now seems fundamentally different, as Yves Hervouet explains:

> The idea that the literature of the past may provide aesthetic models or be exploited for didactic or moral purposes is not new. But, since the end of the nineteenth century, intertextuality has become more conscious and systematic, with the modern literary text overtly proclaiming its relation to a host of other texts.[35]

This is the reason for the focus on intertextuality as an almost ideological battleground for openings. An ending may not immediately evoke another ending, but who can write an opening of a text without being impregnated with the echoes from preceding openings? Even "Once upon a time..." will inevitably resonate in any attempt at beginning a text. When we consider the emphasis that literary studies in the twentieth century have put on the concept of "intertextuality," we can only be surprised to discover that no discussion of the concept has focused on the most intertextual place in a novel, the opening. As we have seen here and in earlier chapters, the opening can hardly escape other texts and will have to either imitate or deliberately circumvent the existing

33 Heath, "The Practice of Writing," 24.

34 Julia Kristeva, *Desire in Language*, quoted in Graham Allen, *Intertextuality*, The New Critical Idiom (London and New York: Routledge, 2000), 50.

35 Yves Hervouet, *The French Face of Joseph Conrad* (Cambridge: Cambridge University Press, 1990), 231.

conventions. Much of the remainder of this chapter will therefore deal with the critical stance of intertextuality in relation to openings.

By being a self-conscious, textual production, modernism has been said in the structuralist nomenclature to "unleash the force of the semiotic" which opens for the intertextual connectivity by exploiting what Kristeva calls the "transpositional" element.[36] The writings of, for instance, Joseph Conrad thus require what Yves Hervouet calls a "relational" reading or what Philippe Lejeune calls a "palimpsestic" reading whereby two or more texts are read simultaneously.[37] This mode of reading relates directly to a particular readerly pleasure, which we find in central critical works like Genette's *Palimpsests* or Barthes's *The Pleasure of the Text*: "If one really enjoys texts, one must surely wish, now and again, to enjoy (at least) two at the same time."[38] The modernist text is in other words characterized as a palimpsestic text. Even quotations at the beginning of a poem have become commonplace since T. S. Eliot, whereas previously, for instance in the romantic period, such quotations and epigraphs would have interfered with the cult of originality.[39]

The palimpsestic text constantly explores and exposes the borderland between itself and the other text, or as Mikhail Bakhtin, one of the forerunners of the intertextual theorists, writes: "Language lies on the borderline between oneself and the other." Language is never entirely its own: "The word in language is half someone else's."[40] As I have discussed elsewhere,[41] modernism has an inherent fascination with otherness, and this facet, although ideological in nature, can be approached through the otherwise seemingly formalistic concept of intertextuality. It could be claimed, for instance, that ideological dominance will attempt to stabilize the relationship between *signified* and *signifier*, that is to say, the relational structure will serve only to propagate the circumscribed "otherness."[42] Theorists who use the concept of intertextuality rather than Bloom's "anxiety of influence" or Bate's "burden of the past," will be able to spell out this ideological authority in more detail.[43] Edward Said's *Beginnings*,

36 Allen, *Intertextuality*, 54.

37 Hervouet, *The French Face of Joseph Conrad*; Philippe Lejeune, "Par où commencer ?," in *Moi aussi* (Paris: Seuil, 1986).

38 Hervouet, *The French Face of Joseph Conrad*, 232.

39 This observation is due to Fiona J. Stafford, *Starting Lines in Scottish, Irish and English Poetry: From Burns to Heaney* (Oxford: Oxford University Press, 2000).

40 Mikhail M. Bakhtin, *The Dialogic Imagination: Four Essays*, trans. Caryl Emerson and Michael Holquist (Austin, TX: University of Texas Press, 2000), 293.

41 Buch-Jepsen, "What Happened to the Author?"

42 See Allen, *Intertextuality*, 33.

43 Harold Bloom, *The Anxiety of Influence: A Theory of Poetry* (New York: Oxford Uni-

which on the face of it appears to be rather abstract and aloof and generally detached from Said's later ideological preoccupations, turns out to develop precisely these dynamics implicitly. For one thing, Said's idea of quotation suggests, as Stafford points out, "a force more spatial than temporal in its progress."[44] To Said, even a passing allusion serves as "a reminder that other writing serves to displace present writing, to a greater or lesser extent, from its absolute, central, proper place."[45] This is, as Fiona J. Stafford fittingly puts it, "the language of conquest rather than inheritance." In Said's view, quotation thus belongs not predominantly to the realm of literary genealogy, but assumes instead the role of a dominant, or even "colonizing," power through its capacity to "displace" and "encroach."[46]

The emphasis on intertextuality challenges, if not replaces, one of most central concepts in traditional comparative literature, namely that of influence. In the nineteenth century, this concept used the etymological image of "flow" (*fluere*) to represent an unhindered passage of certain key components from one work to another.[47] Comparative literature as a discipline, in its continuous focus on literary influences across international frontiers, quickly fostered an obsession with biological concepts such as origins, genesis, and growth, all while positing the organic wholeness of each national culture. The discipline of comparative literature has thus always essentially been a negotiation between, on the one hand, the desire for system and, on the other hand, an international posture. The notion of influence provided precisely the tool for undertaking this constant negotiation.[48]

In the preface to his famous *Manual of the History of French Literature* from 1898,[49] the French critic Ferdinand Brunetière further sharpened the concept of influence by proclaiming that of all the influences that operate in the history of literature, the influence of *works on works* is

versity Press, 1973); W. Jackson Bate, *The Burden of the Past and the English Poet* (Cambridge, MA: Harvard University Press, 1970).

44 Said, *Beginnings*, 22; Stafford, *Starting Lines*, 39.

45 Said, *Beginnings*, 22.

46 Stafford, *Starting Lines*, 39; Hayden White, "Criticism as Cultural Politics," *Diacritics* 6, no. 3 (1976).

47 For the history of comparative literature see Claudio Guillén, *Literature as System: Essays towards the Theory of Literary History* (Princeton, NJ: Princeton University Press, 1970).

48 Ibid.

49 Brunetière quoted in René Wellek, *Concepts of Criticism* (New Haven, CT: Yale University Press, 1963). 44.

the principal one.[50] Beginning with Russian formalism, though, concrete influence of one author upon another began to be seen as a direct *obstacle* to the reader's interaction with the text. Jurij Tynjanov, one of the Russian theorists most directly involved in the twentieth-century reformulation of influence, explains this concern in his famous essay "On Literary Evolution":

> "Influence" can occur at such a time and in such a direction as literary conditions permit. In the case of functional coincidence, whatever influences him provides the artist with elements which permit the development and strengthening of the function. If there is no such "influence," then an analogous function may result in analogous formal elements without any influence.[51]

Tynjanov's exposition is important in its insistence on the fact that literary criticism should not build on vague hypotheses when placing coherences in a historical perspective. His focus on the text's "function" leads him categorically to reject all previous attempts to understand literary evolution: "The evolutionary relationship of function and formal elements is a completely uninvestigated problem."[52] "Influence" can, he claims, only be affirmed when identical functions bring about identical or analogous formal elements (what he calls an "auto-function").[53] A study of literary openings, I do not hesitate to add, would satisfy Tynjanov's methodological requirement.

The concept of intertextuality, although only coined by Kristeva in the 1960s, is a direct development from Tynjanov's theory and tries to set up

50 For a humanist, genealogical conception of influence from author to author, as if they were related, see for instance André Gide, *Conseils au jeune écrivain. De l'influence en littérature* (Paris: Proverbe, 1993).

51 Tynjanov, "On Literary Evolution," 76.

52 Ibid., 71.

53 Ibid., 68. In this passage it is clarified that "the interrelationship of each element with every other in a literary work and with the whole literary system as well may be called the constructional *function* of the given element. On close examination, such a function proves to be a complex concept. An element is on the one hand interrelated with similar elements in other works in other systems, and on the other hand it is interrelated with different elements within the same work. The former may be termed the *auto-function* and the latter, the *syn-function*." This means that the auto-function conditions the syn-function. The structural function changes the author's intention into a catalyst. This is not creative freedom, but creative necessity. Direct influence will be replaced by considerations of evolution viewed as modification of literary works, that is, deformation. This is in line with Jakobson as well as Tynjanov: "The evolution of literature cannot be understood until the evolutionary problem ceases to be observed by questions of episodic, nonsystemic origin, whether literary (for example, so-called 'literary influences') or extraliterary." "On Literary Evolution," 79.

a *positive technique* for the critic to work with other texts. Intertextuality does not evoke an "anxiety" or a "burden" as in the twentieth-century Anglo-American theories based on the writer's perspective: the perspective of intertextuality is invariably that of the reader, not the writer. Although scholars unsurprisingly disagree on the exact meaning and applicability of the term "intertextuality," Michael Riffaterre's broad definition that "the intertext is the reader's perception of relationships between one work and others, which either preceded or followed it," may come closest to a consensus.[54] Yet, more important seems to be the shared assumption that intertextuality challenges any consideration of *origin*. At this point even Tynjanov's dismissal of genesis as an external phenomenon is not radical enough, as Tzvetan Todorov, an important disciple of Barthes and specialist in Russian formalism, avows: "As far back as we trace genesis, we find only other texts, other products of language; and it is difficult for us to conceive their apportionment."[55]

Intertextuality's interest in textual relations does under no circumstances amount to source hunting. The relations between texts are not concrete—one text cannot be antecedent in relation to another; texts are instead seen to occupy an abstract space in which they interact synchronically, or as Jonathan Culler accurately puts it: "Intertextuality is less a name for a work's relation to particular prior texts than an assertion of a work's participation in a discursive space and its relation to the codes which are the potential formalizations of that space."[56] Yet, the real complication is how this works in practice. Intertextual relations are per definition boundless and, as Culler notes, any concrete attempt to work with them will inevitably narrow them down, thereby threatening them to collapse back into precisely the kind of source study that these literary theorists tried to circumvent. Or put differently, the dilemma of intertextuality is the following: either intertextuality remains abstract and limitless—rendering the concept more or less useless from a critical and formalistic point of view[57]—or intertextuality must be narrowed

54 Michael Riffaterre, *La Production du texte* (Paris: Seuil, 1979), 8.

55 Tzvetan Todorov, *Introduction to Poetics* (Brighton: The Harvester Press, 1981), 60.

56 Jonathan Culler, "Presupposition and Intertextuality," *Modern Language Notes* 91 (1976), reprinted in Jonathan Culler, *The Pursuit of Signs: Semiotics, Literature, Deconstruction* (Ithaca, NY: Cornell University Press, 1981), 241. Barthes expresses the same idea quite differently: "l'intertexte: l'impossibilité de vivre hors du texte infini." Roland Barthes, *Le Plaisir du texte*, Collection Tel Quel (Paris: Éditions du Seuil, 1973), 59.

57 My view is here in line with Clayton's: "[Barthes's] radical intertextuality forgoes the possibility of rigor in the discussion of individual texts." Jay Clayton and Eric Rothstein, "Figures in the Corpus: Theories of Influence and Intertextuality," in *Influence and*

down to more concrete relations, with the threat of collapsing it into the otherwise rejected concept of influence.

Culler thus points out the fundamental instability of the concept of intertextuality and the insufficiency of the use to which Barthes puts this concept, for instance in his analysis of Balzac. Sean Burke has even drawn the conclusion that intertextuality cannot break the spell of the traditional, critical practice: "Intertextuality ... as it has been formulated and put into practice returns quite compliantly to notions of influence and revision."[58] Yet, the impulse behind intertextuality is a stout resistance to the idea of origin and a preexisting textual authority: the reader is not bound, the text is boundless, and to read is to *open* the text.

Culler has therefore tried to reformulate the intertextual impulse in the face of its impractical and unstable nature by associating it with *competence* on a par with linguistic mastery: "What makes possible reading and writing is not a single anterior action which serves as origin and moment of plenitude but an open series of acts, both identifiable and lost, which work together to constitute something like a language, discursive possibilities, systems of convention."[59] Culler therefore constructively suggests working with *presupposition* as a model for intertextuality, since presupposition undermines referentiality, but yet limits the set of intertexts for an interpretation to those that are either logically or pragmatically suggested by the text one is studying. Culler's proposal adds methodology and assurance to the critical act, without introducing the rebuked dependence on "moments of authority and points of origin."[60] Characteristically of Culler's work, this way of perceiving intertextuality emphasizes the reader's awareness of *conventions* as central to literary criticism.

Despite the evident usefulness of Culler's proposal, especially as he points out that logical presuppositions are important in opening sentences in novels, I believe that Barthes would remain interested merely in intertextuality as a system of combination and as a logic of composition that would simply ignore the inherent instability of the concept. As indicated earlier in this chapter, Barthes is interested in the space of the opening itself, without concern for the shape that the text develops

Intertextuality in Literary History, ed. Jay Clayton and Eric Rothstein (Madison: University of Wisconsin Press, 1991), 23.

58 Sean Burke, *The Death and Return of the Author: Criticism and Subjectivity in Barthes, Foucault and Derrida* (Edinburgh: Edinburgh University Press, 1992), 173.

59 Culler, *The Pursuit of Signs*, 110.

60 Ibid., 117.

into—and as indicated above this is an ideological stand. Barthes would therefore not be interested in more thorough redefinitions of intertextuality that emerged from American criticism. Moreover, it is unclear to what degree even such an intertextual system can rely on communal conventions and not simply fall back on individual critics' selections and their individual, intellectual competence.[61]

Barthes's Beginnings: Where to Begin?

For Barthes, who was also extremely instrumental in shaping the concept of intertextuality, textual utterances can under no circumstances bear out moments of origin. With his typical intermingling of subjectivity theory and literary theory, Barthes exclaims: "I am not an innocent subject, anterior to the text ... This 'me' which approaches the text is already itself a plurality of other texts, of infinite codes, or more exactly, lost codes (whose origin is lost)."[62] In his famous proclamation of the "death" of the author, it is important to look behind the avant-gardist provocation, which it is often hailed as, and notice that Barthes does not in fact wholly disavow the *author*, but instead the *authority* that we traditionally attach to that concept. The author should no longer be perceived as the *origin* of the writings, and no longer provide a privileged access into them; the author does not exert authority over his or her own fictions. The author may thus, as Barthes himself puts it, "come back" in the text, but only

61 Bloom refers to Barthes's approach as being inspired by the cabala, which would further explain why someone with Barthes's outlook would not try to go beyond the initial state, see also the first chapter's discussion of Jacob Böhme. "One might indeed call Cordovero the first structuralist, an unacknowledged ancestor of many contemporary French theorists of the "human sciences." Bloom, *Kabbalah and Criticism*, 37. Bloom goes on to say: "Gnosis and Kabbalah, as I think we can now begin to see, were the first Modernisms, in our still current sense 'Modernism'. A modern poem begins with a clinamen that depends upon the renunciation of an earlier poem. But this renunciation must be dialectical. The earlier poem (or poet) is concentrated (which means also contracted) and made to vacate part of himself. Since the precursor has been internalized, a crucial mental space in the ephebe is being voided. Creation begins therefore with an element in the self contracting to a primordial point. But this concentration sets up defensive reactions in the self, making the subsequent creation a catastrophe, and rendering tikkun or representation a hopeless quest, since there can come no reparation for an overly-defended self, and least of all from that self." Ibid., 79–80.

62 Roland Barthes, *S/Z* (Paris: Seuil, 1970), 15–16.

as a "guest."[63] In his methodology, Barthes also accepts the notion of "oeuvre," for instance when undertaking parallel readings of an author's different texts, which is a technique that relies precisely on the notion of authorship.[64] The notion of *origin* is the real offender; the notion of author only offends insofar as it is perceived as an origin.

To Barthes, writing is thus a synchronous activity, cut off from considerations of causality, and "the writer can only imitate a gesture that is always anterior, never original."[65] Yet, the dismissal of origin is in reality a relocation of the textual unity: "A text's unity lies not in its origin but in its destination."[66] Edward Said's spatial sense of quotation is also found in Barthes's validation of the reader: "The reader is the space on which all the quotations that make up a writing are inscribed without any of them being lost."[67]

In this readerly accumulation of quotation lies the key to structuralism's underlying intention. In the article "Where to Begin?" that inaugurated the prominent theoretical journal *Poétique*, Barthes portrays structuralism

63 Roland Barthes, "From Work to Text," in *The Rustle of Language* (New York: Hill and Wang, 1986), 61. Compare with Derrida's comment on Rousseau in *Of Grammatology*: "His declared intention is not annulled ... but rather inscribed within a system which it no longer dominates." Jacques Derrida, *Of Grammatology* (Baltimore, MD: Johns Hopkins University Press, 1976), 243.

64 Cf. Raymond Picard's famous critique of Barthes. I also believe that Graham Allen is perfectly right in his observation: "Yet at the very moment that Barthes makes that move he is citing Mallarmé as an authorial point not of origin but at least of conscious determination." Allen, *Intertextuality*, 74. See Barthes's text "Longtemps, je me suis couché de bonne heure," in Barthes, *Œuvres complètes*, V, 459–70. Here Barthes claims that the opening sentence "opens up an episode of some fifty pages which, like the Tibetan mandala, contains all the Proustian work in its view," 461. In this text Barthes also mentions Dante's "Nel mezzo del camin di nostra vita" ("Midway along the journey of our life").

65 "A text is ... a multidimensional space in which a variety of writings, none of them original, blend and clash." Barthes, "La mort de l'auteur." This leads Seymour Chatman to exclaim that "Structuralist poetics takes narrative as a synchronous phenomenon and so is not concerned with its genesis or composition, but only its completed shape." Chatman, "Towards a Theory of Narrative." This characterization is of course ironic when the reader's interest lies in the "writable." Chatman's comment does not seem wholly correct: the concept of genesis is questioned, but an interest in composition does not necessarily stand on the side of genesis. For other structuralist validations of openings, see Genette on beginnings in Proust, in "Discours du récit," 85–89. See also Zoltán Kanyó, "Anmerkungen zur Frage des Textanfangs der literarischen Geschichte," in *Texttheorie und Interpretation. Untersuchungen zu Gryphius, Borchert und Böll*, ed. Arpád Bernáth, Csúri Károly, and Zoltán Kanyó (Kronberg/Ts: Scriptor Verlag, 1975). Kanyó is very structurally founded and treats text as a linguistic system with formulae for different openings. A model for beginnings can be found in Algirdas Julien Greimas, *Sémantique structurale, recherche de méthode*, Langue et langage (Paris: Larousse, 1966).

66 Barthes, "La mort de l'auteur."

67 Said, *Beginnings*, 315. Structuralists are like the "essentialists" also guilty of the myth of the origin. Said does not mythify writing like Barthes does.

as "a science of plurality."[68] This characterization is deliberately meant to defy the French scholastic method of "explication de texte," which attempts to explicate a whole text by analyzing each and every stylistic element occurring in a short textual extract. This institutionalized method seals off the text, whereas, to Barthes, criticism is a question of setting foot in "the plurality of the text in the game of the signifier, in the writing."[69] In this manifesto-like text, the ambivalence, always present in Barthes's thinking, between *science* and *pleasure* stands out particularly well. The "scientific" is set to sustain the playful, and the critical analysis even seems to begin at an arbitrary point: "The analysis begins with a semantic view, either thematic, symbolic or ideological." The beginning is open—and is supposed to be open. Only when one has begun, can science push forward, and still only in the interest of semantic plurality: "On the basis of a condensation the first content must pass through the act of a formal science that seeks plurality."[70] Thus, even in the early "structuralist" Barthes, we sense a limit to the "scientific" impulse, which becomes dominant in his later texts. In Barthes's analysis of an extract from Genesis, for example, considerations of both diachronic origin *and* synchronic structure are undermined in favor of the text's disruptive potential, as textual analysis is now taken as no longer saying "*from where* the text comes (historical criticism), nor even *how* it is made (structural analysis), but how it is unmade, how it explodes, disseminates—by what coded paths it goes off."[71]

Not only does the approach to the text quickly become ideological; certain texts will lend themselves better to that particular readerly approach. What is now called modernist texts allow the reader to become part of the production of meaning,[72] whereas "the classical text ... closes the work, chains it to the letter, rivets it to its signified."[73] The beginning of the work thus plays an instrumental role in opening the work; in the article on the point of departure of textual analysis, "Where to Begin?," Barthes rebukes the openings of Balzac's novels because they open "like a 'painting', a static and synchronic discourse."[74] Yet, in this methodological article, Barthes reflects on the "first act to perform in the presence of the text" and argues

68 Roland Barthes, "Par où commencer ?" *Poétique* 1 (1970): 3–9.

69 Ibid., 3.

70 Ibid. It is, however, not clear how a condensation works with plurality.

71 Roland Barthes, "The Struggle with the Angel: Textual Analysis of Genesis 32: 22–32," in *Image—Music—Text,* trans. Stephen Heath (New York: Hill and Wang, 1971).

72 Cf. Graham Allen's comments on Barthes. Allen, *Intertextuality,* 68.

73 Roland Barthes, "The Theory of the Text," in *Untying the Text: A Post-structuralist Reader*, ed. Robert Young (Boston, MA: Routledge and Kegan Paul, 1981), 33.

74 Barthes, "Par où commencer ?"

that the reader should begin by setting up precisely a "painting" on the basis of the information collected in the opening of the novel.[75]

Barthes exemplifies this piece of advice by reading Jules Verne's *The Mysterious Island* (1875), which he directs away from Verne's otherwise stout fixation on "closure and plenitude" and towards the heroes' early development of tools, which allows their story to begin properly. Being thus a *mise-en-abyme* of the critical process of developing the appropriate tool for the particular (textual) situation, there does not seem to be one overarching method with which to begin the textual interaction. Barthes's recommendation therefore seems disappointing to literary criticism's possible 'scientific' aspirations: as Diana Knight indicates, one simply begins where one wants to begin.[76] In the attempt at decipherment, the critic develops the appropriate tools along the way depending on the point of departure, in a move that Barthes draws up around the word "déchiffrement" (decipherment), which quickly turns into "défrichement" (ground clearing), where the critic employs the improvised tools to clear the ground for his or her impromptu reading.

Barthes's prescription at this point is not so much how to carry out a textual analysis as how to position it from the outset. Barthes does not seem to move beyond the beginning and focuses instead merely on what Knight calls a "pre-criticism," while the full structural analysis "recedes into the future."[77] Knight reads this move as an indication that Barthes is more thematic than formalist in his readings, but this would be to underestimate Barthes's stylistic sensibility. Barthes begins in style and begins with style: "Style is somehow the beginning of writing: even timidly, by committing itself to great risks of recuperation, it initiates ("amorce") the reign of the signifier."[78] "Amorcer" is here a particularly well chosen term (a term discussed in chapter 2): the text puts on "bait" ("amorce") in the form of rich signifiers, which then lure in the reader. This move, however, will inescapably mark a beginning ("amorcer" in the figurative meaning: "to begin"). Text should shun "recuperation" by analysis and instead *open* the doors to the realm of the signifier. To Barthes, textual pleasure is first and foremost to be found in the sovereignty of a text that opens up the reading process and in this way continuously seeks

75 See Knight's illuminating discussion of Barthes's article. Diana Knight, "Where to Begin?" *Yale Journal of Criticism: Interpretation in the Humanities* 14, no. 2 (2001): 494.

76 Ibid., 495.

77 Ibid. Knight interestingly uses this observation to argue that the article "Where to Begin?" may mark Barthes's transition from structural to textual analysis.

78 "Roland Barthes par Roland Barthes," in Barthes, *Œuvres complètes,* IV, 653.

beginnings. There is a particular pleasure in beginnings that Barthes recognizes even in his own writing:

> Liking to find, to write *beginnings*, he [i.e. Barthes himself] tends to multiply this pleasure: that is why he writes fragments: so many fragments, so many beginnings, so many pleasures (but he does not like ends: the risk of the rhetorical clausule is too great: fear of not knowing how to resist the *last word*, the last reply.[79]

Barthes's remark suggests that this multiplication of the pleasure of beginning is not altogether innocent. The bliss of beginning is an ideological question.

The structuralist concept of "text" is often portrayed as having no real boundaries: in principle it is endless and consequently has neither definite beginnings nor endings. Yet, both in Barthes and in associated theorists it appears that the concept of "text" rejects only endings while in fact staying loyal to beginnings. One of the theorists who shaped structuralism into an ideological tool, Claude Duchet, articulates this explicitly in an article on openings in the first issue of *Littérature*: "The word 'text' does not imply any closure."[80] Text is not tied down by an ending, but instead shifts continuously according to the particular study's point of departure: "It is a study object whose nature changes according to the point of view from which it is approached."[81] A text is hence perceived as the potential of its readings, which instigate its very existence: "The end of a text is not its end, but the anticipation of its reading, the beginning of its 'why', of its 'to what'."[82] To Duchet as well as to Barthes, the critic's point of departure is *poetics*, that is, the creation of meaning, which begins with the text's effect on the reader. Theorists like Barthes and Duchet who favor poetics over hermeneutics seem to have a keener interest in openings and the general theme of beginning. Openings make it is easier for them to demonstrate the dynamic generation of meaning, all the while steering clear of the hermeneutic search for preexistent meaning hidden in the text.

79 Ibid., 671. See also Roland Barthes, *Le Grain de la voix* (Paris: Seuil, 1981), 174, and Barthes, *Le Plaisir du texte*, ad passim.

80 Claude Duchet, "Pour un sociocritique, ou variation sur un incipit," *Littérature* 1 (1971): 6.

81 Ibid.

82 Ibid., 7–8.

Refusal of the Beginning: Modernist Critics Make Literature Modernist

Despite the apparent formalism of intertextuality, the concept inevitably gets entangled in a tremendously ideological debate about literature and the role of literary criticism. Although this debate may seem far from the discussion of literary openings, it is neccesary to discuss intertextuality at some length, as I have done, since an approach to openings and an approach to intertextuality in many ways are logically interdependent. Due to the particular nature of the opening, which constantly threatens to fall into the recognizable cliché, the opening both illustrates and challenges the concept of intertextuality as well as challenges both the author and the critic.

The question that I started out addressing more specifically was whether the opening during the modernist period differs fundamentally from its predecessors. As I have already indicated, I believe that this question is inseparable from the question of the literary critic's methodology. Regardless of the formal characteristics of a literary text, the critic will approach it in a particular manner that influences the way that these formal characteristics are perceived. Structuralist critics such as Barthes and Kristeva are no exception, and consequently they are prone to the following difficulty: on the one hand they claim that there is something particular about modernist openings, while, on the other hand, they analyze older openings in such a way that make them appear modernist, thereby undermining their first claim. The modernist critics have strengthened the conviction that one cannot and should not investigate the origin of the text; yet the arguments regarding the abruptness of the modernist text are themselves modernist.[83]

For instance, Kristeva is very explicit in *Le Texte clos* (*The Closed Text*) about the "epistemological rupture of the nineteenth–twentieth century," which liberated the text from a frozen approach that perceives the literary work as "finished in its beginning, closed."[84] Yet, as John Frow has

83 It should be added, as I have explored elsewhere, that the term "modernism" is not used in French literary history, which talks merely of the modern and modernity, Buch-Jepsen, "What Happened to the Author?" Refer to this article for more discussion of how this affects the debate. In the present study, I will simply presuppose that the distinction is as valid in French as it is in English and most other European languages.

84 Julia Kristeva, "Le Texte clos," in *Σημειωτική: recherches pour une sémanalyse* (Paris: Seuil, 1978 [1969]), 58.

also pointed out,[85] the otherwise extremely formalistic Kristeva fails to explain in formalistic terms precisely how the modern novels differ from earlier novels. Kristeva merely reverts to what I have earlier called the "clichés of modernism"—generalizations about a fundamental rupture. So we must ask: has the modernist novel really changed—or is it merely the critic's stance that has changed?

The reason why structuralism runs into this difficulty is also due to the fact that the structuralist critic becomes a sort of writer in his or her own right: "It remains, therefore, for structuralism to be transformed into a 'writer'," [86] thereby setting the critic on a par with the modernist writer. This tendency is especially conspicuous when Barthes manages to analyze Edgar Allan Poe or Balzac with a perfect modern, intertextual approach: how could it be argued that the intertextuality in the form that we recognize emerges in literary works only with the rise of modernism,[87] as Kristeva suggests, when a perfectly intertextual analysis of earlier works can be successfully conducted? This implies either that intertextuality is not after all a defining property of modernist works—or that Kristeva's and Barthes's criticism itself becomes modernist, thereby transforming all literary works through the lens of structuralism/modernism.[88] This would be entirely in the spirit of Barthes, according to whom the linearity of the concept of influence is replaced by the dynamic concept of circulation: "I do not believe in influences. ... That is why the notion of *circulation* seems to me more accurate than that of *influence*; books are more like 'currencies' than 'forces'."[89] So the question as to what is so special about modernism still remains to be answered.

Yet, Barthes operates with the same historical divide as Kristeva: modern literature has an altogether different ambition. Barthes here also reverts to some of the common (Mallarméan and Bergsonian) clichés about modernism: "Modernism begins with the search for a Literature which is no longer possible" and "What must be destroyed [in modern art] is duration."[90] Barthes, despite his inconsistencies, is however profoundly interested in pinning these differences down formalistically and in *S/Z* he introduced the much acclaimed distinction between texts

85 John Frow quoted in Clayton and Rothstein, "Figures in the Corpus," 20.

86 Roland Barthes, "De la science à la literature," in Barthes, *Œuvres complètes,* II, 1267.

87 Cf. Allen, *Intertextuality*, 81.

88 I here equate structuralism and modernism, as I see structuralism as modernism moving into the circle of criticism.

89 Barthes, *Œuvres complètes*, II, 616.

90 "Le Degré zéro de l'écriture," in *Œuvres*, I, 194. Translated in *Writing Degree Zero* (London: Cape Editions, 1967), 44.

that are "scriptible" (writable, focused on the author) and texts that are "lisible" (readable, focused on the reader), a distinction which reminds us of the narratologists' distinction between narrative perspectives.[91] Yet, even this formalistic distinction quickly drifts into the normative, or even the ideological: the "writable" is thus positively associated with "the opening of networks" whereas the texts that are "readable" are negatively "engaged in the Western system of closure."[92]

What is clear from my discussion of Kristeva and Barthes is that the seemingly profoundly formalistic concept of intertextuality cannot avoid being deeply entangled with ideology. Intertextuality is used ideologically, just as the glorification of certain novelistic openings is used ideologically. Intertextuality is a "revolutionary" technique, both formalistically and ideologically, and engrained in the avant-gardism with which modernism is associated.[93] The modernist critic thus also becomes an avant-gardist who participates, through the disruptive technique of intertextuality, in the demolition of the existing rules.[94] Following Peter Bürger's widely accepted definition of the avant-garde as primarily constituting an attack on the institution of art in bourgeois society based on the idea of the artwork's autonomy,[95] it becomes quite clear that intertextuality can be used precisely to reject this autonomy. Through such a critical lens, it is not surprising that Barthes sees modern literature as following "stage by stage the disintegration of bourgeois consciousness."[96]

The French avant-garde critic thereby develops a special relation to intertextuality as well as to openings as the latter represent the future potential of a limitless artistic space. The critic thus becomes prone to what Foucault has analyzed as "the refusal of the beginning," as a particular modern, critical mode.[97]

91 See the previous chapter 2.

92 *S/Z*, in Barthes, *Œuvres complètes*, III, 122–24.

93 Lukács equated the avant-garde with modernism. György Lukács, *The Meaning of Contemporary Realism* (London: Merlin Press, 1963).

94 For instance the early Edward Said of *Beginnings* explicitly defines himself as an avant-garde critic. Edward W. Said, "Interview," *Diacritics* 6, no. 3 (1976).

95 Peter Bürger, *Theory of the Avant-Garde*, trans. Michael Shaw (Minneapolis: University of Minnesota Press, 1984), 86.

96 "Le Degré zéro de l'écriture," in Barthes, *Œuvres complètes*, I, 173. Translated in *Writing Degree Zero*, 11.

97 "The incompleteness of interpretation, the fact that it is always lacerated and that it remains suspended on its own brink, is found once again, I believe, in a somewhat analogous fashion in Marx, Nietzsche, and Freud in the form of the refusal of beginning." Michel Foucault, "Nietzsche, Freud, Marx," in *Nietzsche, Cahiers de Royaumont* (Paris: Editions de Minuit, 1967), 188. Translated by Jon Anderson and Gary Hentzi in Michael Foucault, *Aesthetics, Method and Epistemology* (New York: The New Press, 1998).

Said's *Beginnings*: The Elusive Opening

It is in this discussion that Edward Said's monumental work *Beginnings* (1975) fits in. Drawing primarily on Giambattista Vico, Said differentiates between *origins*, which are divine and mythical, and *beginnings*, which are worldly and humanly produced. Unsurprisingly, Said favors beginnings over origins. Origins have what he calls a "dynastic" structure, which aims to dominate and determine what derives from it. Beginnings, on the contrary, have what we can call a "dynamic" structure, which implies complementarity and adjacency between the beginning and the result.[98] In other words, origins are perceived as passive, beginnings as active.

This distinction is important for our conception of the modernist writer and, in turn, for our conception of the modernist or "avant garde" critic—of which Said himself is a prime example. When, as Foucault argues, the idea of order dissipated by the end of the nineteenth century, the modern writer was left without a clear sense of origins and, for that matter, ends.[99] This loss of origins later turned into a theoretical *critique* of origins; Ferdinand de Saussure's notion of favoring synchrony over diachrony gained ground and, with structuralism and poststructuralism, anti-foundational thinking flourished: the authoritarian—or "dynastic"—concept of *influence* was replaced by the relational concept of *intertextuality*; and the dynastic concept of *author* was buried beneath a relational network of *text*.

Although drawing heavily on the structuralist impulse in France, Said insinuates that the structuralists, in their systematic repression of origins, are just as prone to the myth of the origin.[100] Unlike Barthes, Said does not wish to mythify writing, and by differentiating beginnings from origins, Said finds a place to reinstate authorial will and authorial intentions without having to embrace the eschewed concept of origins. This twist does, however, not revert to a traditional intentionalist criticism, but it simply helps Said insist on a relation between the existence of the author and his or her textual product: "The net result is to understand language as an intentional structure signifying a series of displacements."[101]

This move is important for Said's later, and more, explicitly ideological work, and although *Beginnings* is now probably more cited than read, it

98 Said, *Beginnings*, xii, 373.

99 White, "Criticism as Cultural Politics," 10.

100 Said, *Beginnings*, 315.

101 Ibid., 66.

marked—very appropriately—the beginning of Said's own academic and critical career. *Beginnings* was a beginning for Said, not simply because it established his reputation, but because it cleared the ground for his later works and furthermore justified the appearance on American soil of what he himself calls an "avant-garde" or "French-influenced" critic.[102] Said's reflection on the simultaneous difficulty and potential of beginning is in itself a metareflection on the modern critic's challenges in the absence of an origin in traditional literary criticism:

> So the critics face irregularity on all sides. Because he cannot have recourse to tradition in solving the problems of writers like Joyce, and because his (and Joyce's) references are to other makeshift formalities of knowledge, the critic is aptly characterized in Lukacs' epithet for the novel as being transcendentally homeless. He begins each work as if it were a new occasion. His beginning, as much as any modern writer's beginning, takes up a subject in order to begin it, keep it going, create it.[103]

The dense style and generally non-argumentative structure of *Beginnings* makes Jonathan Culler exclaim: "The expert on beginnings has difficulty getting under way."[104] Yet, this characteristic is precisely, as Culler is very well aware of, what sets the avant-garde critic apart from the "institutionalized" critic.[105] Said consolidates all the problems of the modern, traditionless critic into one fundamental question: "How should [the critic] begin to write?"[106] The modern critic is hence on a par with the modernist writer:

> One way of mitigating this change [in the critic's conditions for writing] and even of enhancing the fact that it has taken place, is to argue that literature itself has gone through the same change. … Thus when one begins to write today one is necessarily more of an autodidact, gathering or making up the knowledge one needs in the course of creating. The influence of the past appears less

102 "Avant-garde critics are mainly French-influenced critics. One can divide critics into French-influenced and non-French influenced. The avant-garde critic claims intertextuality to be the universal condition of text." Said, "Interview," *Diacritics* 6, no. 3 (1976): 30–47.

103 Said, *Beginnings*, 11.

104 Jonathan Culler, "Beginnings: Intention and Method by Edward W. Said," *Modern Language Review* 73, no. 3 (1978): 583.

105 Moreover, modern linguistics began precisely with Saussure's difficulty in beginning, see Knight, "Where to Begin?," 493.

106 Said, *Beginnings*, 6.

> useful and, as two recent critics, W. J. Bate and Harold Bloom, have argued, more likely to produce anxiety. Therefore Roland Barthes, paraphrasing Bachelard, has said that the study—and the production of literature today—is the study and the production of de-formation. To read Joyce we must follow these de-formations, just as Joyce's reading de-formed the traditional curriculum.[107]

Literary criticism thus matches modernist writing in inventiveness and in "the redistribution of textual space." Dismantling the traditionally dynastic relations between authors and between texts, the production of meaning will instead follow a logic of "adjacency": "The [modernist] text itself stands to the side of, next to, or between the bulk of all other works—not in a line with them, nor in a line of descent from them."[108] Any interest in precedence and in the past appears to be simply "improbable," as in the case of Joyce's reference in *Ulysses* to Homer and T. S. Eliot's reference to Dante in *The Waste Land*. The modernist text can consequently be "neither effectively read as commentary nor described by commentary."[109] At this point, Said may not realize that the commendable "adjacency" of modern texts very easily equals a form of textual "solipsism," by which texts fail altogether to communicate and interact. On the other hand, this would only add to the creative importance of the critic whose job it is to associate these texts in an imaginative way.

It is on this background of tradition and creation that Said develops his most useful theoretical distinction, that between "authority" and "molestation." The author constantly mediates between his or her own authority and an external pressure, or as Jonathan Culler fittingly puts it:

> The novelist desires to be a beginning, the source of an authoritative fictional world, but he knows that his authority is 'molested' both by the tradition of the novel, which precedes and guides his activity, and by the independent authority of the world to which he seeks to relate. Novels display the tension between the novelist's authoritative assertion of self in creating a continuation of

107 Ibid., 8.

108 Ibid., 10.

109 Ibid. This is one point where Said, despite his French-inspired approach, seems to differ from the French critics; according to Barthes, a text is always a comment, and the French tend to see the novel as always related to society. The experimental Philippe Sollers concurs: "The novel is the way in which this society speaks, the way in which the individual must live in order to be accepted. It is therefore essential that the "romantic" point of view be omnipresent, evident, untouchable." Philippe Sollers, *Logiques*, Collection Tel Quel (Paris: Editions du Seuil, 1968), 228.

> life and the threats to that authority posed by all the independent agents of mediation: language, tradition, verisimilitude.[110]

Molestation makes the reader aware that the work is always comparable to reality and with other novels, and therefore can be found to be an illusion. Said's distinction may therefore, as Homer Brown has suggested, be more illuminative than the realist vs. non-realist contrast.[111]

The distinction furthermore helps us understand *Beginnings*, despite its hermetic appearance, as essentially a political allegory, as for instance claimed by Hayden White.[112] The dynamics between authority and molestation makes the smallest reference remind us "that other writing serves to displace present writing, to a greater or lesser extent, from its absolute, central, proper place."[113]

This, however, is also the point that sets Said most apart from the structuralist inspiration. Writing testifies to the author's existence by manifesting his or her struggle for authority in the face of the threat of molestation. As Culler has pointed out, Said simply fails to address the complication stemming from the text's establishment of a fictional self, which could undermine the empirical author of any authority.[114] Thus, when Said relies rigidly on the foucauldian distinction between beginnings as active and origins as passive, he runs a risk of simplifying the fundamental problems underlying *both* these concepts. In other words, Said runs the risk of rendering origins "pathologically fictive" and beginnings "restrictively and preclusively performative," as Vance Smith puts it.[115] This makes Said neglect the very formal construction of beginnings, which in turn would explain his peculiar failure concretely to analyze literary beginnings. Only rarely does Said actually concretely discuss the beginnings of novels in his voluminous study.[116]

Due to its reputation, Said's *Beginnings* is difficult simply to ignore,

110 Culler, "Beginnings: Intention and Method by Edward W. Said," 583–84.

111 Homer Obed Brown, "Review of Beginnings: Intention and Method," *MLN* 91, no. 5 (1976). Also see my discussion of the distinction between realism and non-realism in chapter 2.

112 White, "Criticism as Cultural Politics," 8.

113 Ibid., 22.

114 Culler, "Beginnings: Intention and Method by Edward W. Said." Yet, one could question whether Culler is entirely right in his objection. Could one not say that the empirical author has the authority over the fictional self? The author, for example, has a right to create as many fictional selves as the work requires, as in the case of the Portuguese writer Fernando Pessoa. The empirical author needs to create a fictional self—that is part of the fictional game.

115 Smith, *The Book of the Incipit*, 218. Also, see Said, *Beginnings*, 24.

116 Said, *Beginnings*, 43, 46, 50, 84, 89.

which is why I engage it in the discussion of intertextuality, influences, and origin. Yet the work is in fact not very useful when it comes to the real intent of the book, namely the understanding of the formal dynamics of novelistic beginnings.

Conclusion: Modernism as a Shift in the Communicative Model

We have seen that the modernist critics are extremely preoccupied with beginnings and openings. Yet, the strange thing is that, by closer inspection, these critics refrain from discussing openings concretely. It therefore becomes extremely difficult to pin down any indication that there is indeed something particular about the modernist opening. Even in the most intelligent attempts, it is difficult to distinguish clichés about modernism from formalistic observations about modernism. Since Hegel talked of the "modern embarrassment about the beginning,"[117] this uneasiness about the beginning has been incredibly difficult to pin down. In the previous chapter I tried to show some of the formal characteristics of modernist openings, and in my view this examination must inevitably be statistical-grammatical in order to have credence.

We must therefore be on guard against loose, unsubstantiated claims such as George Steiner's: "We have no more beginnings."[118] This sort of speculation is at best ambiguous, first of all because it does not distinguish between ontology and epistemology: Is this a claim about the world—or a claim about how we perceive the world?

The inability of critics to make concrete observations about modernist openings demonstrates, in my view, that modernism is itself another narrative (in fact a narrative of a beginning without an end: most theorists do not describe the end of the period, only its inception). As I have shown in the case of the structuralist critics, the approach to the opening is very much an ideological question, which threatens to obscure the concrete discussion rather severely.

Yet, at the level of narrative, the modernist designation of origin as

117 Quoted in George Steiner, *Grammars of Creation*, 196.
118 Ibid., 1.

the deprivation of beginning often takes the shape of a formal principle. David Lodge claims that "the modernist novel has no real 'beginning', since it plunges us into a flowing stream of experience."[119] According to this logic, the beginning of the modernist work becomes a question of "where we decide to join the flow."[120] The challenge is how to direct this generalization about stream of consciousness in the direction of a concrete, formal observation. One common approach is to involve the temporal experience of literary works. Joseph Frank for example claims that modern works suspend the "process of individual reference temporarily until the entire pattern of internal references can be apprehended as a unity."[121] In so doing, modern literature locks past and present "in a timeless unity" and achieves a "transformation of the historical imagination into myth—an imagination for which time does not exist."[122] Yet, these temporal observations are generalizations, which may be difficult to trace in concrete observations about openings.

Since modernist criticism has turned modernism into a narrative in itself and thereby has made it difficult to approach modernism itself, I propose to analyze it through a communicative approach, just like I did in the case of the Gricean cooperative principle in the previous chapter. I was originally inspired to this approach by Edgar Allan Poe who, as early as 1846, complained about the literary tradition's tight focus on the *dénouement.*[123] In his provocative explanation of the creative process underlying one of his most famous poems, "The Raven," Poe announces that the raven's rather unmotivated repetition of "nevermore" is the very pivot of the poem. In this seemingly intentionless refrain, "the poem may be said to have its beginning at the end, where all works of art should begin."[124] Behind Poe's irony and willingness to astound, we apprehend that the author and his reader are likely to embark on *exact opposite routes* in order to get to the artwork. This is an insight obviously at play in Poe's other artistic production where suspense remains a central component in the crime narrative.

With inspiration in Poe, we can therefore explicate the confusion in

119 David Lodge, *The Modes of Modern Writing* (London: Hodder Arnold, 1977), 45.

120 Steven G. Kellman, "Grand Openings and Plain: The Poetics of First Lines," *Sub-Stance* 17 (1977): 147.

121 Frank, "Spatial Form in Modern Literature," 13.

122 Ibid., 60.

123 Edgar Allan Poe, "The Philosophy of Composition," in *The Norton Anthology of Theory and Criticism*, ed. Vincent B. Leitch (New York: W.W. Norton & Company, 2001 [1846]), 746–47.

124 Ibid.

the debate over the modernist opening by postulating that there are two opposing models of communication at play: that of the writer and that of the reader.[125] According to the first model, the author has an intention or a meaning to transpose through the literary work, which has then been grasped when the intention is received and understood. According to the second model, the comprehension of the work is not driven teleologically by a preexisting intention. As Thomas Docherty writes:

> Attention instead is on the process of producing meanings, and the active reader shares in this never-ending activity. The former model has plots and characters presented as finalized products, semantic facts to be assimilated or consumed by a subservient reader; the latter model has fictions, semiotic processes, which the reader helps produce, as he or she helps produce plots and characters.[126]

The observations about a modernist shift in temporality can thus be explained by means of a shift in the communicative model of literature. The question is simply which communicative model to prioritize. What we expect of literature will naturally change if the communicative model surrounding literature changes, and with the communicative model in mind we can precisely ask such questions as posed by Porter Abbott's: "Are we not becoming ... less keenly focused on the end of the story, more prone to want to cruise around [?]"[127] Approaching the question as a question of communicative model also helps explain why the temporal axis seems to become less conspicuous in modernist novels: "Many novels try to present the reader only with the present action of reading the novel."[128]

Having explored the theoretical concept of intertextuality and its impact on the critical approach to openings, the next chapter explores more concretely the intertextuality of a particular opening.

125 Cf. Thomas Docherty, "From Ends to Beginnings: Time and the Plot," in *Reading (Absent) Character: Towards a Theory of Characterization in Fiction* (Oxford: Clarendon Press, 1983), 133–34.

126 Ibid.

127 Abbott, "The Future of All Future Narratives," 531.

128 Docherty, "From Ends to Beginnings," 138.

CHAPTER 4

Intertextuality of the Novelistic Opening: A Practice of Openings

Almost all art consists in making the reader forget his personal power of intervention
PAUL VALÉRY, preface to *Histoires brisées*[1]

Paul Valéry's Opening and the Disappearance of the Marquise

"The marquise went out at five o'clock. Where the heck have I read that!?" asks the narrator himself in the opening of Julio Cortázar's novel *The Winners.*[2] And, indeed, this question is frequently asked. "The marquise went out at five o'clock" ("La Marquise sortit à cinq heures") is no doubt Paul Valéry's most frequently cited sentence and some may know it as a skit of a novelistic opening, meant to encapsulate his critical attitude towards the genre. The sentence, however, turns out to have become a dictum in itself and immediately takes us beyond Valéry's specific claims; it has become, as we shall see, the little motto we find inside an entire cultural rumination on the French novel.[3]

1 Valéry, *Œuvres*, I, 407.

2 Julio Cortázar, *Los premios* (Buenos Aires: Editorial Sudamericana, 1960). In the short story "Click" by John Barth, the same line is equally unknown by the two characters, see John Barth, "Click," *The Atlantic Monthly* 280, no. 6 (December 1997). This chapter is based on my French article, Niels Buch Leander, "L'intertextualité de l'incipit romanesque," in *Intertextualité, interdiscursivité et intermédialité*, ed. Louis Hébert and Lucie Guillemette (Québec, Canada: Presses de l'Université Laval, 2009). I thank the Presses de l'Université Laval for permission to draw on that article in the present book.

3 It is noteworthy that a large number of central contemporary authors like Éric Chevillard, Georges Baudouin, Daniel Oster, and Bernard Magné make reference to Valéry's marquise. Éric Chevillard, "La Marquise toujours recommencée," *Le Nouveau recueil. Revue*

Cover of Claude Mauriac, *La marquise sortit à cinq heures* (Paris: Éditions Albin Michel, 1961).

When the imagined marquise appears in Cortázar's novel from 1960, she already serves as the perfect example of a sentence we know so well that we may in fact never have read it. In fact, the effectiveness of *The Winners*' opening lies in the apparently ignorant evocation of a famed epitome of an unsuccessful opening, whose origin in any case evades us. Chilean author José Donoso thus wrote his whole *A House in the Country* (1978) in response to this sentence, yet, without knowing its origin: "Somebody said, and I don't know who it was, that you can't write novels that begin: The marquise went out at five o'clock ... And then I set out to

trimestrielle de littérature et de critique 64 (2002); Georges Baudouin, "La Marquise sortit à cinq heures," in *Contes à rebours, contes et nouvelles* (Paris: Buchet / Chastel, 1994); Daniel Oster, "'Je ne suis pas de ceux qui aiment les livres pour les livres'," in *Monsieur Valéry* (Paris: Seuil, 1981), 9. Writer and theorist Bernard Magné presents the phrase as a central paradigm in the theorization of the novel: "These aristocrats, especially when they go out at five o'clock, play in the history of literary theory as important a role as the bald kings of France in the theory of the sign." Bernard Magné, "Esquisse d'une typologie de la littérature combinatoire," http://perso.club-internet.fr/magneb/professionnel/typologie-combi/typ-combi.html. The "bald kings of France" is a reference to Bertrand Russell's famous example in his groundbreaking article on "empty descriptions," which defined propositional logic and hence started analytic philosophy. Bertrand Russell, "On Denoting," *Mind* 14 (1905).

prove that novels can be written in that way."[4] Like Donoso we may know this sentence—we just do not know why we know it.[5]

The origin of the marquise has therefore been the cause of fierce interrogation, with critics frequently going to great lengths to locate this very sentence within Valéry's works. These quests have, however, been to no avail. In a letter of 1959 to the Valéry scholar André Berne-Joffroy, the *Services culturels de SVP* symptomatically quails: "All Valéry specialists know this sentence, but not *one* could tell us where in his oeuvre one can find it."[6]

We can quickly explain this repeated state of scholarly frustration by the simple fact that this sentence actually appears nowhere in Valéry's works.[7] Yet, such was the state of confusion that Berne-Joffroy (in 1959) and Michel Butor (in 1964) saw it necessary to point out that the mocking Marquise cannot be found in Valéry's work.[8] The sentence exists only as reported in the *Surrealist Manifesto* of 1924, where André Breton writes: "Paul Valéry ... speaking of novels, assured me that, so far as he was concerned, he would continue to refrain from writing: 'The marquise went out at five o'clock'."[9] Through this seminal, surrealist text, the marquise was hence propelled into the general literary *ethos*. Strangely enough, Valéry in fact never *wrote* his most often quoted sentence.

4 Ricardo Gutierrez Mouat, "Beginnings and Returns: An Interview with José Donoso," *The Review of Contemporary Fiction* 12, no. 2 (Summer 1992).

5 Symptomatically, a French website of novelistic openings begins by citing "La Marquise sortit à cinq heures," referring to it as a "slice of life" and then notes the sentence's author as "anonymous." See http://christian.mathis.perso.sfr.fr/incipit.html.

6 André Berne-Joffroy, "La Marquise sortit à cinq heures," *Nouvelle Revue Française* 81 (1959): 556.

7 Comparable sentences do, however, occur in Valéry's notebooks *Cahiers*, which were published later only as facsimile and transcribed by the I.T.E.M. group at C.N.R.S. in Paris. In the 1960s these notebooks were thus not included as part of Valéry's "official" oeuvre. These fragments will be discussed below.

8 Berne-Joffroy, "La Marquise sortit à cinq heures"; Michel Butor, *Répertoire*, vol. II (Paris: Minuit, 1964), 11.

9 André Breton, *Manifeste du surréalisme; Poisson soluble* (Paris: Éditions du Sagittaire, 1924). It may be objected that the sentence about the marquise does not necessarily have to be an example of an *opening*, but could just as well be an example of an arbitrary sentence. The marquise, however, is mentioned in a context of an anthology of openings, and in any case the sentence has intuitively been understood as an opening and has played its role as such.

Valéry, Breton, and the Arbitrarity of the Novel

The story of the marquise could therefore end here—and often it does. Valéry scholars are still constantly asked about the origin of the sentence, but once the marquise has been revealed to reside only in this peculiar verbal alliance between Breton and Valéry, critical interrogation seems to come to a halt, or as Michel Raimond testifies: "The sentence on the marquise was only a reported statement, a bad thought that one could expel."[10] But why should we heed the function of the marquise *less* just because it results not from Valéry's written works, but from a *discussion* between two of the greatest literary authorities at the time? Would this not rather be an indication of the existence of a literary problem that extends beyond each of them?[11]

Admittedly, there may be something initially implausible about this union of the biblioclastic Breton and the venerable Valéry. In a century that was soon to hail both the artistic and commercial triumph of the novel, the Breton–Valéry alliance quickly comes to stand out as being nothing but an amusing oddity of French literary history: "It is one of those happy encounters in literary history that this conjunction of two generations [Breton and Valéry] and two opposing views had the same intransigence with regard to compromises in which literature could deteriorate."[12] The two figures seem to belong to opposite sides of the literary spectrum, almost seeming to belong to two different centuries. Yet, the periods of their creative summits overlap rather strikingly. Valéry had been a mentor for the young Breton and even when Breton leaped into dadaism and surrealism and had all the institutional and positional reasons to renounce Valéry's phantom, he did not.[13] Valéry on the other hand was far from absorbed in his protected position as France's official poet, but kept up to date with the developments amongst the youngest poets. Valéry was informed about the surrealist activities, and he is reported to have been a frequent visitor at the Surrealist Research Office in

10 Michel Raimond, *La Crise du roman. Des lendemains du naturalisme aux années vingt* (Paris: José Corti, 1966), 132.

11 One must not forget either that the remark about the marquise is also an intervention in a more general debate about the novel, taking place in Paris in the years 1924–25. See for instance René Boylesve, "Un genre littéraire en danger: le roman," *Revue de France* 5 (1924); François Fosca, "Apologie pour le roman," *Revue hebdomadaire* (1925).

12 Raimond, *La Crise du roman*, 124.

13 In a ranking of poets that Breton made in the journal *Littérature*, Valéry received the grade "15" on a scale from -25 to 20. That grade was even higher than most of the surrealist poets, including Duchamp and Ernst. See Herbert S. Gerschman, "Valéry and Breton," *Yale French Studies* 44 (1970).

rue de Grenelle. Even the title of their journal, *Littérature*, was apparently proposed by Valéry.[14] For someone who does not typically comment on literary figures in his *Cahiers*, it is striking here to find no less than four references to surrealism. Valéry acclaims provocatively that surrealism is "salvation through waste,"[15] but affirms on a different occasion: "I have seen in me the birth of all possible heresies. The incomplete developed."[16] Despite obvious reservations, the surrealist project enters into Valéry's field of imagination.[17] Not only does he share their mathematical interest; when making "a clean slate of all human acquit," their ideas of the creative activity look strikingly similar.

Nevertheless, except for a few comments by Albert Thibaudet, Jean Cassou, and Alexandre Embiricos, few critics of the period have noticed these connections.[18] On the contrary, Valéry's status as a conservative authority is only reinforced over time. The more Valéry is portrayed as the official "enemy of the novel," a view of himself he acquiesces to,[19] the more the novel appears to stand out as the modern genre *par excellence.* Asked about the crisis of the novel, the young novelist Joseph Delteil exclaims: "I love the novel passionately! It is the great modern genre. ... And whatever Valéry thinks of it, I write without the slightest shame: 'the princess [sic!] went out at five o'clock'."[20]

14 "We [Soupault, Breton, Aragon] decided one fine day to publish a magazine whose title was proposed to us by Paul Valéry: Littérature." Philippe Soupault, "Déposition," *Les Cahiers du mois* 21–22 (1926).

15 *Cahiers* XII, 742. This comes after the text fragment: "Modern literature—A B [André Breton] etc.—Maximum ease and maximum scandal—produce the maximum of scandal by the maximum of ease." His sceptism is also expressed in *Cahiers* XX: "There are secrets that only have their virtue as secrets, and unveiled are nothing—such is the case of the substitution effects of the surrealists ... crosswords," 76.

16 Valéry, *Cahiers*, XXIII, 656. See also Paul Valéry, *Cahiers*, vol. I (Paris: CNRS), 420, where Valéry takes an "anti-paranoid" position with regard to literature.

17 This observation has also been made by Jacqueline Chénieux-Gendron: "These effects of slow motion and this [Breton's] science of ruptures apparently fit into the Valéryan perspective," Jacqueline Chénieux-Gendron, *Le Surréalisme et le roman, 1922–1950* (Lausanne, Suisse: Age d'homme, 1983), 92.

18 Alexandre Embiricos, "La Galerie des contemporains," *La Revue nouvelle* 1, no. 6 (15 May 1925). Albert Thibaudet recognizes the existence of a conceptual bond between Valéry and the surrealists notably in their mathematical preoccupations which leads them to see "literary problems under a figure of abstraction, of theoretical limit, of purity." Moreover, Thibaudet stresses that for both Valéry and the surrealists "the thought is a movement or a result, let us not take one for the other: it is understood that I here give only movement and not a result." Albert Thibaudet, "Réflexions sur la littérature—du surréalisme," *Nouvelle Revue Française* XXIV, no. 138 (1925): 138. Jean Cassou equally refers to this rapprochement between Valéry and the surrealists. Jean Cassou, "Propos sur le surréalisme," *Nouvelle Revue Française* XXIV (1 January 1925).

19 "I have been turned into the enemy of the novel." Valéry, *Œuvres*, I, 1835.

20 Frédéric Lefèvre, "Une heure avec M. Joseph Delteil, poète de Jeanne d'Arc," *Les*

At the time of the publication of the surrealist manifesto, Valéry's reservations about the novel were thus widely known. When Jean Cocteau in 1924 sent him a copy of his novel *Le Grand écart* ("The Big Gap"), his dedication—"In the hope that you will read this one"—perhaps suggests that Valéry did not necessarily read the novels he received from different authors.[21] Simultaneously, in the magazine *La Renaissance*, Professor Fortunat Strowski at the Sorbonne referred generally to the anti-novelistic attitude of the period as "Valérysm." Yet, his article "Valérysm against the Novel" surprisingly does not discuss Valéry at all, but rather Pierre Lafue's anti-novelistic attitude, simply taking for granted that the readers of the magazine are familiar with Valéry's position.[22] In a follow-up article, "Pour le valérysme," Strowski attempts to justify the use of the term by merely accepting that "valérysm" may have little to do with Valéry, but may serve heuristically: "Some names are more than denominations. They play a symbolic role; they allow the spirits to unite, without holding them back within the narrow limits of an idea. ... This word, this name, it seems to me, is due to the radiance that surrounds the work and the person of Paul Valéry. Hence 'Valérysm'."[23] In other words, at this point Valéry has already become shorthand for an outmoded literary predisposition, leading, for instance, novelist Edmond Jaloux to dismiss Valéry's anti-novelistic grievance as nothing but symbolist discrimination.[24] In his seminal work on the French novel, *The Novel's Crisis*, Michel Raimond can finally mollify the debate by nullifying the *Manifesto*'s provocation: "The marquise was merely a joke. It proceeded from an insufficient reflection on the true nature of the novel."[25]

Underplaying Valéry's alliance with Breton may, however, mean that we do not grasp the full extent of his preoccupation with the question of prose.[26] Admittedly, in his less generous moments, Valéry compares

Nouvelles littéraires (16 May 1925).

21 This dedication appears in Valéry's personal library that I worked on in 2001–2002 for the University of Newcastle and the I.T.E.M. group at the C.N.R.S. This dedication proved futile, however, as it appears from the state of the book that Valéry did not read even this novel by Cocteau.

22 Fortunat Strowski, "Le Valérysme contre le roman," *La Renaissance: Politique, littéraire, artistique* (2 May 1925).

23 Fortunat Strowski, "Pour le Valérysme," *La Renaissance: Politique, littéraire, artistique* (23 May 1925).

24 "This scrupulousness is a phenomenon peculiar to the symbolist generation ... The current outcry against the novel has no other meaning." Edmond Jaloux, "L'Esprit des livres. Pierre Louÿs," *Les Nouvelles littéraires* (13 June 1925).

25 Raimond, *La Crise du roman*, 136.

26 A preoccupation which has been convincingly demonstrated in Michel Jarrety, *Valéry devant la littérature. Mesure de la limite*, 1 ed., Ecrivains (Paris: Presses universitaires poetry with *sound* and the novel simply with *noise*. Yet, his discontent with the novel, which is instrumental in provoking the debate of 1924–25 in which Delteil and Jaloux intervened, also reveals a genuine preoccupation precisely with prose that pivots around the problem of opening the literary work.[27] The marquise was thus, according to Breton, associated with a whole anthology of novelistic openings that Valéry hoped to gather: "For want of purification, Paul Valery recently proposed to assemble an anthology of as many openings of novels as possible, an inanity for which he had high hopes. The most famous authors were to contribute."[28] In spite of this sarcasm, the marquise will in fact emerge as a technical challenge to be met by subsequent novelists.[29] Contrary to Strowski's premonition about the destructive nature of "valérysm," Valéry's dissatisfaction with the novel appears to have helped to bring about a reform of the genre precisely by adding "its inner reflection to this art of composing," thus providing a prerequisite for the formulation of a new kind of novel.[30] Valéry appears not as the archenemy of the novel, but in fact as a theorist of prose, which may help us explain why Jorge Luis Borges—to everyone's surprise—characterizes Valéry as first and foremost a prose writer.[31]

The French novel has lived a much more turbulent life than modern readers imagine. Despite its growing commercial success and fairly consistent artistic achievement, the novel had been regarded with suspicion by the Parisian intellectual milieu since the seventeenth-century

de France, 1991); Silvio Yeschua, "La Marquise sortit à cinq heures," in *Valéry, le roman et l'œuvre à faire* (Paris: Minard, 1976).

27 Paul Valéry, *Ego Scriptor. Poèmes et petits poèmes abstraits* (Paris: NRF Gallimard, 1992), 136.

28 Breton, *Manifeste du surréalisme*.

29 In addition to the novelists that I discussed in the first part of this chapter, I could mention Walter Lewino's book, which proclaims to fulfill Valéry's project of collecting an anthology of openings. Walter Lewino, *Longtemps je me suis couché de travers. Incipit* (Paris: Maurice Nadeau, 1994). Jean Ricardou's question in his article "Le nouveau roman est-il valéryen?" in *Entretiens sur Paul Valéry*, ed. Émilie Noulet-Carner (Paris / La Haye: Éditions Mouton & Co., 1968) also comes to mind.

30 "Madame Bovary is the masterpiece of classical 'composition'. It is in this sense that Valérysm can reform the novel, adding its inner reflection to this art of composing. But he would waste his time if he was hoping to destroy it [the novel]." Strowski, "Le Valérysme contre le roman," 18.

31 "Poet insignia and still better prose writer Paul Valéry is currently doing a poetic art course at the Collège de France." Jorge Luis Borges, "'Introduction à la poétique' de Paul Valéry," in *Œuvres* (Paris: Gallimard, 1938), 1154. In the debate concerning Valéry's marquise, it had in fact been insinuated by Pierre Lièvre and Léon Pierre-Quint that Valéry was a better prose writer than poet, see for instance Léon Pierre-Quint, "Lectures," *Revue de France* VI, no. 2 (1 April 1926): 531ff.

poetologist Nicolas Boileau dismissed the novel as a ridiculous and easy genre, inferior in its literary structure and implausible as a mimetic project. Despite a nineteenth century saturated by novelists like Balzac, Stendhal, Flaubert, Maupassant, and Zola, the anti-novelistic bias in Paris at the beginning of the twentieth century was no less than substantial. In fact, the talk even of a "crisis" in the novel was altogether pervasive, especially after the editor of the influential *Nouvelle Revue Française*, Jacques Rivière, in 1913 made this crisis "official."[32] In 1924, when the surrealist manifesto appeared, the novel was only just on the brink of breaking through as a genre as the so-called modernist novelists emerged, represented most notably in France by Marcel Proust. However, the critique of the novel seemed almost to grow proportional with the genre's success. In the interwar period, the German aesthetician William Bonsels held his anti-novelistic conferences in France to which a special issue of *les Nouvelles littéraires* appearing in the first months of 1924 was entirely devoted.[33] When Breton's anti-novelistic *Manifesto* was published later that year, certainly more than simple provocation was at stake. The time was more than ripe for various French literary magazines, in particular the ubiquitous *Nouvelles littéraires*, to face the debate and invite contemporary novelists to comment on and—typically—refute Valéry's marquise in their ambition to circumvent the prevailing "Valérysm" of the intellectual elite.

In these literary interviews, however, the novelists all seem to forget Valéry's exact phrase, for instance when Delteil, in his passion for the novel, elevates the marquise's aristocratic standing when confirming—as we saw—that he would "feel no shame whatsoever" in writing "the princess went out at five o'clock."[34] And Edmond Jaloux turns the opening on its head when he writes that "The marquise returned home at five o'clock," an opening actually far more perplexing than Valéry's.[35] Even one year after the emergence of the surrealist manifesto, the marquise opening lost its origins in the permutations of polemics and became a sentence without a clear origin.

These permutations, however, precisely reflect one of Valéry's reser-

32 Jacques Rivière, "Le Roman d'aventure," *Nouvelle Revue Française* 5, no. 53–55 (May/June/July 1913). For further discussion of this crisis, see Raimond, *La Crise du roman*. Moreover, see my article on the adventure genre and the development of the modern French novel, Niels Buch Leander, "The Colonial Metropolis and Its Artistic Adventure: Conrad, Congo, and the *Nouvelle Revue Francaise*," *Romanic Review* 99, no. 1–2 (2008).

33 *Les Nouvelles littéraires*, 19 January 1924.

34 Delteil, "Interview menée par Lefèvre."

35 Jaloux, "L'Esprit des livres. Pierre Louÿs."

vations about the novel; its so-called "contingency." Playing in his notebooks with a "countess" who "took the 8 o'clock train" and a marquise who "took the 9 o'clock train," Valéry adds, "I can thus vary indefinitely."[36] It is the fact that one can change this sentence—that it is "arbitrary"—that bothers him. As a young man, he writes in his *Cahiers*: "I could only write a novel if I had a servant to write down in my place all that it would require of arbitrary observations."[37] And this bias would remain with him throughout his life. In a late letter touching on his view of the novel, he expands on this discontent with the possible arbitrariness of novelistic sentences:

> [Novels] must therefore refrain from arousing the faculty of invention which in every reader is as powerful as that of the author, and which could at any moment divert the reader in a devilish way into modifying the text and causing intervention from the infinite possibilities of substitutions that any narrative admits without any noticeable alteration of its theme...[38]

With Valéry's emphasis on the possibilities of substitution, it is consequently rather paradoxical that people are so eager to find the precise wording in Valéry's works.

The concepts of the "contingent" and the "necessary" have already been evoked by critics investigating Valéry's qualms about the novel.[39] To associate "contingency" with the novel and "necessity" with poetry does, however, seem too schematic a dichotomy and may obfuscate the context of Valéry's ideas about the novel. More generally, Valéry defies the novelistic idea of reality, or rather the idea that the novel *captures* reality: on the very same page as his small Marquise permutations, Valéry notes: "Novels ... As arbitrary as reality."[40] In other words, it can be claimed that Valéry's reservation regarding the novel works in parallel with his even better-known reservation about history.[41]

36 Paul Valéry, *Cahiers*, vol. V (Paris: CNRS), 101.

37 Ibid., I, 744.

38 Valéry, *Œuvres*, I, 1835.

39 For instance by Gérard Genette, "Littérature comme telle," in *Figures I* (Paris: Seuil, 1966), 255.

40 Valéry, *Cahiers*, V, 101.

41 This point is further supported by the abovementioned letter (note 38), in which Valéry simultaneously discusses his discontent with the novel and with history.

The Illusory Origin of the Story

We therefore need to address the problem of *origins* as a foundation both of history and of a story. If history consists in a search for chronology, causality, and origins, typically as the ambition of elucidating a present state, such an enterprise cannot take us far since, according to Valéry, the very concept of origins is questionable: "The origin is altogether imaginary."[42] An origin cannot be but an act of imagination, an arbitrary choice, and, if meant to secure constancy or a foundation, surely an "illusion": "Some try to extend back beyond the origin, which is the concurrence of presence and the *initial* event—and try in that gap to find gold, diamonds."[43] Such a quest for the chronological foundations of history is conceptually flawed—and can be nothing but history *as* story—precisely because it will inescapably contain the present moment as its reference frame, as discussed in chapter 1: "All thought of the origin of things is only a reverie of their present disposition, a way of degenerating reality, a variation on what is."[44] The past is, in other words, a pure product of the present: "For *what was* is spirit and has no properties that are not spiritual."[45] This mental projection about the past can then only lead to the idea of the individual's present potentiality; and any imagination of origin can serve only as a creative beginning, which explains Valéry's famous, but enigmatic aphorism "In the beginning was the fable," and which showed that the past is staged in the creative mind.[46]

A beginning can therefore never be a foundation, but will follow as a consequence of an imaginative enterprise, even when appearing to consist of chaos: "This inconceivable chaos is ordered by my intention to conceive. I myself have shuffled the cards in order to rearrange them."[47]

This devotion to the extreme potential is what refrains Valéry from venturing into prose: "This sensation of possibilities is very strong in me and has always diverted me from the path of the narrative."[48] The traditional novel precisely pretends that everything follows from a par-

42 Valéry, *Cahiers*, XXIII, 592.

43 Valéry, *Cahiers* XV, 526, quoted by Martin Rueff, "Robinson, une vue de l'esprit (À propos du *Robinson* de Paul Valéry)," *Critica del testo: rivista quadrimestrale* 2 (2002). Compare with "origin is an illusion," Valéry, *Œuvres*, II, 1451.

44 "Au sujet d'Eureka," in Valéry, *Œuvres*, I, 863.

45 "Au commencement était la fable," in Valéry, *Œuvres*, I, 394.

46 In a small manuscript by Valéry from 1921, the creativity of Orpheus is described as beginning only when the past fades entirely and becomes inconceivable. Valéry, "Commencement d'Orphée."

47 Valéry, *Œuvres*, I, 863.

48 Preface to "Histoires brisées," Valéry, *Œuvres*, II, 408.

ticular beginning—that its beginning is absolute. Whereas poetry is privileged by being "all the time a beginning,"[49] a novel suffers from the same flaw as any historical narrative: quite simply, it begins only once. Yet, the possible permutations of opening lines ("the marquise took the train at 8 o'clock," etc.) indicate that the beginning of any story is itself a story in its own right—"in the beginning was the fable."

The Opening and the Renewal of the Novel

Valéry's proposal to gather an anthology of openings of novels may not be as sarcastically meant as Breton's manifesto insinuates. What if the beginnings became continuous? What if a novel constantly started all over? What if a novel contained nothing but beginnings? This reflection seems to shape precisely one of Valéry's only prose projects, the peculiar *Histoires brisées*. These "broken" or "shattered" story lines (or histories, for that matter) are written by means of a method that testifies to a genuine fascination with the potentiality of the novelistic opening: "I write a tale as if it were the beginning of a work ... After a few lines or a page, I give up, having caught in the writing only what surprised, amused, intrigued me."[50]

These stories thus remain open-ended and take on a virtual quality, which to Valéry preserves their appeal: "I know that the work will not exist, I feel that I do not know where it would go, and that boredom would seize me if I applied myself to carrying it to some well-determined end."[51] What disturbs Valéry about a completed novel is its sense of determination, that is to say, its pretence that its elements are predetermined, that from the beginning "things" could not have been otherwise: "Any novel could have one or more endings that are quite different from the one it actually has."[52] It is not so much the fact that a novel *can* be modified, but

49 *Cahiers* XXIV, 862. Quoted by Jarrety, *Valéry devant la littérature*, 119.

50 Valéry, *Œuvres*, II, 407. In his *Cahiers*, Valéry described the consistency and fidelity of the opening: "I look at a text I wrote in 1894 and recognize myself in it in 1938—that is to say 44 years later—in the way that I form the beginning—in the way the 'subject' is presented—in the way that I introduce myself and lead this beginning to positions that would allow me to retrieve myself in this indeterminate region—the area of a given subject." *Cahiers* XXI, 379. See also Jeannine Jallat, "Le Reste et l'incipit. Sur la genèse d'un commencement valéryen," *Littérature* 64 (December 1986).

51 Valéry, *Œuvres*, II, 407.

52 Ibid., 407–8.

the fact that the novel, and presumably the realistic novel in particular, *pretends* that it cannot be modified. A novel pretends to be determined by its beginning, and in this manner tries to hide what is *necessarily contingent* behind its own logic of necessity.

The reflection on the opening seems to instill in Valéry a vision of a work that escapes such determination:

> To create just once a work which would show, in each of its nodes, the diversity which can be presented to the mind, and from which it chooses the unique sequence which will be given in the text. This would be to substitute the illusion of a single and imitative determination of reality with that of the possible-at-every-moment, which seems to me far more genuine.[53]

Reading the *Cahiers*, we thus notice that it is precisely in the year of the dispute over the marquise that Valéry begins to imagine writing—a novel. In 1925 he writes to himself: "I *ought* to create a novel. Every man creates one, like a bygone tragedy" and even specifies how he will begin writing it: "Look for names and start there. With caution."[54] At times Valéry simply accepts the limitations of the genre, for instance when noting: "In novels, 'descriptions' play, whether you like it or not, the role of musical parts. So, if you create a novel be concious of this and blame the limitations of the possible on this trait."[55] Most often, however, Valéry seems interested in circumventing the conventions of the genre in the light of his own poetics: "I dreamt of a novel that would deliberately go *against reality* in the novelists' sense. But consisting of *constructed* characters and situations."[56]

This novel was obviously never written. Yet, the formulation of a new kind of novel is in the shaping: "Why couldn't a 'novel' be the diary of someone's day? ... An incoherent sequence and yet a sequence of substitutions of moments and phases,"[57] a description that fits surprisingly well with two major novels appearing in English in this period: James Joyce's *Ulysses* (1922) and Virginia Woolf's *Mrs Dalloway* (1925). One could in fact claim to see the contours of such a novelistic journal in Valéry's cycle of prose poems, *Alphabet*, as a modern book of hours structured around the letters of the alphabet. Beginning with the letter A as "Au commencement sera le sommeil" ("In the beginning will be sleep")—an evident reference

53 Valéry, *Œuvres*, I, 1497. Quoted by Genette, "Littérature comme telle," 255–56.
54 *Cahiers* XI, 299. Quoted by Jarrety, *Valéry devant la littérature*, 342.
55 Valéry, *Cahiers* VII, 192.
56 *Cahiers* XVII, 699. Quoted by Jarrety, *Valéry devant la littérature*, 331.
57 Ibid.

to his much discussed aphorism—the temporal renewal under each letter here seems to allow Valéry to maintain that level of continual beginning that his verse would usually create.

The Anti-Naturalist Opening from Huysmans to Queneau

This aspect of temporal sequencing seems to be what fascinates Valéry in the handful of novels he did read and appreciate. He thus describes the novels of J.-K. Huysmans as a "flow of intact moments" and his annotations in *Against the Grain* (1884) emphasize his particular way of appreciating the prose of Huysmans.[58] Whereas he hardly ever made annotations in the few novels he read, Valéry marked a keyword in the beginning of each chapter of *Against the Grain.*[59] These keywords do not touch on what "happens" in Huysmans's novel (admittedly, very little does happen in this novel); they evoke simply a sensation of each chapter as if each chapter was independent and had its own beginning.

If we put Valéry's tenet that an origin is illusory aside for a moment and insist on finding the real origin of Valéry's Marquise, it is precisely in Huysmans that we ought to look. In his famous critique of Zola in the 1903 preface to *Against the Grain*, Huysmans indicates that the naturalist novel simply prolongs an obsession with social relations that has characterized the genre since the libertine novel:

> Whatever one came up with, the novel could be summed up in a few lines: to know why Monsieur So-and-So committed or did not commit adultery with Madame This-or-That. If you wanted to be distinguished and stand out as a writer of good breeding, you made the fleshly act take place between a marquise and a count; if, on the other hand, you wanted to be a popular author, a prose writer in the know, you set it between a lover from the slums and

58 In Valéry's article from 1898 in the *Mercure de France*. See Raimond, *La Crise du roman*, 58. Notice also the numerous references to Huysmans throughout the work of Valéry: Valéry, *Œuvres*, I, 663m, 742b-56, 57m, 81b-83; Valéry, *Œuvres*, II, 802m, 1001b, 186h, 204m, 327h.

59 Paul Valéry's personal library (unpublished).

> some whore; only the setting was different. … *[The reader] continues to savour the hesitations of the marquise…*[60]

In this light, the "five o'clock" of Valéry's marquise appears precisely to be a mockery of the openings of Émile Zola's novels. No less than six of Zola's novels open with a similar temporal indication, for instance *The Downfall* (1892) that begins by informing the reader that "it was about five o'clock when they had come in from Belfort" and *The Joy of Life* (1884) that opens: "When the cuckoo-clock in the dining-room struck six, Chanteau lost all hope."[61] It is thus hardly a coincidence that *The Vatard Sisters* (1879), a novel that Huysmans wrote under the influence of Zola, opens like this: "A bell tolled. It was 2.00 AM." The temporal indication was a naturalist stigmatization that he was later to renounce.[62]

Julio Cortázar's reference to Valéry's marquise, with which this chapter began, thus serves as an indication of how the critique of the traditional novel was articulated through an exposition of the novelistic mode of opening. Experimental novelists of the postwar period thus seem to transform Valéry's discontent with the novel into a well-defined artistic challenge. The writer-critic Julien Gracq thus attempts to justify the noveslistic opening with a delay in the construction of meaning: "The truth is that the novelist cannot say: 'The marquise went out at five o'clock': at this stage of the reading, such a sentence is not even perceived; it leaves only, in a night not yet illuminated, an accessory of the scene which is destined to become meaningful later, when the curtain will be lifted for real."[63]

Queneau's *The Sunday of Life* (1951) had initiated a mockery of temporal indications by beginning a chapter by "It was five o'clock in October," and his later *Zazie in the Metro* (1959) and *The Blue Flowers* (1965) seem further to expose Zola's clichéd openings in ways that remind us of Valéry's imagined opening: "Five o'clock struck at the village church" and "four o'clock struck at the bell tower of a nearby church."[64] Evidence of Queneau's direct inspiration from Valéry can be found in his combinational poem *Cent mille milliards de poèmes* (1961) in which precisely 10 percent

60 Joris-Karl Huysmans, *Against the Grain*, trans. Brandan King (Cambs, UK: Dedalus, 2008), added emphasis. *À rebours* (Paris: Argenteuil, 1924 [1884]).

61 Émile Zola, *Œuvres complètes* (Paris: Cercle du livre précieux, 1966).

62 Joris-Karl Huysmans, *Les Soeurs Vatard* (Paris: G. Charpentier, 1879).

63 Julien Gracq, *En lisant en écrivant* (Paris: Corti, 1981), 119.

64 Raymond Queneau, *Le Dimanche de la vie* (Paris: Gallimard, 1951), 68; Raymond Queneau, *Les Fleurs bleues* (Paris: Gallimard, 1965), 163; Raymond Queneau, *Zazie dans le métro* (Paris: Gallimard, 1959), 114.

of the sonnets begin with "It was at five o'clock that the marquise left."[65] In the very same year, Claude Mauriac took Valéry's sentence as the very guiding principle of his novel, completing the irony by naming the novel *La Marquise sortit à cinq heures* (1961). Like Cortázar's novel from the year before, Mauriac's novel opens with this sentence without being determined by it.[66] The marquise who went out at five o'clock thus comes to serve as a theoretical motto that condenses the direction that the French novel was to take after the Second World War when breaking with the constraints of the traditional novelistic opening.

65 Raymond Queneau, *Cent mille milliards de poèmes* (Paris: NRF Gallimard, 1961).

66 Claude Mauriac, *La Marquise sortit à cinq heures; roman* (Paris: Albin Michel, 1961). See also his *Dinner in Town* that can be opened anywhere since it is nothing but one long dinner conversation. Claude Mauriac, *Le Dîner en ville* (Paris: Albin Michel, 1959).

EPILOGUE

Beginning without End?

Everything that happens keeps on being a beginning
RAINER MARIA RILKE, *Letters to a Young Poet*, letter six

Openings as Relations to Conventions

As I observed in chapter 2, the pre-modern novel drew little attention to its beginnings. This was paradoxically achieved, I argued, by making the opening stand out from the body of text while abiding by conventional generic rules for beginning: the reader can *see* that it is a beginning. The inherent challenge is that a beginning cannot be "natural" in its own right; it is only by fulfilling certain conventional expectations that a novel's beginning will seem natural. I showed in chapter 1, for instance, that a beginning cannot lend its naturalness from its analogy with that of a birth; in the discussed examples, such an opening strategy tends to poke fun at precisely the *artificiality* of this naturalness.

The textual conventions of what constitutes a proper beginning will, however, change over time. Supported by linguistic studies, I pointed out how there had been a shift away from the use of existential openings, which was common prior to the nineteenth century (e.g. Diderot's "Here were two men"). In the nineteenth century, the use of proper names instead became frequent in the openings, and in the twentieth century even unintroduced pronouns, such as "he," could open a novel, thereby adding increasingly higher levels of what I call "perspectival abruptness." This perspectival abruptness is to be understood in its contrast to the temporal abruptness that we know as *in medias res*.

I have also argued that a change in the opening will change the conditions for the novel's possible resolution. Narratologists have demonstrated, for instance, that openings that use a reflector-character will tend to be abrupt and open, and that open beginnings will also create *open-ended* stories that do not easily find a *dénouement*.

What constitutes a literary opening is in other words historically determined and will reflect a whole range of cultural aspects. Some periods and some authors will favor an opening that also appears chronologically—to be a beginning; that is to say, where "story" and "presentation" (*fabula* and *sjuzét*) overlap chronologically as much as possible, which I discussed in chapter 2. A beginning belongs to the abstract level of the story whereas an opening belongs to the concrete level of the presentation; a literary opening is simply where the reader embarks or is supposed to embark on the text. This distinction is important, but what is even more important is the fact that literary works ostensibly question literary openings' dependency on the concept of beginnings by casting doubt on the solidity of beginnings themselves. As A. D. Nuttall puts it, there is an underlying suspicion that all natural beginnings could thus simply be cultural fictions.[1] If beginnings can never be truly "natural," the work that remains is to instate the text's own authority by a forceful opening—which explains much of the abruptness of the modern literary opening.

With a contemporary perspective, my assertion is that beginnings are precisely important to study because they highlight the "randomness" of the composition. The divergence between "story" and "presentation" that I discussed in chapter 2 is distinctive of the text, and an opening fully radicalizes the choice of presentation: the opening becomes a rich manifestation of authorial choice. The more the textual scenario is open, the more a choice of beginning becomes indicative of the author's choice of one approach rather than another. As I illustrated in chapter 3 and 4 on intertextuality, the opening is the point at which the author constitutes a space for the *text* before it constitutes a space for the *story*. This separation between *story* and *presentation* is most radicalized in the opening of a novel due to the divergence between opening and beginning. To express it in positive terms: the opening is what best highlights the very *littérarité* of a novel. Recalling the quotation from Italo Calvino in my prologue, it is indeed the "lieu littéraire par excellence."[2]

1 Nuttall, *Openings*, 195.
2 Calvino, "Appendice: cominciare e finire."

French vs. American Criticism

One of the central pillars in the present study has been the great schism between Anglo-American and French (and to some extent also German) criticism. Specifically French criticism seems preoccupied with openings and the symbolism of beginnings, whereas Anglo-American criticism on the same subject is practically non-existent. I further substantiate this claim in the appendix where I chronologically list the critical texts that have dealt with openings. As the appendix, as well as chapter 3, make clear, English-speaking critics are generally little concerned with beginnings, but are strikingly more likely to discuss the very opposite: endings. This generalization does seem to be substantiated by the observation that the few Anglo-American scholars who are interested in openings are often Romance scholars inspired by Continental methodologies.[3] Moreover, the few Americanists who are interested in openings are often of French nationality.[4]

I am well aware that my generalization on the basis of national critical traditions cannot avoid being schematic, as there will be numerous exceptions to such a generalization. Yet, my contention is that the schematism nevertheless generates insights which would otherwise not be noticed.

The way that a literary work is written obviously also determines the way that it will be read. Some works are written in a way that encourages a more "open" reading and some a more "closed" reading. This open or closed nature can be detected in formal traits, for instance when perspectival abruptness is used to enhance the impression of openness, as I discussed in chapter 2. But whatever the formal traits of the literary work, the critic's perception of an opening also determines the reception of the work.

It seems fair to say that French criticism has traditionally been more

3 For instance, David R. Ellison, "Proust and Kafka: On the Opening of Narrative Space," *Modern Language Notes* 101, no. 5 (1986); Graham Falconer, "L'entrée en matière chez Balzac. Prolégomènes à une étude sociocritique," in *La Lecture sociocritique du texte romanesque* (Toronto: Stevens & Hakkert, 1975); Freeman G. Henry, *Beginnings in French Literature*, French Literature Series (Amsterdam and New York: Rodopi, 2002). See the appendix for further references.

4 Jean-Claude Marimoutou, "Ulysse, Jacques, la Muse et le grand Rouleau," in *Représentation de l'origine: littérature, histoire, civilisation* (Saint-Denis (Réunion): Publications de l'université de la Réunion, 1987); André Topia, "Incipit joyciens. Le Fœtus et le dictionnaire," in *L'incipit. Actes Du Colloque De Poitiers 29–30 mars 1996*, ed. Liliane Louvel (Poitiers: La Licorne, 1997); Carola Veit, "The Evolution of Samuel Beckett's 'nouvelle écriture'," in *Commencements du roman: Conférences du séminaire de littérature comparée de l'université de la Sorbonne Nouvelle*, ed. Jean Bessière (Paris: Honoré Champion, 2001). See the appendix for further references.

concerned with literature's formal aspects, and this could be expected also to be the case when it comes to a formal unit like the literary opening. Part of the explanation of this difference is to be found in the fact that the two critical traditions have been differently influenced by the hermeneutic and the phenomenological lines of thought, which inescapably determines the approach to such critical concepts as interpretation and authorial intentionality. Yet, this cannot be the whole explanation of the French preoccupation with openings since Anglo-American critics readily discuss another formal unit: the ending. It can therefore be concluded that the schism is not simply a question of formal priorities, but a question of the approach to the literary field as a whole.

My point is that value or even ideology is attached to the notion of the literary opening. Simply put, one can react to openness in either a positive or negative way, and this attitude to openness is again reflected in the critics' approach to openings. The discussion of openings is intrinsically related to grander considerations such as the very role of literature in society. Is the overall role of literature fundamentally to offer a static *description* of society, or is it instead dynamic and aimed at *transforming* society? The schism between French and American criticism with regard to openings is partly due to this difference in the *ideological* perception of the role of literature in society. In this way, the French avant-garde preoccupation with openings relates to an overarching critical stance that generally perceives the text as interacting directly with society.[5] By contrast, to perceive the literary as an *autonomous* object, which is to be analyzed in its *own right*, is indeed characteristic of an American branch of criticism like New Criticism, which did show interest in openings despite its formal interests. Schematically speaking, openness in the American tradition has a negative ideological connotation as it is by default associated with nonresolution.

It is thus characteristic that central Paris-based critics (e.g. Philippe Hamon and Andrea del Lungo) perceive the opening as "liminal," as an act of transgression itself, as if it were or would be a political object. Moreover, there is a clear tendency to perceive the narrative not as a structuring unit, but as a potential trap, which threatens to capture the reader. "The narrative is a trap," as Aragon exclaims in his seminal text *Les incipit*. The French tradition is therefore skeptical with regard to the possibility of interacting directly with the opening without a prejudiced

5 See note 109 on page 23. There are of course many exceptions to this generalization, as one could not claim that for instance the criticism of Gérard Genette or the journal *Poétique* is concerned with society.

or predefined mind. The French critics are less prone to adopt what could be called "the myth of close reading," according to which "nothing is given from the beginning."[6] The French stance is very appropriately expressed by the following extract from *Finnegans Wake*: "The idea of the 'erste Akt' can only ever be a fiction; innocence is always already lost."[7]

It is important to note that this difference in the approach to the textual beginning mirrors a grander schism between Continental and Anglo-American philosophy. This schism concerns the possibility of perceiving the world as if nothing is given from the beginning, as British empiricism postulates, whereas French and Continental philosophers like Descartes and Kant postulate that the mind is pre-defined with concepts that structure our perception already from the outset (the so-called "innate ideas"). This symmetry between philosophical traditions and literary criticism is not coincidental. It shows how minute literary preoccupations are shaped by larger philosophical and ideological movements. The literary opening is no exception in this regard.

Criticism and the Opening as "Epitaph"

Victor Brombert begins his article on opening signals by quoting Samuel Beckett's declaration that "the end is in the beginning."[8] This epigraph also evokes T.S. Eliot's use of Mary Stuart's famous motto in his *East Coker*, which is the second of his *Four Quartets*: Eliot begins the poem with the words "In my beginning is my end" and ends it with "in my end is my beginning." Brombert's choice of this epigraph for his article suggests that openings are mainly an object of study because they can tell us something about the *end* of the work and thus about its resolution. Openings merely send us "signals," as Brombert's title suggests, of what is to come or of what could come. The focus is still the *telos* and the resolution, and the study of beginnings is, in other words, just a more economical way of studying a work.

T.S. Eliot made sure to use the above motto as the epitaph on his grave

6 Shlomith Rimmon-Kenan, *Narrative Fiction: Contemporary Poetics* (London: Routledge, 1983).

7 James Joyce, *Finnegans Wake* (London: Penguin, 1999 [1939]), 28.

8 Brombert, "Opening Signals in Narrative"; Samuel Beckett, *Endgame* (New York, NY: Grove Press, 1958).

in *East Coker*. This provides us with an image of the Anglo-American approach to openings: the opening can serve not only as the "epigraph" of the text, but also as the "epitaph" of a text, that is to say, it is already presumed that the work is closed or concluded; or at least that it will be concluded—that the text will come to an end, to a resolution.

To view the opening as an "epitaph" obviously constitutes a powerful critical instrument. For one thing it aims at giving us an interpretation of the work as a whole on the basis of the beginning. This Aristotelian *inductive* reminiscence could easily be compatible with the scholarly provision of interpretations of *single* works, which has been the main preoccupation of Anglo-American criticism before its late turn to the "pursuit of signs," which Jonathan Culler calls the linguistically inspired critical orientation.

When speculating about the differences between the critical traditions, it is relevant to remember Wolfgang Iser's comment about the antagonism between fiction's interpretative openness and fiction's illusion-making ability: "The polysemantic nature of the text and the illusion-making of the reader are opposed factors."[9] This means in principle that although the reader can accept a high level of polysemantism, there is a limit where the polysemantic nature of the text threatens to lose the reader.

These two opposing factors seem also to be at play in the opposition

FIGURE 9. The nature of literature

between the Anglo-American and the French critical traditions. In his analysis of Proust, Gérard Genette is for instance preoccupied with the formal techniques of "multiplication," through which he identifies no less than five beginnings in Proust.[10] The French approach to beginnings is very well reflected in the glorification of this polysemantism, and the strong emphasis on intertextuality is an effective way of breaking down the linearity of the text.[11] This goes surprisingly well hand-in-hand with the following stance by Kermode: "We are in a world of which it needs to be said *not* that plural readings are possible (for this is true of

9 Wolfgang Iser, "The Reading Process: A Phenomenological Approach," *New Literary History* 3 (1972): 279–99.

10 Genette, "Discours du récit," 85–89.

11 Laurent Jenny quoted in Allen, *Intertextuality*, 113.

all narrative) but that *the illusion of the single right reading is possible no longer.*"[12] While this stance does place the level of illusion-making in the background, it does pose a problem for the reader. As Kermode puts it, the reader's "difficulties are those of falsified expectation or hermeneutic deception; of incomplete closure; and of a failure to understand the preferential treatment given to latent as against manifest significance."[13] We recognize that reading involves "unconscious complicity with arbitrary authority,"[14] but reading also requires a competence which cannot be achieved without the instability of the narrative progression. It does not help to erect the prejudiced expectations of the ordinary reader into rules based on Austin's ideas of illocutionary acts, as Richard Ohmann attempted (as discussed earlier). The glorification of the illusion-making of the reader simply does not entail that narrative confusion and lack of closure are necessarily breaches of the narrative "contract"—to Kermode this non-linearity is actually an indispensable feature of narrative.

Kermode is important because despite his strong focus on the ending, he does not presuppose a linear narrative and a "closed" interpretation. The recursive method of Kermode (and Brooks) leaves open at least the reader's game of interpretation: "Whatever the constraints of a particular culture or a particular period, plurality is in the nature of narrativity."[15] Kermode is therefore able to situate the polysemantic nature of the text within the author's illusion-making act. Yet, Kermode's approach is unmistakably "Anglo-American" in its core when it comes to the directed nature of the narrative: the narrative may be plural and it may be non-linear, but it is bound for resolution and progresses accordingly.

The French stance that I have attempted to schematize is much more radical because it thwarts the possibility of resolution. We can here recall Aragon mentioning that "a path does not necessarily have an end."[16] Another example which also uses the metaphor of the path can be attributed to the novelist Claude Simon, who in his Nobel speech explains the nature of the modern novel:

> The path then followed will be very different from that of the novelist who, starting out from a "beginning," reaches an "ending." This other way, which it costs an explorer of an unknown country

12 Kermode, "Novels: Recognition and Deception," 111.

13 Ibid., 117.

14 Ibid., 120.

15 Ibid., 119. Barthes by contrast often seems deliberately to limit recursiveness by going left to right in his analyses.

16 Aragon, *Les Incipit*, 90.

> such pains to find (losing himself, retracing his steps, guided or led astray by resemblances between different places, the same place's different aspects) will constantly call for rechecks, pass across crossroads already crossed.[17]

The striking thing is that Simon's explorer does not have an endpoint in mind whatsoever: "This journey's end may well be that he comes back to his point of departure." According to this view, the literary text is in a semantic flux, an inherent interpretative instability, as exemplified by Paul Claudel's important poetics: "Nothing is created once and for all. It does not cease; it continues to be produced, it expresses a state of permanent tension of the effort which brought it about."[18]

With this semantic non-linearity, it becomes very difficult, if not impossible, for two different readers to interact with literature in the same fashion. Yet, even Derrida is willing to admit that a certain level of linearity is a necessary characteristic of literature: "The end of linear writing is indeed the end of the book."[19] Nevertheless, the communicative model of literature is difficult to establish if the interpretative structure is in constant flux. This stance which is typical of French criticism is further strengthened by the last decades of experimental, formal openings by authors such as Georges Perec, Marcel Bénabou, Marie NDiaye, Jean-Philippe Toussaint, Yves Navarre, Walter Lewino, Éric Chevillard, Emmanuel Carrère, Renaud Camus, Georges Baudouin, Claude Simon, and Antoine Volodine.

A Final Word about Conventions and Cooperative Literature

It is no coincidence that these experimental openings and the critics' non-linear approach to textual interpretation fall within the same period as the emergence of computer-inspired or even computer-generated literature. With hyperlinks and interaction the computer-inspired liter-

17 Simon, "Discours à Stockholm."

18 Paul Claudel, *Art Poétique*, quoted by Poulet, *Le Point de départ*, 29.

19 Jacques Derrida, *De la grammatologie* (Paris: Éditions de Minuit, 1967), 129. Translated in *Of Grammatology* (Baltimore, MD: Johns Hopkins University Press, 1976), 86.

ature highlights the reader's various routes through the text. Inspired by Valéry's "The marquise went out at five o'clock," the experimental writer John Barth has precisely called this phenomenon the "Marquise in the Machine."[20] With an interactive text, the opening may not be predictable, yet this is no guarantee that the text will move beyond the clichéd openings mocked by Valéry.

This computer-inspired or computer-assisted literature does, however, exemplify that the importance of narrativity in the last fifty years has changed and that it becomes more and more challenging to maintain the illusion-making of traditional literature. The critic's challenge is therefore that conventions of reading seem to have compartmentalized into group-based or even individual "conventions" that make it hard to establish a common ground of interpretation or interaction. In literature as well as more generally speaking, we could say, as does Porter Abbott, that we are "becoming, culturally, even globally, more participatory, less keenly focused on the end of the story."[21]

On the basis of this shift in openings, the question is to which degree it makes sense to establish a generalized communicative model for literature. However, by pointing to the cooperative principle, which I introduced in chapter 2, I argued that the cooperative principle has merely changed its focus. The change in how this principle is applied concerns the areas that I discussed at length in chapters 1–4, namely the emergence of what I have called "perspectival abruptness" (chapter 2) as well as the emergence of a high level of consciousness concerning the text's intertextuality (chapter 3 and 4). As I illustrated in chapter 4 on Valéry and the marquise, intertextuality becomes merely a set of conventions that needs to be respected in order for the literary exchange between the author and the reader to be successful.

Literary openings are an effective tool for registering these historical shifts in both the formal characteristics of literature of a particular period and the critics' ideological efforts of interpretation. This is why we need our sense of a beginning.

20 Barth, "Click."

21 Abbott, "The Future of All Future Narratives," 531.

APPENDIX

Approaching the Text: A Criticism of Openings

As my first chapter showed, people have always thought about beginnings, and cosmologies have never failed to approach concepts like "origin," "conception," and "end." Considering the obvious parallels between such cosmological concepts and the ones used to describe literary creation, it is surprising to discover that literary critics generally do not seem to concern themselves much with beginnings. As I ponted out in chapter 1, in 1980 Victor Brombert signaled that the field "still remains uncharted territory" and, overall, this assessment holds true today.[1] Critical texts on literary openings have indeed appeared fairly regularly since 1965, but always as rather isolated and singular contributions to the discipline, for instance when elucidating a particular text or a certain author's methods. Only rarely have texts on openings entered into dialogue with each other: they have not established their own discursive space in criticism, at least not in the English-speaking world. When we think of the importance of the concept of intertextuality, which so easily lends itself to openings, and which precisely makes way for "dialogue" amongst texts, it becomes even more striking.

This book is far from being the first critical text ever to discuss the literary opening. Yet, it claims to be the first work in English that aims at a comprehensive understanding of the literary opening as a tool for

1 Brombert, "Opening Signals in Narrative," 493.

criticism.[2] Given this comprehensive approach, it is beneficial to include a survey of how critics until now have worked on openings, thereby attempting to situate these previous approaches in an overall critical narrative. The principal purpose of the survey is to help and encourage the intellectual navigation in the slowly growing collection of critical texts on the topic. In the process, however, I demonstrate that ordering, categorizing, and synthesizing these various approaches will enable us to arrive at a workable and dynamic concept of the literary opening. In other words, I also establish a discursive space for these critical texts—to jump to a metacritical level where these texts start interacting.

Such a metacritical survey has the advantage of revealing particular preoccupations amongst critics in different periods, expounding on their various ideas about how we approach—or should approach—literary texts. My approach is to portray the literary opening in the critical chronology and as systematically as possible without, however, pretending that there could be one universal approach. Rather, I show how the use of the opening varies according to the critical priorities of the period. By getting these priorities to enter into a dialogue with each other by focusing on a single formal unit such as the beginning, I suggest one effective way of elucidating the bends in literary criticism's itinerary across movements and languages. This will further serve to illustrate what my previous chapters have already argued: that one's approach to the opening reflects one's general approach to literature.

At the end of this chronological itinerary, I will hope to have illustrated further my contention that the study of the literary opening illuminates a great divide between the Anglo-American and the French (as well as the German) approach to literature. As I have already delineated in the previous chapters, the opening has been neglected amongst critics in the Anglo-American critical tradition, which will be further substantiated in this appendix. Although one may suspect that this asymmetry between the critical traditions is to be found in French criticism's stronger preoccupation with the formal aspects of literature, I here argue that the difference in the approach to the beginning extends beyond simply the question of formal priorities. The difference in the approach to the opening points to a difference in the approach to the literary text as a

2 Some dissertations have used openings from a particular author as the dissertation's guiding principle, but the insight to be gained is on the side of the author, not on openings themselves. Nancy Ezer, "The Opening as a Master-Narrative of the Political Unconscious" (Villanova University, 1988); Mary Isobel Rosner, "Novel Beginnings: A Rhetorical Analysis of Ouvertures in Nineteenth-Century Fiction" (Ohio State University, 1978).

whole; literary texts occupy an altogether different function in the Anglo-American literary tradition.

I will make reference to some texts which have already been discussed in previous chapters, but the idea is to place these texts within a different perspective—namely that of elucidating the chronology of the criticism of openings. In other words, some references from previous chapters will be brought to bear again, but the purpose of this is to assemble a comprehensive guide to the critical field on the topic, and also to look at these references within a new setting.

For the sake of comprehensiveness and chronology let us begin by going all the way back to the Ancient Greeks, because here as in many other areas the main schism is already brought out. In other words, I begin—quite appropriately—at the beginning.

Greek Reason and Natural Beginnings

Since the professional literary critic is a modern invention, a historical survey of older, critical texts on openings can be made very quickly indeed. Criticism, however, has existed since ancient times, but generally in the form of either philosophers' aesthetic ontologies or authors' reflections on the creative process.

As discussed in chapter 1, Greek reason since Hesiod views narratives—typically epics and tragedies—as being committed to beginning "at the beginning." The *logos* that we have come to know as the Greek sense of rationality also refers to a presupposition of a certain direction in a narrative. As Rémi Brague points out: "What we lazily call 'Greek reason' first of all consists in telling what has happened, and to do it in a certain way."[3] Using the *logos* and speaking "straight" involves the speaker's commitment to telling how the "whole thing" started. To Hesiod, it is only by beginning at the beginning that a speaker will be able to summarize what has happened in a way that will present the chain of events in its various dimensions without leading the speaker astray. Yet, it is only when deciding not to hide or distort anything that a speaker will be able to set out from the affair itself and avoid obfuscating the narrative by beginning with his or her own perspective. In other words, to speak in public

3 Brague, "Le Récit du commencement," 23.

involves explaining how the current situation *came about*: the current state will need to be presented in the light of its "natural" beginning.[4]

Hesiod's line continues through Aristotle's celebrated thoughts on the structure of tragedy. Having described "a whole" as "that which has a beginning, a middle and a conclusion,"[5] the *Poetics* defines a beginning as "that which itself does not of necessity follow something else, but after which there naturally is, or comes into being, something else." In other words, the beginning cannot be deduced from what preceded it. The middle and the conclusion, however, should follow from the beginning, and nothing else should follow the conclusion. These logical boundaries of the artwork establish a "cosmological" parallel that renders mimetic representation possible. A plot must therefore not begin "from a random point"—the beginning ought to be "natural," as I discussed in chapter 1. Aristotle's ultimate interest, however, lies in the *telos*, in the "final cause" and its means of persuasion as effected through emotion, style as well as through argumentation. The *logos* serves the artwork's resolution: "The end is most important of all."

Yet, the Greeks themselves were aware that the commitment to "natural" beginning, despite its commonsensical appeal, contains a logical obstacle. Going back to a state of affairs prior to the present involves logically restoring things as they physically were. This exercise is not easy—and for two reasons: first, it would practically require the speaker to relinquish his or her present perspective. Yet, it is only when keeping the present perspective that the speaker will be able to focus on the direction and move through the sequence of events as they happened. Second, when locating a beginning one could theoretically extend the search infinitely backwards. A storm in the Alps could in principle be explained as being caused by a butterfly flapping its wings in China. And we could then start telling the life story of this butterfly, and so on. A "natural" beginning is in fact not very "natural": as I have already argued in chapter 1, it must rely on a pragmatic decision about where to begin.

This holds true of even the most "natural" of beginnings: birth. Texts that have tried to trace origins by describing the protagonist's birth immediately have an air of artificiality about them. The implausibility of the perspective is illustrated when David Copperfield begins his narrative by announcing "I am born." Yet, once this search is started, one ought to extend back still further and describe the moment of one's *conception*—

4 Hesiod, *Theogony*, vv. 156, 203, 408, 25, 52.

5 Aristotle, *Poetics*, 96.

as Tristram Shandy famously does. Although philosophers recommend providing "natural" beginnings, literature has profound difficulties in complying with this, as seen in chapter 1.

It is therefore symptomatic that the oldest example of a critical assessment of a specific literary opening addresses precisely this problem of "natural" beginnings. In his *Ars Poetica*, Horace extends back before High Classical Greek reasoning and eulogizes Homer for opening *in medias res* with "Sing, goddess, of the Wrath…." What makes Homer the greatest of poets in Horace's eyes is precisely that "he doesn't … begin the Trojan war from the twin egg [that is, of the twins Clytemnestra and Helen]."[6] Inception is not conception is the lesson. And an opening is not a beginning. Instead, the midway becomes the measure for the whole work: the poet "tells his fables and mixes truth with falsehoods in such a way that the middle squares with the beginning and the end with the middle."

Pre-Modern Creation and the Incipit

Generally, and perhaps not surprisingly, Horace's lesson has been honored more by literary craftsmen than by theorists. Dante Alighieri famously begins his *Divine Comedy* (1320) with "Nel Mezzo del Cammin…" ("Halfway on the journey of my life…"). The narrative begins precisely at the halfway mark of the character Dante's life, with nothing but allusions to what came before, to what led the protagonist astray and into the journey of the fiction. This principle is echoed by Pierre de Ronsard in his *Brief on the Art of French Poetry* (1565), where he asserts that "great poems never begin at the first of the action."[7] He consequently gives the following piece of advice to poets: "Begin in the middle," allowing only one exception: lyrical odes may begin "abruptly." In other words, the principle of the midway opening signifies not abruptness, but, on the contrary, poetic harmony.

In the medieval period in general, the incipit is an important marker of the poem and is used centrally to classify poems, as a sort of catalogue in honor of God.[8] An important incipit of the period is "Je a cest mien

6 Horace, *Ars Poetica*, 127.
7 Ronsard, *From a Brief on the Art of French Poetry*.
8 See Smith, *The Book of the Incipit*.

commencement" ("I have my beginning"), which exploits precisely the literary parallel to cosmology to the fullest.[9]

The very first "stylistic" analysis of an opening appeared in 1612 by the German cabalistic mystic Jacob Böhme, whom I also discussed in chapter 1. In his work with the regenerative title of *Aurora*, Böhme sketches the power of the combinational cabala. An entire section is devoted to "an exposition of the first verse of the first chapter of Genesis, according to the language of Nature" and consists in a peculiar, "semantic" analysis of the phonetics of the words of Genesis. The analysis is based simply on the German Bible, and apparently Böhme does not seem to be concerned with the fact that these "words of God" sound different in their "original" Hebrew/Greek form. This cabbalistic approach was to return later, as structuralism of the twentieth century would adopt some important features from cabbalism, as has been pointed out by Harold Bloom, one of the central theorists of influence of the twentieth century.

1850–1920: Modern Provocation and the Potential of Beginnings

As previous chapters have revealed, modern literature tends to interrogate norms such as the conventional identification of reader and writer in literary activity. The increasingly provocative mode of literary poetics results from this loosening link between reader and writer, as Siegfried Jüttner puts it: "The authors feel free from personal ties to the reader, whom they do not even know, and deny the binding nature of norms."[10] For many modern authors, tradition is under attack and the method consists in provoking the reader to be more responsive to the opening.

Openings illustrate quite well this change in the literary perception. From the mid-nineteenth century, the descriptions of openings sometimes turn playful and somewhat "provocative." In his seminal text on the opening line as the very generative principle of his novels, Aragon

9 Arthur Långfors, *Les Incipit des poèmes français antérieurs au XVIe siècle: Répertoire bibliographique* (Genève: Slatkine Reprints, 1977), 175.

10 Siegfried Jüttner, "Der beschimpfte Leser. Zur Analyse der literarischen Provokation," *Romanische Forschungen* 86 (1974): 95.

explains: "I considered the nineteenth century to be the century that broke away from tradition."[11]

Aragon points to Gobineau's *Scaramouche* from 1843, which opens by suggesting different clichéd openings in order only to express to the reader an exasperation with the vulgarity of the beginning (as discussed in chapter 2 and 3): "Well, no! All these beginnings are vulgar and boring, and since I do not have enough imagination to throw you into my narrative in a somewhat new way, I prefer not to start at all." In this refusal to begin, Aragon locates the new attitude to literary convention: "Thus, the young Gobineau manifests the anxiety which necessarily seizes the writer in front of the conventional character who seems necessarily to take the primer, the opening of all writing, any sentence that seems to initiate the mental ceremony—be it a tale or novel—which will make up the undertaken narrative."[12]

Almost simultaneously with Gobineau, Edgar Allan Poe protests (in 1846) against the literary tradition's tight focus on the *dénouement*.[13] In his provocative explanation of the creative process underlying his "The Raven," Poe announces the raven's rather unmotivated repetition of "nevermore" as the pivot of the poem. In this seemingly intentionless refrain "the poem may be said to have its beginning—at the end, where all works of art should begin." Behind Poe's irony and willingness to astound, however, we apprehend that the author and his reader are likely to embark on exact opposite routes in order to get to the artwork. This is an insight obviously at play in Poe's other artistic production where suspense remains a central component in the crime narrative.

This frustration with a conventional opening is partly a product of the modern era's shift in genre from recital to *récit* (narrative). In the nineteenth century the novel gradually came to dominate the literary scene, both commercially and creatively, threatening the work with banality as the novelistic opening became increasingly institutionalized. The nineteenth-century openings are recognizable and classifiable according to the individual author, as Aragon points out: "Under the apparent diversity of the openings of the Romantic novel, I began to rediscover a simple uniformity, that of the man, the author. There was the style of Balzac, that of Hugo, that of Flaubert. And so forth."[14]

The post-realist authors therefore increasingly found that the opening

11 Aragon, *Les Incipit*, 37.

12 Ibid., 75.

13 Poe, "The Philosophy of Composition," 746–47.

14 Aragon, *Les Incipit*, 37.

constrained the author's creative possibilities as well as the plausibility of the story. With the advent of the twentieth century, writers have pointed out the impossibility for the narrator to comprehend the entire story,[15] and the way of beginning therefore becomes essential. Proust's narrator does not pretend to perceive the entire *In Search of Lost Time*; on the contrary, the opening of the novel reveals a dynamic between the narrator's two first persons—a dynamic between "référent" (referent) and "référé" (reference)—without which the work could not even have been generated. As Fontane explained in 1880, the opening page becomes a key to the work that will unfold in the light of it: "The first chapter is always the key thing and in the first chapter it is the first page. ... With the right structure, the germ of the whole thing must be present on the first page."[16]

In the 1920s a polemic crusade against the banality of the novel took shape in France precisely through a reflection on the novelistic opening. In chapter 4 of this book I pursued the peculiar united front of Paul Valéry and André Breton, which summed up their discontent with the novel through a mockery of the sentence "La Marquise sortit à cinq heures" ("The marquise went out at five o'clock"). With the surrealist "phrase de réveil" ("sentence of awakening") and Valéry's impatience, it became a defined artistic challenge to begin.

The rise of academic criticism at the beginning of the twentieth century actually did not spur any considerable debate specific to literary openings. It is remarkable that comments on openings came exclusively from the authors themselves. There is one exception, however: a critical work devoted exclusively to openings in German literature did appear as early as 1913 in a doctoral dissertation submitted at the University of Giessen.[17] This work, which I have not, however, been able to retrieve in any library, is really the first critical work on the topic. The war, however, seemed to impede critics' interest in formal measures and no work on the topic was to appear for the next almost half a century.

15 Nuttall, *Openings*, 194.

16 Theodor Fontane, 18 August 1880, cited in Hertling, *Theodor Fontanes Irrungen, Wirrungen, Die 'Erste Seite' als Schlüssel zum Werk*, 7.

17 Fritz, "Erzähleingänge in der deutschen Literatur" (Giessen, 1913).

1960s: The Beginnings of the Criticism of Openings

In 1958, however, the young American critic J. Hillis Miller wrote a chapter based on the opening of Charles Dickens's *Bleak House.*[18] In 1960 the study of the opening turned to stylistics with Ian Watt's article on the first paragraph of Henry James's *The Ambassadors.*[19] Watt here managed to exhibit the narrative strategies of James through a close look at the descriptive density and grammatical repetitiveness of James's late prose. Watt's article was later translated into French and appeared in the central French journal *Poétique*, to which I shall return below. Later, in 1967 and 1974, Frank Kermode was to publish his two important contributions to the topic, his *The Sense of an Ending* and his related article "Sensing Endings."[20] Yet, as I argued in chapter 3, the preoccupation is fundamentally different from that of the German and the French critics during the same period.

A flourish of publications on the topic would then appear in German. The first article on the literary opening as a general poetic consideration appeared in 1961 when Hermann Piwitt published his article "Zum Problem des Romaneingangs,"[21] which would be followed by the first critical collection on openings appearing in 1965.[22] Despite the subtitle of this collection—"Attempt at a Poetics of Novels"—the ideas presented here did not amount to a systematic approach: "In any case a systematic exposition could not and should not emerge from this, as this would with the current state of research only lead to a barren and irrelevant schematism."[23] Just as the literary discipline started using methodic tools often borrowed from linguistics, time worked against the idea of developing a system: "It seems today that even if you cannot do away with systems altogether then at least you do not entirely rely upon them any longer."[24] Yet, the collection contains important suggestions for the study of the

18 Hillis Miller, "Chapter VI: Bleak House."

19 Ian Watt, "The First Paragraph of *The Ambassadors*: An Explication," in *Henry James: The Ambassadors* (New York, NY: Norton, 1994).

20 Kermode, *The Sense of an Ending*; Frank Kermode, "Sensing Endings," in *Narrative Endings*, ed. Alexander Welsh. Special issue, *Nineteenth-Century Fiction* 33, no. 1 (1978).

21 Hermann Peter Piwitt, "Zum Problem des Romaneingangs," *Akzente* 8 (1961).

22 *Romananfänge. Versuch zu einer Poetik des Romans*, ed. Norbert Miller (Berlin: Literarisches Colloquium, 1965).

23 Ibid., 7–8.

24 Ibid.

opening, for instance by being the first to propose that the opening may reveal central historical shifts in the creative imagination.[25]

In French literature of the 1960s, a group of authors with a keen, critical sensibility pursued the potentiality of the literary opening in their ambition to renew the novelistic genre. In 1961, Alain Robbe-Grillet toyed with the idea of a novel that following its conception became self-generative.[26] In chapter 4, I discussed how Claude Mauriac uses Paul Valéry's mockery of the novel in the very title of his novel, *La Marquise sortit à cinq heures*. These novelists' primary target is the conventional novel's artificial concordance between historical time and story time. Raymond Jean efficiently summed up the French *nouveau roman* thus: "Everything happens almost always as if the break, the initial rupture of the narrative, indicated that this narrative had already begun elsewhere and took over from an earlier text rather than from a referential, pre-existing reality."[27]

These reflections on the part of authors were closely related to the nascent structuralism, which was to predominate in the 1970s.

1970s: French Structuralism and the Open Poetics

Right from the beginning of the 1970s, the French journal *Poétique* was instrumental in putting literary openings on the critical agenda in France. Ian Watt's article in English and Weinrich's article in German were translated and published in *Poétique* and a number of critics published through this organ as well as the *Poétique* book series at Seuil during the 1970s and 1980s. Important contributions were featured by prominent theorists such as Roland Barthes, Julia Kristeva, Gérard Genette, Philippe Hamon as well as specialized contributions from Dominique Lancereux, Boris Uspenski, Jacques Dubois, Dorrit Cohn, Jean-Louis Morhange, and

25 See in particular Klotz's article, which pursues the disappearance of the muse from the epic with the consequence that the beginning itself becomes increasingly thematized. Volker Klotz, "Muse und Helios—Über epische Anfangsnöte und -weise," in *Romananfänge. Versuch zu einer Poetik des Romans*, ed. Norbert Miller (Berlin: Literarisches Colloquium, 1965).

26 Robbe-Grillet, "Un roman qui s'invente lui-même."

27 Raymond Jean, "Ouvertures, Phrases-Seuils," *Critique* XXVII, no. 288 (1971): 431.

Sophie Rabau.[28] The journal's commitment to the theme of openings has remained steadfast in recent decades, where one of the central theorists of openings, Andrea del Lungo, published his initial article in *Poétique* and later published his book at the same publishing house, Minuit.[29]

The "openness" of the opening was an obvious tool for structuralism, which defined itself as a "science of plurality," taking the side of writing rather than treading, as I explained in chapter 3. Realism was often targeted by structuralism, which accused realism of being "pseudo-realist" with its concrete references to time and space. Inspired by linguistic tools, the adopted approach was to focus on the creation of meaning instead. Unsurprisingly, linguists are instrumental in maintaining a tight focus on openings, all the way from Juryi Tynjanov and Roman Jakobson to Joseph M. Backus (1965), with more recent contributions by Ann Banfield (1987), Ronald Carter (1987), Svetlana Vogeleer (1987), J. F. Duchan (1995), and Gilles Philippe (1998).[30]

In the midst of this formalistic period of the 1970s, several of the French critics, such as Julia Kristeva and Claude Duchet, turned the formal concern into societal critique.[31]

28 Barthes, "Par où commencer ?"; Philippe Hamon, "Clausules," *Poétique* 24 (1975); Philippe Hamon, "Texte littéraire et métalangage," *Poétique* 31 (1977); Dorrit Cohn, "K fait son entrée au Château: A propos du changement d'instance narrative dans le manuscrit de Kafka," *Poétique* 61 (1985); Gérard Genette, "Le Statut pragmatique de la fiction narrative," *Poétique* 78 (1989); Kristeva, "Le Texte clos"; Dominique Lanceraux, "Modalités de la narration dans 'La Route des Flandres'," *Poétique* 14 (1973); Boris Uspenski, "Poétique de la composition," *Poétique* 9 (1972); Jacques Dubois, "Surcodage et protocole de lecture dans le roman naturaliste," *Poétique* 16 (1973); J.-L. Morhange, "Incipit narratifs. L'entrée du lecteur dans l'univers de la fiction," *Poétique* (1995); Sophie Rabau, "La Première phrase du premier roman," *Poétique* 82 (1990).

29 Andrea del Lungo, "Pour une poétique de l'incipit," *Poétique* 94 (1993); Andrea del Lungo, *L'Incipit romanesque*.

30 Tynjanov, "On Literary Evolution"; Roman Jakobson and Jurij Tynjanov, "Problems in the Study of Literature and Language," in *Readings in Russian Poetics: Formalist and Structuralist Views*, ed. Ladislav Matejka and Krystyna Pomorska (Ann Arbor: Michigan Slavic Publications, 1978 [1928]); Backus, "'He came into her line of vision walking backward'"; Ann Banfield, "'Describing the Unobserved': Events Grouped around an Empty Center," in *The Linguistics of Writing: Arguments between Language and Literature*, ed. Nagal Fabb, Derek Attridge, Alan Durant, and Colin MacCabe (Manchester: Manchester University Press, 1987); Ronald Carter, "The Placing of Names: Sequencing in Narrative Openings," *Leeds Studies in English* 18 (1987); Svetlana Vogeleer, "Le Concept de point de vue et son application aux phrases existentielles qui ouvrent un texte narratif," *Le Langage et l'homme* XXII, no. 1 (1987); J. F. Duchan, G. A. Bruder, and L. E. Hewitt, *Deixis in Narrative: A Cognitive Science Perspective* (Hillsdale, NJ: Lawrence Erlbaum Associates Inc., 1995); Philippe, "Les Démonstratifs et le statut énonciatif des textes de fiction."

31 Duchet, "Pour un sociocritique, ou variation sur un incipit"; Claude Duchet, "Idéologie de la mise en texte [Premières phrases des 'Rougon-Macquart'],"*La Pensée* 215 (1980).

1970s: Structuralism *à l'américaine*

It is in many ways striking that, in spite of their close readings, the American New Critics never seemed particularly interested in openings, which were not particularly pertinent to their method. This may have been attributable to the fact that American New Criticism viewed the work of art as an autonomous object. Consequently, criticism on openings in the English-speaking world was virtually non-existent until the winds of structuralism blew across the Atlantic. The only mention of openings up until the 1970s was thus Hillis Miller's and Ian Watt's above-mentioned articles. It should be noted that Hillis Miller's methodology was strongly inspired by Georges Poulet and the so-called Geneva School, so the English-speaking criticism is strictly speaking only represented by Ian Watt's article.

Structuralism focused new attention on openings, a theme which was discussed throughout the 1970s. Edward Said's important book *Beginnings*, which I discussed in chapter 3, appeared in 1975, but we also see contributions from Philip Stevick (1970), W.R. Martin (1973), Jonathan Culler (1975, 1976, 1980), Seymour Chatman (1975), James Bennett (1976), Steven Kellman (1977), Meir Sternberg (1978), Victor Brombert (1980), and Thomas Docherty (1983).[32] What is common to all these critics is that they are all inspired by French criticism and French methodology.

1970s: American Endings

As I discussed at greater length in chapter 3, the focus in English-speaking criticism is rather on the ending, the two most eminent examples being Frank Kermode's *The Sense of an Ending* and Peter Brooks's *Reading for*

32 Philip Stevick, "Beginnings," in *The Chapter in Fiction: Theories of Narrative Division* (Syracuse, NY: Syracuse University Press, 1970); W.R. Martin, "Beginnings and Endings in Conrad," *Conradiana* 5, no. 1 (1973); Jonathan Culler, "Defining Narrative Units," in *Style and Structure in Literature: Essays in the New Stylistics*, ed. Roger Fowler (Oxford: Basil Blackwell, 1975); Culler, "Presupposition and Intertextuality"; Jonathan Culler, "Prolegomena to a Theory of Reading," in *The Reader in the Text: Essays on Audience and Interpretation*, ed. Susan R. Suleiman and Inge Crosman (Princeton, NJ: Princeton University Press, 1980); Chatman, "Towards a Theory of Narrative"; James R. Bennett, "Beginning and Ending: A Bibliography," *Style* 10 (1976); Kellman, "Grand Openings and Plain: The Poetics of First Lines"; Sternberg, *Expositional Modes and Temporal Ordering in Fiction*; Brombert, "Opening Signals in Narrative"; Docherty, "From Ends to Beginnings: Time and the Plot."

the Plot. The same period brought other important contributions on endings by David Richter (1974), Marianna Torgovnick (1981), Neil Hertz (1985), D.A. Miller (1981), Joyce Rowe (1988), Barbara Smith (1968), and Alexander Welsh (1978).[33]

1980s: The Breakthrough of Narratology

In the 1970s there was an obvious schism between "mainstream" critics who worked with endings and structuralist critics (before these in turn became "mainstream") who worked with beginnings. This schism was to dissolve in the 1980s as the discipline of narratology gathered momentum and picked up on the usefulness of discussing openings. Narratology is more internationally well-founded than any of the previous literary methodologies and we see a broad group of scholars interested in openings, from Gérard Genette and Stanzel to Jaap Lintvelt (1984), Norman Springer (1987), Ina Ferris (1988) and Gerd Driehorst (1988).[34] This interest was more or less constantly sustained throughout the subsequent decades all the way up to the anthology *Narrative Beginnings* (2008), edited by Brian Richardson, and to which I contributed with an essay.[35]

33 Richter, *Fable's End*; Torgovnick, *Closure in the Novel*; Neil Hertz, *The End of the Line: Essays on Psychoanalysis and the Sublime* (New York: Columbia University Press, 1985); Miller, *Narrative and its Discontents*; Joyce A. Rowe, *Equivocal Endings in Classic American Novels* (Cambridge: Cambridge University Press, 1988); Barbara H. Smith, *Poetic Closure* (Chicago: University of Chicago Press, 1968); Alexander Welsh, "Opening and Closing *Les Misérables*," in *Narrative Endings*, ed. Alexander Welsh. Special issue, *Nineteenth-Century Fiction* 33, no. 1 (1978).

34 Stanzel, *A Theory of Narrative*; Jaap Lintvelt, "L'ouverture du roman: procédures d'analyse," in *Recherches sur le roman II 1950–1970: Cahiers de recherche des instituts néerlandais*, ed. Charles Grivel and Frans Rutten (Groningen: Institut de Langes Romanes, 1984); Norman Springer, "The Language of Literary Openings: Hemingway's *Cat in the Rain*," in *Narrative Poetics: Innovations, Limits, Challenges*, ed. James Phelan (Columbus, OH: Center for Comparative Studies in the Humanities, 1987); Ina Ferris, "The Historical Novel and the Problem of Beginning: The Model of Scott," *Journal of Narrative Technique* 18, no. 1 (1988); Gerd Driehorst and Katharina Schlicht, "Textuale Grenzsignale in narrativer Sicht. Zum Problem von Texteingang und Textausgang. Forschungsstand und Perspektiven," in *Sprache in Vergangenheit und Gegenwart*, ed. Wolfgang Brandt (Marburg: Beiträge aus dem Institut für Germanistische Sprachwissenschaft der Philipps-Universität Marburg, 1988).

35 Richardson, *Narrative Beginnings*.

1990s: Genetic Studies and the Fragile Opening

In the 1990s the literary methodology (generally as well as specifically in the case of openings) splits up more equally where a multitude of "schools" or "orientations" co-exist side by side. The fragility of opening becomes an object of study for poetic and genetic studies, notably in the French tradition where the opening becomes a point of fixture almost regardless of the predominant theoretical orientation of the time. This period also saw the emergence of poetic and genetic studies based on openings by Jean-Louis Morhange (1995), Andrea del Lungo (1993), Daniel Ferrer (1993), Frédérique Chevillot (1993), and Umberto Eco (1994), who uses it to discuss the concept of fictionality.[36]

1990s: Openings and the Insight into History

A different trend in the 1990s brought openings to the critic's attention as a tool for unraveling variations in and across historical periods, that is, as a tool for insight into history. This approach was started earlier by Norbert Miller (1968) and Volker Klotz (1965) and peaked around 1990 with the works of A. D. Nuttall (1991 and 1992), Rémi Brague (1987), Francis M. Dunn and Thomas Cole (1992), Michael Mandelartz (1993), and Pierre Rodriguez (1990).[37] With a few exceptions, notably A. D. Nuttall, who I discussed in chapter 1, and who also uses openings as insights into historical variations in metaphysics, the German and French critics tend to predominate. The shared belief in these critical works is that, as Rodriguez puts it, it is pos-

36 Morhange, "Incipit narratifs. L'entrée du lecteur dans l'univers de la fiction"; del Lungo, "Pour une poétique de l'incipit"; Daniel Ferrer and Bernhild Boie, eds., *Genèse du roman contemporain. Incipit et entrée en écriture* (Paris: CNRS Editions, 1993); Chevillot, *La Réouverture du texte*; Eco, "Fictional Protocols."

37 Norbert Miller, *Der empfindsame Erzähler. Untersuchungen an Romananfängen des 18. Jahrhunderts* (Munich: Hanser, 1968); Klotz, "Muse und Helios—Über epische Anfangsnöte und -weise"; A. D. Nuttall, "Some Shakespearean Openings: *Hamlet, Twelfth Night, The Tempest*," in *The Arts of Performance in Elizabethan and Early Stuart Drama: Essays for G. K. Hunter*, ed. Murray Biggs, Philip Edwards, Inga-Stina Ewbank, and Eugene M. Waith (Edinburgh: Edinburgh University Press, 1991); Nuttall, *Openings*; Brague, "Le Récit du commencement"; Francis M. Dunn and Thomas Cole, "Beginnings in Classical Literature," *Yale Classical Studies* 29 (1992); Michael Mandelartz, "Der Textanfang als kosmologischer Entwurf: die Motive des Musenanrufs und des Waldes," *Euphorion* 87 (1993); Pierre Rodriguez and Michele Weil, eds., *Topique des ouvertures narratives avant 1800* (Montpellier: Centre d'Étude du Dix-Huitième Siècle de Montpellier, Univ. Paul Valery Montpellier, 1990).

sible to establish "a theme of universal beginning, or as least common to an era." As argued in chapter 3, such an approach would, however, need a very well-described linguistic focus if it is not to turn into generalizations.

Within this trend there is an increasing interest in what I call "generic" beginnings, represented by such critics as Sophie Rabau (1990), Jean Bessière (2001), Helmut Kreuzer (1993), and Wolfgang Haubrichs (1995).[38] These critics use openings as units that define the literary genres and the inauguration of a particular genre. Again French and German critics predominate, but the English-speaking criticism is here importantly represented by Sheldon Sacks, who may have been the first American critic to acknowledge the signals of literary openings by talking about tragedy in terms of sequence. Through this analysis he reveals that modern tragedy *begins* with the tragedy, making it more of a "blunder" (Lord Jim, Tess) from which one needs to fight back rather than being an inevitable endpoint of the story as in Greek tragedy.[39]

1990s: Diversion with Openings: Pedagogy and Memorization

A third trend in the 1990s is the more informal use of openings as a tool for teaching and canonization of novels. For instance, Jean Verrier (1992) and Hélène Sabbah (1991) use openings as a pedagogical tool for introducing literary considerations to a high-school audience.[40] Simon Leys (2001) and Amos Oz (1999) use openings as an ordering principle within their own poetics.[41] Moreover, openings began to be classified, at least informally,

38 Bessière, ed. *Commencements du roman*; Rabau, "La Première phrase du premier roman"; Helmut Kreuzer, "Anfänge des Romans," *LiLi. Zeitschrift für Literaturwissenschaft und Linguistik* 23, no. 89 (1993); Wolfgang Haubrichs, ed., "Anfang und Ende," *LiLi. Zeitschrift für Literaturwissenschaft und Linguistik* 25, no. 99 (1995).

39 Sheldon Sacks, "Some Psychological Implications of Generic Distinctions," *Genre* 1 (1968); Sheldon Sacks, "Golden Birds and Dying Generations," *Comparative Literature Studies* 6 (1969); Sheldon Sacks, "Clarissa and the Tragic Traditions," in *Irrationalism in the Eighteenth Century*, ed. Harold E. Pagliaro (Cleveland: The Press of Case Western Reserve University, 1972).

40 Jean Verrier, *Les Débuts de romans* (Paris: Bertrand-Lacoste, 1992); Hélène Sabbah, *Les Débuts de roman* (Paris: Hatier, 1991).

41 Simon Leys, "Ouvertures," in *Protée et autres essais* (Paris: Gallimard, 2001); Amos Oz, *The Story Begins: Essays on Literature* (New York: Harcourt Brace & Company, 1999).

by a variety of popular anthologies on openings, which serve further to canonize certain works.[42] It is also a period in which the advent of the Internet increased the possibilities of this collective memorization of openings, which the anthologies started. In any case, a number of websites devoted to openings began to appear within the later part of the decade. In the same period, the German critic Helmut Bonheim also begins with a professional classification according to genres and distinguishes between openings 1) with comment, 2) with description, 3) with report, 4) with speech.[43]

Within this category falls also the use of openings as a tool to write. We thus see Friedrich Pfäfflin create a writing manual beginning with the title "The White Page—Or How to Begin?" and Marge Piercy and Ira Wood also devote a prominent section of their writer's manual to the techniques of the novelistic opening.[44]

2000s: Openings and the Metaphor of the Millennium

It is characteristic throughout the critical tradition that whenever there is a symbolic use of beginnings there is also a stronger critical interest in the opening—as if they mutually justify or strengthen each other. We saw this in the studies of Sophie Rabau and Francis M. Dunn in whose works the beginning at the symbolic level occupies a central ordering principle.[45] It is therefore hardly surprising that there was a further surge in critical texts that deliberately used the turn of the millennium as an ordering principle for the discussion of transitions, including literary

42 Donald Newlove, *First Paragraphs: Inspired Openings for Writers and Readers* (New York: St. Martin's Press, 1992); Bruce L. Weaver, *Novel Openers: First Sentences of 11,000 Fictional Works, Topically Arranged with Subject, Keyword, Author, and Title Indexing* (Jefferson, NC: McFarland & Co., 1995); Baird W. Whitlock, *From these Beginnings: Openings of Fifty Major Literary Works* (New Nork, NY: Schocken, 1985); Georgianne Ensign, *Great Beginnings and Endings: Opening and Closing Lines of Great Novels* (New York: Harper Perennial, 1996).

43 Bonheim, "How Stories Begin."

44 Friedrich Pfäfflin, Ludwig Harig, and Schiller-Nationalmuseum, *Das weisse Blatt, oder, Wie anfangen?* Vom Schreiben (Marbach am Neckar: Deutsche Schillergesellschaft, 1994); Piercy and Wood, *So You Want To Write.*

45 Rabau, "La Première phrase du premier roman"; Dunn and Cole, "Beginnings in Classical Literature."

beginnings. In this period we thus see the works of Liliane Louvel (1997), Annette Retsch (2000), Rolf Vollman (2000), Jean Bessière (2001), Andrea del Lungo (2003), Peter Childs (2001), Simon Leys (2001), George Steiner (2001), and Freeman G. Henry (2002).[46] Bessière, for instance, edited a whole anthology that appeared in 2001, and during the same period a reprint of Kermode's *The Sense of an Ending* also appeared, which included a new epilogue that was written specifically on the occasion of the turn of the millennium.[47] Later appeared also the aforementioned book edited by Brian Richardson.[48] Although the occasion of the millennium may seem arbitrary from a literary viewpoint, the volume of critical works on openings in the last fifteen years has helped mature the field, especially with Andrea del Lungo's contribution, which condensed and systematized a lot of the Francophile preoccupation with openings since the emergence of the journal *Poétique*.

2010s: Openings in the Era of Computers

In the period 1985–1995, it became common for leading French writers to use highly formal openings. I am here thinking of such authors as Georges Perec, Marcel Bénabou, Marie NDiaye, Jean-Philippe Toussaint, Yves Navarre, Walter Lewino, Éric Chevillard, Emmanuel Carrère, Renaud Camus, Georges Baudouin, Claude Simon, and Antoine Volodine. These formal openings indicate the changing medium of literature in an age where the computer has become an instrument that not only supports the creative act, but also interferes with the act and shapes it. The emergence in the past decade of computer-generated texts and the framework of the hypertext has only made the critical investigation into intertextuality and structural components more pertinent. It is the "Marquise in the Machine," as John Barth calls it.[49]

46 Liliane Louvel, ed. *L'Incipit. Actes du colloque de Poitiers 29–30 mars 1996* (Poitiers: La Licorne, 1997); Annette Retsch, *Paratext und Textanfang* (Würzburg: Königshausen & Neumann, 2000); Rolf Vollman, "Was war am Anfang?," *Die Zeit* 2000; Bessière, *Commencements du roman*; del Lungo, *L'Incipit romanesque*; Peter Childs, *Reading Fiction: Opening the Text* (Houndsmills, UK: Palgrave, 2001); Leys, "Ouvertures"; Steiner, *Grammars of Creation*; Henry, *Beginnings in French Literature.*

47 Frank Kermode, *The Sense of an Ending: Studies in the Theory of Fiction, with a new epilogue* (Oxford and New York: Oxford University Press, 2000).

48 Richardson, *Narrative Beginnings.*

49 See note 20 on page 153.

Structuring Critical Approaches to Openings

What is evident from this *tour d'horizon* through the critical use of openings is that the critical approaches to openings are very varied. Yet it is possible to structure critics, as I have tried to do above, into rough categories according to their methodologies and different periods. Another way to structure them would be to classify their texts according to their object of analysis. According to this classification, I suggest the following categories, according to what the critic wishes to elucidate:

» Author/oeuvre approach (examples are Wilhelm Füger, Gunter Hertling, Gilbert Lascault, Hans-Joachim Müllenbrock, Viktor Zmegac, Barbara Hardy, Bernhard Joly, W.R. Martin, Christina Mazzoni)[50]

» Single-text approach (examples are Jean-Louis Cornille, Danielle Constantin, Laurence Dahan-Gaïda, Jean Deurbergue, Claude Duchet, Horst Enders, Alex Lascar, Terence Martin)[51]

50 Wilhelm Füger, "Zur Kunst des Erzählanfangs bei Charles Dickens," in *Charles Dickens. Sein Werk in Lichte neuer deutscher Forschung*, ed. Heinz Reinhold (Heidelberg: Carl Winter Universitätsverlag, 1969); Hertling, *Theodor Fontanes Irrungen, Wirrungen, Die 'Erste Seite' als Schlüssel zum Werk*; Gilbert Lascault, "Commencements de Dumas," *L'Arc* 71 (1978); Heinz-Joachim Müllenbrock, "Modes of Opening in the Work of E.M. Forster: A Contribution to the Poetics of his novels," *Modern Philology* 70 (February 1973); Viktor Zmegac, "Zum Problem des Erzähleinsatzes bei Thomas Mann," *Filologija (Zagreb)* 4 (1964); Barbara Hardy, "The Relationship of Beginning and End in George Eliot's Fiction," *Cahiers victoriens et édouardiens* 26 (1987); Bernard Joly, "La Première phrase dans les Contes et Nouvelles de Maupassant," *Cahiers naturalistes* 57 (1983); Martin, "Beginnings and Endings in Conrad"; Christina Mazzoni, "(Re)constructing the incipit: Narrative Beginnings in Calvino and Freud," *Comparative Literature Studies* 30, no. 1 (1993).

51 Jean-Louis Cornille, "Blanc, semblant et vraisemblance. Sur l'incipit de 'L'Étranger'," *Revue Romane,* 11 (1976); Danielle Constantin, "'Le Seul véritable problème est bien évidemment de commencer': Sur le travail prérédactionnel et l'entrée en écriture de *La Vie: Mode d'emploi* de Georges Perec," in *Beginnings in French Literature*, ed. Freeman G. Henry, French Literature Series (Amsterdam and New York: Rodopi, 2002); Laurence Dahan-Gaïda, "'D'où, chose remarquable, rien ne s'ensuit': Un incipit sans qualités," in *L'Incipit. Actes du colloque de Poitiers 29–30 mars 1996*, ed. Liliane Louvel (Poitiers: La Licorne, 1997); Jean Deurbergue, "The Opening of Victory," *Cahiers d'etudes et de recherches victoriennes et edouardiennes* 2 (1975); Duchet, "Pour un sociocritique, ou variation sur un incipit"; Horst Enders, "Der doppelte Beginn mit Hans Castorp: Zu Thomas Manns 'Der Zauberberg'," in *Romananfänge. Versuch zu einer Poetik des Romans*, ed. Norbert Miller (Berlin: 1965); Alex Lascar, "Le Début de la Maison du chat-qui-pelote: de la seconde ébauche à L'édition Furne," *L'Année balzacienne* 10 (1989); Terence Martin, "Beginnings and Endings in the *Leatherstocking Tales*," in *Narrative Endings*, ed. Alexander Welsh. Special issue, *Nineteenth-Century Fiction* 33, no. 1 (1978).

- » Poetics approach (examples are Frédérique Chevillot, Jacques Dubois, Peter Erlebach, Willi Hirdt, Raymond Jean, Roland Harweg, Steven Kellman, Maggi Keulen, Jean-Jacques Lecercle)[52]
- » Movement/period approach (examples are Norbert Miller and Geza von Molnar)[53]

The advantage of structuring the critics according to their methodological approaches and periods rather than their object of study (author, single-text, poetics, period), as I have done, is that the historical shifts in orientations are highlighted across the national boundaries, which is the traditional focus of comparative literature.

The purpose of the exposition of critical approaches is also to show to what extent this book rests upon quite a substantial amount of critical predecessors. This book is obviously far from being the first work of criticism on the topic, but its comprehensive survey of the entire field of previous critical approaches to openings will hopefully provide fertile soil for future research on the theme.

52 Peter Erlebach, *Theorie und Praxis des Romaneingangs. Untersuchungen zur Poetik des englischen Romans* (Heidelberg: Carl Winter Universitätsverlag, 1990); Chevillot, *La réouverture du texte*; Dubois, "Surcodage et protocole de lecture dans le roman naturaliste"; Willi Hirdt, "Incipit. Zu einer Poetik des Romananfangs," *Romanische Forschung* LXXXVI (1974); Jean, "Ouvertures, Phrases-Seuils"; Raymond Jean, "Commencements romanesques," in *Positions et oppositions sur le roman contemporain. Actes du colloque organisé par le centre de Philologie et littératures romanes de Strasbourg, avril 1970*, ed. Michel Mansuy (Paris: Klincksieck, 1971); Harweg, *Pronomina und Textkonstitution*; Kellman, "Grand Openings and Plain: The Poetics of First Lines"; Maggi Keulen, "Where is Here? or: The Importance of First Sentences in Novels," in *Near Encounters: Festschrift for Richard Martin*, ed. Hanjo Berressem and Bernd Herzogen-Rath (Frankfurt: Peter Lang, 1995); Jean-Jacques Lecercle, "Combien coûte le premier pas? Une théorie annonciative de l'incipit," in *L'Incipit. Actes du colloque de Poitiers 29–30 mars 1996*, ed. Liliane Louvel (Poitiers: La Licorne, 1997).

53 Norbert Miller, "Die Rolle des Erzählers—Zum Problem des Romansanfangs im 18. Jahrhundert," in *Romananfänge. Versuch zu einer Poetik des Romans*, ed. Norbert Miller (Berlin: Literarisches Colloquium, 1965); Geza von Molnar, "Iconic Closure and Narrative Opening in Lessing, Kant, Goethe, and Novalis," *Historical Reflections* 18, no. 3 (1992).

BIBLIOGRAPHY

Abbott, H. Porter. "The Future of All Future Narratives." In *A Companion to Narrative Theory*, edited by James Phelan and Peter J. Rabinowitz, 529–41. Oxford: Blackwell Publishing, 2005.

Allen, Graham. *Intertextuality*. The New Critical Idiom. London and New York: Routledge, 2000.

Aragon, Louis. *Je n'ai jamais appris à écrire ou les incipit*. Paris: Skira, 1969.

Aristotle. *Poetics*. In *The Norton Anthology of Theory and Criticism*, edited by Vincent B. Leitch, 90–117. New York: W.W. Norton & Company, 2001.

Augustine. *The Confessions of St. Augustine*. Translated by E.B. Pusey. London: J.M. Dent & Sons, 1907.

Austin, John L. *How to Do Things with Words*. The William James Lectures 1955. Cambridge, MA: Harvard University Press, 1962.

Backus, Joseph M. "'He Came into Her Line of Vision Walking Backward': Nonsequential Sequence-Signals in Short Story Openings." *Language Learning* XV, no. 1/2 (1965): 67–83.

Bakhtin, Mikhail M. *The Dialogic Imagination: Four Essays*. Translated by Caryl Emerson and Michael Holquist. Austin, TX: University of Texas Press, 2000.

Banfield, Ann. "'Describing the Unobserved': Events Grouped around an Empty Center." In *The Linguistics of Writing: Arguments between Language and Literature*, edited by Nagal Fabb, Derek Attridge, Alan Durant, and Colin MacCabe, 265–85. Manchester: Manchester University Press, 1987.

Barth, John. "Click." *The Atlantic Monthly* 280, no. 6 (December 1997): 81–96.

———. *Lost in the Funhouse*. London: Secker & Warburg, 1969.

Barthes, Roland. "From Work to Text." In *The Rustle of Language*, 56–64. New York: Hill and Wang, 1986.

———. "La Mort de l'auteur." In *Œuvres complètes II*, edited by É. Marty, 491–95. Paris: Seuil, 1994 [1968].

———. *Le Grain de la voix*. Paris: Seuil, 1981.

———. *Le Plaisir du texte*. Collection Tel Quel. Paris: Éditions du Seuil, 1973.

———. *Œuvres complètes*. 5 vols. Paris: Seuil, 2002.

———. "Par où commencer ?" *Poétique* 1 (1970): 3–9.

———. *Roland Barthes par Roland Barthes*. Paris: Seuil, 1975.

———. *S/Z*. Paris: Seuil, 1970.

———. "The Struggle with the Angel: Textual Analysis of Genesis 32: 22–32." In *Image—Music—Text*,125–41. Translated by Stephen Heath. New York: Hill and Wang, 1971.

———. "The Theory of the Text." In *Untying the Text: A Post-Structuralist Reader*, edited by Robert Young, 31–47. Boston, MA: Routledge and Kegan Paul, 1981.

Bate, W. Jackson. *The Burden of the Past and the English Poet*. Cambridge, MA: Harvard University Press, 1970.

Baudouin, Georges. "La Marquise sortit à cinq heures." In *Contes à rebours, Contes et nouvelles*, 260–65. Paris: Buchet / Chastel, 1994.

Beckett, Samuel. *Comment c'est*. Paris: Minuit, 1961.

———. *Endgame*. New York, NY: Grove Press, 1958.

Benjamin, Walter. "The Storyteller." In *Theory of the Novel: A Historical Approach*, edited by Michael McKeon, 77–93. Baltimore, MD: Johns Hopkins University Press, 2000.

Bennett, James R. "Beginning and Ending: A Bibliography." *Style* 10 (1976): 184–88.

Berne-Joffroy, André. "La Marquise sortit à cinq heures." *Nouvelle Revue Française* 81 (1959): 556–61.

Bessière, Jean, ed. *Commencements du roman: Conférences du séminaire de littérature comparée de L'université de la Sorbonne Nouvelle*. Paris: Honoré Champion, 2001.

Bloom, Harold. *The Anxiety of Influence: A Theory of Poetry*. New York: Oxford University Press, 1973.

———. *Kabbalah and Criticism*. New York: Seabury Press, 1975.

Bonheim, Helmut. "How Stories Begin: Devices of Exposition in 600 English, American, and Canadian Stories." *The Yearbook of R.E.A.L.* 1 (1982): 191–226.

Borges, Jorge Luis. "'Introduction à la Poétique' de Paul Valéry." In *Œuvres*, 1154–55. Paris: Gallimard, 1938.

Boylesve, René. "Un genre littéraire en danger: Le roman." *Revue de France* 5 (15 October 1924): 826–31.

Brague, Rémi. "Le récit du commencement. Une aporie de la raison grecque." In *La Naissance de la raison en Grèce: Actes du colloque de Nice mai 1987*, edited by Jean-François Mattéi, 23–31. Paris: PUF, 1990.

Breton, André. *Manifeste du surréalisme; Poisson soluble*. Paris: Éditions du Sagittaire, 1924.

Brombert, Victor. "Opening Signals in Narrative." *New Literary History* 11, no. 3 (1980): 489–502.

Brooks, Peter. *Reading for the Plot: Design and Intention in Narrative*. Cambridge, MA: Harvard University Press, 1992.

Brown, Homer Obed. "Review of Beginnings: Intention and Method." *MLN* 91, no. 5 (1976): 1141–49.

Buch-Jepsen, Niels. "Georges Poulet." In *Encyclopedia of Modern French Thought*, edited by Christopher John Murray, 535–37. New York and London: Fitzroy Dearborn, 2004.

———. "Le nom propre et le propre auteur – qu'est-ce qu'une fonction-auteur?" In *Une histoire de La fonction-auteur est-elle possible?*, edited by Nicole Jacques-Lefévre, 49–64. Saint-Etienne: Publications de l'Université de Saint-Etienne, 2001.

———. "What Happened to the Author? Modernist Impersonality and Authorial Selfhood." In *From Homer to Hypertext: Studies in Narrative, Literature and Media*, edited by Hans Balling and Anders Klinkby Madsen, 77–94. Odense: University Press of Southern Denmark, 2002.

Bulwer-Lytton, Edward George. *Paul Clifford*. New York: Printed by J. & J. Harper, 1830.

Burke, Sean. *The Death and Return of the Author: Criticism and Subjectivity in Barthes, Foucault and Derrida*. Edinburgh: Edinburgh University Press, 1992.

Butor, Michel. *Répertoire*. Vol. II. Paris: Minuit, 1964.

Bürger, Peter. *Theory of the Avant-Garde*. Translated by Michael Shaw. Minneapolis: University of Minnesota Press, 1984.

Byron, Lord. *Don Juan*. London: John Lehmann, 1949.

Böhme, Jacob. *The Aurora*. London: Watkins, 1960 [1612].

Cain, Kate. "Text Comprehension and Its Relation to Coherence and Cohesion in Children's Fictional Narratives." *British Journal of Developmental Psychology* 21 (2003): 335–51.

Calvino, Italo. "Appendice: Cominciare E Finire." In *Saggi 1945–1985*, edited by M. Barenghi, 734–53. Milan: Mondadori, 1995.

Carroll, Lewis. *Alice in Wonderland*. New York: Norton, 1992 [1865].

Carter, Ronald. "The Placing of Names: Sequencing in Narrative Openings."

Leeds Studies in English 18 (1987): 89–100.

Cassou, Jean. "Propos sur le surréalisme." *Nouvelle Revue Française* XXIV (1 January 1925): 30–34.

Chambers, Ross. *Story and Situation: Narrative Seduction and the Power of Fiction*. Minneapolis: University of Minnesota Press, 1984.

Chatman, Seymour. "Towards a Theory of Narrative." *New Literary History* 11 (1975): 295–318.

Chénieux-Gendron, Jacqueline. *Le surréalisme et le roman, 1922–1950*. Lausanne: Age d'homme, 1983.

Chevillard, Éric. "La Marquise toujours recommencée." *Le nouveau recueil – revue trimestrielle de littérature et de critique* 64 (2002): 77–81.

Chevillot, Frédérique. *La Réouverture du texte. Balzac, Beckett, Robbe-Grillet, Roussel, Aragon, Calvino, Bénabou, Hébert*. Saratoga, CA: Anma Libri, 1993.

Childs, Peter. *Reading Fiction: Opening the Text*. Houndsmills, UK: Palgrave, 2001.

Clayton, Jay, and Eric Rothstein. "Figures in the Corpus: Theories of Influence and Intertextuality." In *Influence and Intertextuality in Literary History*, edited by Jay Clayton and Eric Rothstein, 3–36. Madison: University of Wisconsin Press, 1991.

Coetzee, John Maxwell. *Life and Times of Michael K*. London: Secker & Warburg, 1983.

Cohn, Dorrit. "K fait son entrée au château: A propos du changement d'instance narrative dans le manuscrit de Kafka." *Poétique* 61 (1985): 111–27.

Concise Oxford Dictionary. Oxford: Oxford University Press.

Conrad, Joseph. "Henry James: An Appreciation." In *Notes on Life and Letters*. London: Dent, 1924 [1905].

———. *Lord Jim*. Edinburgh and London: Blackwood's Magazine, 1899–1900.

———. *The Nigger of the 'Narcissus'*. London: The New Review, 1897.

Constantin, Danielle. "'Le seul véritable problème est bien Évidemment de commencer': Sur le travail prérédactionnel et l'entrée en Écriture de *La Vie mode d'emploi* de Georges Perec." In *Beginnings in French Literature*, edited by Freeman G. Henry. French Literature Series. Amsterdam and New York: Rodopi, 2002.

Cornille, Jean-Louis. "Blanc, semblant et vraisemblance. Sur l'incipit de 'L'étranger'." *Revue Romane* 11 (1976): 210–19.

Cortázar, Julio. *La Vuelta al día en ochenta mundos*. La Creación Literaria. México: Siglo Veintiuno Editores, 1967.

———. *Los premios*. Buenos Aires: Editorial Sudamericana, 1960.

Culler, Jonathan. "Beginnings: Intention and Method by Edward W. Said." *Modern Language Review* 73, no. 3 (1978): 582–85.

———. "Defining Narrative Units." In *Style and Structure in Literature: Essays in the New Stylistics*, edited by Roger Fowler, 123–42. Oxford: Basil Blackwell, 1975.

———. "Presupposition and Intertextuality." *Modern Language Notes* 91 (1976): 1380–96.

———. "Prolegomena to a Theory of Reading." In *The Reader in the Text: Essays on Audience and Interpretation*, edited by Susan R. Suleiman and Inge Crosman, 46–66. Princeton, NJ: Princeton University Press, 1980.

———. *The Pursuit of Signs: Semiotics, Literature, Deconstruction*. Ithaca, NY: Cornell University Press, 1981.

Cummings, Michael. "The Role of Theme and Rheme in Contrasting Methods of Organization in Texts." In *The Dynamics of Language Use: Functional and Contrastive Perspectives*, edited by Christopher Butler, Maria A. Gomez-Gonzalez,

and Susana Ma. Doval Suarez, 129–53. Pragmatics & Beyond. Amsterdam and Philadelphia: J. Benjamins Pub., 2005.
Curtius, Ernst Robert. "Mittelalter-Studien." *Zeitschrift für Romanische Philologie* 63 (1943).
Dahan-Gaïda, Laurence. "'D'où, chose remarquable, rien ne s'ensuit': Un incipit sans qualités." In *L'incipit. Actes du colloque de Poitiers 29–30 mars 1996*, edited by Liliane Louvel, 149–65. Poitiers: La Licorne, 1997.
Dante. *Inferno*. Translated by Allen Mandelbaum. New York: Bantam Books, 1982.
Danto, Arthur. *Analytical Philosophy of History*. Cambridge: Cambridge University Press, 1965.
Darwin, Charles. *On the Origin of Species by Means of Natural Selection*. London: J. Murray, 1859.
Daudet, Alphonse, and Paul Arène. "L'homme á la cervelle d'or." In *Lettres de mon moulin*. Folio Plus. Paris: Gallimard, 1996 [1860].
del Lungo, Andrea. *L'incipit Romanesque*. Paris: Seuil, 2003.
———. "Pour une poétique de l'incipit." *Poétique* 94 (1993): 131–52.
Derrida, Jacques. *De la grammatologie*. Paris: Éditions de Minuit, 1967.
———. "La Structure, le signe et le jeu dans le discours des sciences humaines." In *L'écriture et la différence*, 409–28. Paris: Seuil, 1967.
———. *Limited Inc*. Collection la Philosophie en effet. Paris: Galilée, 1990.
———. *Of grammatology*. Baltimore, MD: Johns Hopkins University Press, 1976.
———. "Qual quelle – les sources de Valéry." In *Marges de la philosophie*, 325–63. Paris: Minuit, 1972.
Deurbergue, Jean. "The Opening of Victory." *Cahiers d'etudes et de recherches victoriennes et edouardiennes* 2 (1975): 239–70.
Dickens, Charles. *Bleak House*. Cambridge: Riverside Press, 1869 [1852–1853].
———. *Pickwick Papers*. New York: Penguin, 2000 [1836–1837].
Docherty, Thomas. "From Ends to Beginnings: Time and the Plot." In *Reading (Absent) Character: Towards a Theory of Characterization in Fiction*, 127–55. Oxford: Clarendon Press, 1983.
Dostoevsky, Fyodor. *Crime and Punishment*. New York: W.W. Norton, 1989 [1866].
———. *The Idiot*. London: Penguin, 1955 [1868–1869].
Doubrovsky, Serge. *La Place de la madeleine: Ecriture et fantasme chez Proust*. Paris: Mercure de France, 1974.
Douglas, Jane Yellowlees. *The End of Books – or Books without End? Reading Interactive Narratives*. Ann Arbor: University of Michigan Press, 2000.
Driehorst, Gerd, and Katharina Schlicht. "Textuale Grenzsignale in narrativer Sicht. Zum Problem von Texteingang und Textausgang. Forschungsstand und Perspektiven." In *Sprache in Vergangenheit und Gegenwart*, edited by Wolfgang Brandt, 250–69. Marburg: Beiträge aus dem Institut für Germanistische Sprachwissenschaft der Philipps-Universität Marburg, 1988.
Dubois, Jacques. "Surcodage et protocole de lecture dans le roman naturaliste." *Poétique* 16 (1973): 491–98.
Duchan, J.F., G.A. Bruder, and L.E. Hewitt. *Deixis in Narrative: A Cognitive Science Perspective*. Hillsdale, NJ: Lawrence Erlbaum Associates Inc., 1995.
Duchet, Claude. "Idéologie de la mise en texte [Premières phrases des 'Rougon-Macquart']." *La Pensée* 215 (1980): 95–108.
———. "Pour un sociocritique, ou variation sur un incipit." *Littérature* 1 (1971): 5–14.
Dunn, Francis M., and Thomas Cole. "Beginnings in Classical Literature." *Yale Classical Studies* 29 (1992).

Durrell, Lawrence. *Mountolive*. New York: Penguin, 1991 [1958].

Eco, Umberto. "Fictional Protocols." In *Six Walks in the Fictional Woods*, 117–40. Cambridge, MA: Harvard University Press, 1994.

Eliot, George. *Daniel Deronda*. New York, NY: Modern Library, 2002 [1876].

Ellison, David R. "Proust and Kafka: On the Opening of Narrative Space." *Modern Language Notes* 101, no. 5 (1986): 1135–67.

Embiricos, Alexandre. "La Galerie des Contemporains." *La Revue nouvelle* 1, no. 6 (15 May 1925): 27–32.

Enders, Horst. "Der doppelte Beginn mit Hans Castorp: Zu Thomas Manns 'Der Zauberberg'." In *Romananfänge. Versuch zu einer Poetik des Romans*, edited by Norbert Miller, 289–316. Berlin, 1965.

Ensign, Georgianne. *Great Beginnings and Endings: Opening and Closing Lines of Great Novels*. New York: Harper Perennial, 1996.

Erlebach, Peter. *Theorie und Praxis des Romaneingangs. Untersuchungen zur Poetik des englischen Romans*. Heidelberg: Carl Winter Universitätsverlag, 1990.

Ezer, Nancy. "The Opening as a Master-Narrative of the Political Unconscious." Villanova University, 1988.

Falconer, Graham. "L'entrée en matière chez Balzac. Prolégomènes à une ètude sociocritique." In *La Lecture sociocritique du texte Romanesque*. Toronto: Stevens & Hakkert, 1975.

Ferrer, Daniel, and Bernhild Boie, eds. *Genèse du roman contemporain. Incipit et entrée en écriture*. Paris: CNRS Editions, 1993.

Ferris, Ina. "The Historical Novel and the Problem of Beginning: The Model of Scott." *Journal of Narrative Technique* 18, no. 1 (1988).

Fielding, Henry. *The History of Tom Jones, a Foundling*. London: A. Millar, 1749.

Fish, Stanley. *Is There a Text in This Class?* Cambridge, MA: Harvard University Press, 1982.

Fludernik, Monika. *Towards a 'Natural' Narratology*. London: Routledge, 1996.

Ford, Ford Madox. *Critical Writings*. Regents Critics Series. Lincoln: University of Nebraska Press, 1964.

———. *The Good Soldier; a Tale of Passion*. New York: J. Lane, 1915.

Forster, E. M. *Howards End*. New York: Penguin Books, 2000 [1910].

Fosca, François. "Apologie pour le roman." *Revue hebdomadaire* (23 May 1925).

Foucault, Michel. *Les mots et les choses*. Paris: Gallimard, 1966.

———. "Nietzsche, Freud, Marx." In *Nietzsche*. Cahiers de Royaumont. Paris: Editions de Minuit, 1967.

———. *The Order of Things: An Archaeology of the Human Sciences*. Translated by Alan Sheridan. Routledge Classics. London: Routledge, 2001.

Frank, Joseph. "Spatial Form in Modern Literature." In *The Widening Gyre: Crisis and Mastery in Modern Literature*. New Brunswick, NJ: Rutgers University Press, 1963.

Frisby, David. *Fragments of Modernity: Theories of Modernity in the Work of Simmel, Kracauer and Benjamin*. Cambridge: Polity Press in association with Basil Blackwell, Oxford, 1985.

Fritz. "Erzähleingänge in der deutschen Literatur." University of Giessen, 1913.

Fuentes, Carlos. *Cristóbal Nonato*. Mexico City: Fondo de Cultura Económica, 1987.

Füger, Wilhelm. "Zur Kunst des Erzählanfangs bei Charles Dickens." In *Charles Dickens. Sein Werk im Lichte neuer deutscher Forschung*, edited by Heinz Reinhold, 103–18. Heidelberg: Carl Winter Universitätsverlag, 1969.

Genette, Gerard. *Introduction à l'architexte*. Poétique. Paris: Seuil, 1979.

Genette, Gérard. "Discours du récit." In *Figures III*, 67–282. Paris: Seuil, 1972.
———. *Fiction et diction*. Poétique. Paris: Seuil, 1991.
———. "Le Statut pragmatique de la fiction narrative." *Poétique* 78 (1989): 237–49.
———. "Littérature comme telle." In *Figures I*, 253–65. Paris: Seuil, 1966.
———. *Nouveau discours du récit*. Paris: Seuil, 1983.
———. *Palimpsestes. La littérature au second degré*. Paris: Seuil, 1982.
———. *Seuils*. Paris: Seuil, 1987.
Gerschman, Herbert S. "Valéry and Breton." *Yale French Studies* 44 (1970): 199–206.
Gide, André. *Conseils au jeune écrivain – de l'influence en littérature*. Paris: Proverbe, 1993.
"Godard Only Knows...." *The Observer*, 26 November 2000.
Goethe. *Faust*. Ware: Wordsworth Editions, 1999.
Gracq, Julien. *En lisant en écrivant*. Paris: Corti, 1981.
Greimas, Algirdas Julien. *Sémantique structurale, recherche de méthode*. Langue et langage. Paris: Larousse, 1966.
Grice, Paul. "Logic and Conversation." In *Studies in the Way of Words*, edited by Paul Grice, 22–40. Cambridge, MA: Harvard University Press, 1989.
Guillén, Claudio. *Literature as System: Essays towards the Theory of Literary History*. Princeton, NJ: Princeton University Press, 1970.
Hamon, Philippe. "Clausules." *Poétique* 24 (1975): 495–526.
———. "Texte littéraire et métalangage." *Poétique* 31 (1977): 261–84.
Hardy, Barbara. "The Relationship of Beginning and End in George Eliot's Fiction." *Cahiers victoriens et édouardiens* 26 (1987): 7–19.
Hardy, Thomas. *Jude the Obscure: An Authoritative Text, Backgrounds and Contexts, Criticism*. A Norton Critical Edition. 2nd ed. New York: W.W. Norton, 1999.
Harweg, Roland. *Pronomina und Textkonstitution*. Munich: Wilhelm Fink Verlag, 1968.
Haubrichs, Wolfgang, ed. "Anfang und Ende." *LiLi. Zeitschrift für Literaturwissenschaft und Linguistik* 25, no. 99 (1995).
Heath, Stephen. "The Practice of Writing." In *The Nouveau Roman: A Study in the Practice of Writing*, 15–42. Philadelphia, PA: Elek, 1972.
Hemingway, Ernest. *The Complete Short Stories of Ernest Hemingway*. New York: Simon & Schuster, 1987.
Henry, Freeman G. *Beginnings in French Literature*. French Literature Series. Amsterdam and New York: Rodopi, 2002.
Hertling, Gunter H. *Theodor Fontanes Irrungen, Wirrungen, Die 'Erste Seite' als Schlüssel zum Werk*. Frankfurt am Main: Peter Lang, 1985.
Hertz, Neil. *The End of the Line: Essays on Psychoanalysis and the Sublime*. New York: Columbia University Press, 1985.
Hervouet, Yves. *The French Face of Joseph Conrad*. Cambridge: Cambridge University Press, 1990.
Hesiod. *Theogony*. Translated by Hugh G. Evelyn-White. In *The Theogony, Works and Days, and the Shield of Heracles*. Stilwell, KS: Digireads, 2008.
Hirdt, Willi. "Incipit. Zu einer Poetik des Romananfangs." *Romanische Forschung* LXXXVI (1974): 419–36.
Hollier, Denis. *Against Architecture: The Writings of Georges Bataille*. Cambridge, MA: MIT Press, 1989.
Horace. *Ars Poetica*. In *The Norton Anthology of Theory and Criticism*, edited by Vincent B. Leitch, 124–35. New York: W.W. Norton & Company, 2001.
Hultberg, Peer. *Præludier*. Copenhagen: Gyldendal, 1990.

Huysmans, Joris-Karl. *À rebours*. Paris: Argenteuil, 1924 [1884].

———. *Against the Grain*. Translated by Brandan King. Cambs, UK: Dedalus, 2008.

———. *Les soeurs vatard*. Paris: G. Charpentier, 1879.

Jabès, Edmond. *Le livre des questions*. Paris: Gallimard, 1963.

Jakobson, Roman, and Jurij Tynjanov. "Problems in the Study of Literature and Language." In *Readings in Russian Poetics: Formalist and Structuralist Views*, edited by Ladislav Matejka and Krystyna Pomorska, 79–81. Ann Arbor: Michigan Slavic Publications, 1978 [1928].

Jallat, Jeannine. "Le reste et l'incipit. Sur la genèse d'un commencement valéryen." *Littérature* 64 (December 1986): 62–70.

Jaloux, Edmond. "L'Esprit des livres. Pierre Louÿs." *Les Nouvelles littéraires* 3–4 (13 June 1925).

———. *L'Age d'or*. Paris: Vald. Rasmussen, 1926.

———. *Le Démon de la vie*. Paris: Stock, 1908.

James, Henry. *Selected Short Stories: Edited with an Introduction by Quentin Anderson*. Rinehart Editions, 31. New York: Rinehart, 1950.

Jarrety, Michel. *Valéry devant la littérature. Mesure de la limite*. Ecrivains. Paris: Presses universitaires de France, 1991.

Jarry, Alfred. *Le surmâle*. Paris: Bernard Grasset, 1902.

Jean, Raymond. "Commencements romanesques." In *Positions et oppositions sur le roman contemporain. Actes du colloque organisé par le centre de philologie et littératures romanes de Strasbourg, Avril 1970*, edited by Michel Mansuy, 129–42. Paris: Klincksieck, 1971.

———. "Ouvertures, Phrases-Seuils." *Critique* XXVII, no. 288 (1971): 421–31.

Joly, Bernard. "La Première phrase dans les contes et nouvelles de Maupassant." *Cahiers naturalistes* 57 (1983).

Joyce, James. *Finnegans Wake*. London: Penguin, 1999 [1939].

Jüttner, Siegfried. "Der beschimpfte Leser. Zur Analyse der literarischen Provokation." *Romanische Forschungen* 86 (1974): 95–116.

Kant, Immanuel. *Prolegomena to Any Future Metaphysics*. Cambridge Texts in the History of Philosophy. Revised ed. Cambridge: Cambridge University Press, 2004.

Kanyó, Zoltán. "Anmerkungen zur Frage des Textanfangs der literarischen Geschichte." In *Texttheorie und Interpretation. Untersuchungen zu Gryphius, Borchert und Böll*, edited by Arpád Bernáth, Csúri Károly, and Zoltán Kanyó, 89–128. Kronberg/Ts: Scriptor Verlag, 1975.

Kellman, Steven G. "Grand Openings and Plain: The Poetics of First Lines." *Sub-Stance* 17 (1977): 139–47.

Kermode, Frank. "Novels: Recognition and Deception." *Critical Inquiry* 1 (September 1974): 103–21.

———. *The Sense of an Ending*. New York: Oxford University Press, 1967.

———. *The Sense of an Ending: Studies in the Theory of Fiction. With a New Epilogue*. New ed. Oxford and New York: Oxford University Press, 2000.

———. "Sensing Endings." In *Narrative Endings*, edited by Alexander Welsh. Special issue, *Nineteenth-Century Fiction* 33, no. 1 (1978): 144–58.

Keulen, Maggi. "Where Is Here? Or: The Importance of First Sentences in Novels." In *Near Encounters: Festschrift for Richard Martin*, edited by Hanjo Berressem and Bernd Herzogen-Rath. Frankfurt: Peter Lang, 1995.

Klotz, Volker. "Muse und Helios. Über epische Anfangsnöte und -Weise." In

Romananfänge. Versuch zu einer Poetik des Romans, edited by Norbert Miller, 11–36. Berlin: Literarisches Colloquium, 1965.

Knight, Diana. "Where to Begin?" *Yale Journal of Criticism: Interpretation in the Humanities* 14, no. 2 (Fall 2001): 493–501.

Kreuzer, Helmut. "Anfänge des Romans." *LiLi. Zeitschrift für Literaturwissenschaft und Linguistik* 23, no. 89 (1993).

Kripke, Saul A. *Naming and Necessity*. Cambridge, MA: Harvard University Press, 1980.

Kristeva, Julia. "Le texte clos." In *Σημειωτική: Recherches pour une sémanalyse*, 52–81. Paris: Seuil, 1978 [1969].

Lanceraux, Dominique. "Modalités de la narration dans 'La route des Flandres'." *Poétique* 14 (1973): 234–49.

Lane, William R. "The Initiation of Creation." *Vetus Testamentum* 13 (1963): 63–73.

Larbaud, Valery. *Amants, heureux amants*. Paris: NRF Gallimard, 1921.

———. *Fermina Márquez*. Paris: Gallimard, 1926 [1911].

Lascar, Alex. "Le début de la Maison du chat-qui-pelote: De la seconde ébauche à l'édition furne." *L'Année balzacienne* 10 (1989): 43–59.

Lascault, Gilbert. "Commencements de Dumas." *L'Arc* 71 (1978): 4–8.

Lawrence, D.H. *Women in Love*. New York: Quality Paperback Book Club, 1920.

Le Clézio, Jean-Marie Gustave. *Le livre des fuites: Roman d'aventures*. Paris: Gallimard, 1969.

———. *Le procès verbal*. Paris: NRF Gallimard, 1963.

Le Roy, Eugène. *Jacquou le Croquant*. Paris: Calmann-Lévy, 1981.

Leander, Niels Buch. "The Colonial Metropolis and Its Artistic Adventure: Conrad, Congo, and the *Nouvelle Revue Francaise*." *Romanic Review* 99, no. 1–2 (January–March 2008): 87–102.

———. "L'intertextualité de l'incipit romanesque." In *Intertextualité, interdiscursivité et intermédialité*, edited by Louis Hébert and Lucie Guillemette, 117–25. Québec, Canada: Presses de l'Université Laval, 2009.

———. "To Begin with the Beginning: Birth, Origin, and Narrative Inception." In *Narrative Beginnings: Theories and Practices*, edited by Brian Richardson, 15–28. Frontiers of Narrative. Lincoln: University of Nebraska Press, 2008.

Lecercle, Jean-Jacques. "Combien coûte le premier pas? Une théorie annonciative de l'incipit." In *L'incipit. Actes du colloque de Poitiers 29–30 mars 1996*, edited by Liliane Louvel, 7–17. Poitiers: La Licorne, 1997.

Lefèvre, Frédéric. "Une heure avec M. Joseph Delteil, poète de Jeanne d'Arc." *Les Nouvelles littéraires*, 16 May 1925, 15–17.

Lejeune, Philippe. "Par où commencer ?" In *Moi Aussi*, 224–45. Paris: Seuil, 1986.

Levert, Paule. *L'idée de commencement*. Paris: Aubier, 1961.

Lewino, Walter. *Longtemps je me suis couché de travers. Incipit*. Paris: Maurice Nadeau, 1994.

Lewis, David K. *Convention: A Philosophical Study*. Cambridge, MA: Harvard University Press, 1969.

Leys, Simon. "Ouvertures." In *Protée et autres essais*. Paris: Gallimard, 2001.

Lintvelt, Jaap. "L'ouverture du roman: Procédures d'analyse." In *Recherches sur le roman II 1950–1970: Cahiers de recherche des Instituts Néerlandais*, edited by Charles Grivel and Frans Rutten, 40–48. Groningen: Institut de Langues Romanes, 1984.

Lodge, David. *The Modes of Modern Writing*. London: Hodder Arnold, 1977.

Louvel, Liliane, ed. *L'incipit. Actes du colloque de Poitiers 29–30 mars 1996*. Poitiers: La Licorne, 1997.

Lukács, György. *The Meaning of Contemporary Realism*. London: Merlin Press, 1963.

Långfors, Arthur. *Les incipit des poèmes français antérieurs au xvie siècle: Répertoire bibliographique*. Genève: Slatkine Reprints, 1977.

Macherey, Pierre. *Pour une théorie de la production littéraire*. Théorie, 4. Paris: F. Maspero, 1966.

Magné, Bernard. "Esquisse d'une typologie de la littérature combinatoire." http://perso.club-internet.fr/magneb/professionnel/typologie-combi/typcombi.html.

Mandelartz, Michael. "Der Textanfang als kosmologischer Entwurf. Die Motive des Musenanrufs und des Waldes." *Euphorion* 87 (1993): 420–37.

Mann, Thomas. *Das Gesetz: Erzählung*. Stockholm: Bermann Fischer Verlag, 1944.

———. *Der Zauberberg*. Berlin: S. Fischer, 1924.

Marimoutou, Jean-Claude. "Ulysse, Jacques, la Muse et le grand Rouleau." In *Représentation de l'origine: Littérature, histoire, civilisation*. Saint-Denis (Réunion): Publications de l'université de la Réunion, 1987.

Martin, Terence. "Beginnings and Endings in the *Leatherstocking Tales*." In *Narrative Endings*, edited by Alexander Welsh. Special issue, *Nineteenth-Century Fiction* 33, no. 1 (1978): 69–87.

Martin, W.R. "Beginnings and Endings in Conrad." *Conradiana* 5, no. 1 (1973): 43–51.

Maupassant, Guy de. *Pierre et Jean*. Paris: Gernier Freres, 1959.

Mauriac, Claude. *La Marquise sortit à cinq heures; Roman*. Paris: Albin Michel, 1961.

———. *Le Dîner en ville*. Paris: Albin Michel, 1959.

Mazzoni, Christina. "(Re)Constructing the Incipit: Narrative Beginnings in Calvino and Freud." *Comparative Literature Studies* 30, no. 1 (1993): 53–68.

Mill, John Stuart. *System of Logic; Ratiocinative and Inductive*. New York: Elibron Classics, 2005.

Miller, D.A. *Narrative and Its Discontents*. Princeton, NJ: Princeton University Press, 1981.

Miller, J. Hillis. *Ariadne's Thread: Story Lines*. New Haven, CT, and London: Yale University Press, 1992.

———. "Chapter VI: Bleak House." In *Charles Dickens: The World of His Novels*, 160–224. Cambridge, MA: Harvard University Press, 1958.

———. "Literature as Virtual Reality." In *On Literature*, 24–45. London and New York: Routledge, 2002.

Miller, Norbert. *Der empfindsame Erzähler. Untersuchungen an Romananfängen des 18. Jahrhunderts*. Munich: Hanser, 1968.

———. "Die Rolle des Erzählers. Zum Problem des Romansanfangs im 18. Jahrhundert." In *Romananfänge. Versuch zu einer Poetik des Romans*, edited by Norbert Miller, 37–91. Berlin: Literarisches Colloquium, 1965.

———, ed. *Romananfänge. Versuch zu einer Poetik des Romans*. Berlin: Literarisches Colloquium, 1965.

Milton, John, and Gordon Teskey. *Paradise Lost: Authoritative Text, Sources and Backgrounds, Criticism*. A Norton Critical Edition. New York: W.W. Norton, 2005.

Molnar, Geza von. "Iconic Closure and Narrative Opening in Lessing, Kant, Goethe, and Novalis." *Historical Reflections* 18, no. 3 (1992): 95–110.

Montherlant, Henry de. *Les Célibataires*. Paris: Grasset, 1934.

Morhange, J.-L. "Incipit narratifs. L'entrée du lecteur dans l'univers de la fiction." *Poétique* (1995): 387–410.

Mouat, Ricardo Gutierrez. "Beginnings and Returns: An Interview with José

Donoso." *The Review of Contemporary Fiction* 12, no. 2 (Summer 1992).

Muschg, Walter. *Gespräche mit Hans Henny Jahnn*. Frankfurt am Main: Europäische Verlagsanstalt, 1967.

Müllenbrock, Heinz-Joachim. "Modes of Opening in the Work of E.M. Forster: A Contribution to the Poetics of His Novels." *Modern Philology* 70, no. 3 (1973): 216–30.

Navarre, Yves. *Premières pages. Roman*. Paris: Flammarion, 1983.

NDiaye, Marie. *Comédie classique*. Paris: P.O.L., 1987.

Nemesio, Aldo. "La definizione dell'incipit." *Annali d'Italianistica* 18 (2000): 29–48.

Newlove, Donald. *First Paragraphs: Inspired Openings for Writers and Readers*. New York: St. Martin's Press, 1992.

Nuttall, A.D. *Openings: Narrative Beginnings from the Epic to the Novel*. Oxford: Clarendon Press, 1992.

———. "Some Shakespearean Openings: *Hamlet, Twelfth Night, The Tempest*." In *The Arts of Performance in Elizabethan and Early Stuart Drama: Essays for G.K. Hunter*, edited by Murray Biggs, Philip Edwards, Inga-Stina Ewbank, and Eugene M. Waith, 84–95. Edinburgh: Edinburgh University Press, 1991.

Ohmann, Richard. "Speech, Action, and Style." In *Literary Style: A Symposium*, edited by Seymour Chatman, 241–59. New York: Oxford University Press, 1971.

Oster, Daniel. "'Je ne suis pas de ceux qui aiment les livres pour les livres'." In *Monsieur Valéry*, 132–34. Paris: Seuil, 1981.

Oz, Amos. *The Story Begins: Essays on Literature*. New York: Harcourt Brace & Company, 1999.

Pagnol, Marcel. *La Gloire de mon père*. Paris: Pastorelly, 1957.

Perec, Georges. *Je suis né*. Paris: Seuil, 1990.

Pessoa, Fernando. "Notes on a Non-Aristotelian Aesthetics." In *Always Astonished: Selected Prose*. 70–73. San Francisco, CA: City Lights Books, 1988.

Petit Robert. Paris: Dictionnaires Le Robert, 1994.

Pettazzoni, R. "Myths of Beginning and Creation Myths." In *Essays on the History of Religion*, 24–36. Leiden: E.J. Brill, 1954.

Pfäfflin, Friedrich, Ludwig Harig, and Schiller-Nationalmuseum. *Das weisse Blatt, oder, Wie anfangen?* Vom Schreiben. Marbach am Neckar: Deutsche Schillergesellschaft, 1994.

Philippe, Gilles. "Les démonstratifs et le statut Énonciatif des textes de fiction. L'exemple des ouvertures de roman." *Langue Française* 120 (1998): 51–65.

Piercy, Marge, and Ira Wood. *So You Want to Write: How to Master the Craft of Writing Fiction and the Personal Narrative*. Wellfleet, MA: Leapfrog Press, 2001.

Pierre-Quint, Léon. "Lectures." *Revue de France* VI, no. 2 (1 April 1926): 531–32.

Pinget, Robert. *Mahu ou le matériau*. Paris: Minuit, 1952.

Piwitt, Hermann Peter. "Zum Problem des Romaneingangs." *Akzente* 8 (1961): 229–43.

Poe, Edgar Allan. "The Philosophy of Composition." In *The Norton Anthology of Theory and Criticism*, edited by Vincent B. Leitch. New York: W.W. Norton & Company, 2001 [1846].

Poulet, Georges. *Le Point de départ*. Paris: Plon, 1964.

Queneau, Raymond. *Cent mille milliards de poèmes*. Paris: NRF Gallimard, 1961.

———. *Le Dimanche de la vie*. Paris: Gallimard, 1951.

———. *Les Fleurs bleues*. Paris: Gallimard, 1965.

———. *Zazie dans le métro*. Paris: Gallimard, 1959.

Rabau, Sophie. "La Première phrase du premier roman." *Poétique* 82 (1990): 131–44.

Raimond, Michel. *La Crise du roman: Des lendemains du naturalisme aux années vingt*. Paris: José Corti, 1966.

Retsch, Annette. *Paratext und Textanfang*. Würzburg: Königshausen & Neumann, 2000.

Ricardou, Jean. "Le Nouveau roman est-il valéryen?" In *Entretiens sur Paul Valéry*, edited by Émilie Noulet-Carner. Paris / La Haye: Éditions Mouton & Co., 1968.

Richardson, Brian, ed. *Narrative Beginnings: Theories and Practices*. Frontiers of Narrative. Lincoln: University of Nebraska Press, 2008.

Richter, David H. *Fable's End: Completeness and Closure in Rhetorical Fiction*. Chicago: University of Chicago Press, 1974.

Riffaterre, Michael. *La Production du texte*. Paris: Seuil, 1979.

Rilke, Rainer Maria. *Das Stunden-Buch*. Teddington, Middelsex: The Echo Library, 2008 [1899].

Rimmon-Kenan, Shlomith. *Narrative Fiction: Contemporary Poetics*. London: Routledge, 1983.

Rivière, Jacques. "Le Roman d'aventure." *Nouvelle Revue Française* 5, no. 53–55 (May/June/July 1913).

Robbe-Grillet, Alain. "Un roman qui s'invente lui-même." In *Pour un nouveau roman*, 108–12. Paris: Minuit, 1963 [c. 1961].

Rodriguez, Pierre, and Michele Weil, eds. *Topique des ouvertures narratives avant 1800*. Montpellier: Centre d'Étude du Dix-Huitième Siècle de Montpellier, Univ. Paul Valery Montpellier, 1990.

Ronsard, Pierre de. "From a Brief on the Art of French Poetry." In *The Norton Anthology of Theory and Criticism*, edited by Vincent B. Leitch, 179–86. New York: W.W. Norton & Company, 2001 [1565].

Rosner, Mary Isobel. "Novel Beginnings: A Rhetorical Analysis of Ouvertures in Nineteenth-Century Fiction." Dissertation, Ohio State University, 1978.

Rowe, Joyce A. *Equivocal Endings in Classic American Novels*. Cambridge: Cambridge University Press, 1988.

Rueff, Martin. "Robinson, une vue de l'esprit (À propos du *Robinson* de Paul Valéry)." *Critica del testo: rivista quadrimestrale* 2 (2002): 498–540.

Russell, Bertrand. "On Denoting." *Mind* 14 (1905): 479–93.

Sabbah, Hélène. *Les Débuts de roman*. Paris: Hatier, 1991.

Sacks, Sheldon. "Clarissa and the Tragic Traditions." In *Irrationalism in the Eighteenth Century*, edited by Harold E. Pagliaro, 195–221. Cleveland, OH: The Press of Case Western Reserve University, 1972.

———. "Golden Birds and Dying Generations." *Comparative Literature Studies* 6 (1969): 274–91.

———. "Some Psychological Implications of Generic Distinctions." *Genre* 1 (1968): 106–15.

Said, Edward W. *Beginnings: Intention and Method*. New York: Basic Books, 1975.

———. "Interview." *Diacritics* 6, no. 3 (1976): 30–47.

Salinger, J.D. *The Catcher in the Rye*. London: Hamilton, 1951.

Sartre, Jean-Paul. *La Nausée*. Paris: Gallimard, 1938.

Searle, John. "Reiterating the Differences: A Reply to Derrida." *Glyph* I (1977): 172–208.

Searle, John R. *Speech Acts: An Essay in the Philosophy of Language*. London: Cambridge University Press, 1969.

Simon, Claude. "Discours à Stockholm." Nobel Media AB, www.nobel.se.

Smith, Barbara H. *Poetic Closure*. Chicago: University of Chicago Press, 1968.

Smith, D. Vance. *The Book of the Incipit: Beginnings in the Fourteenth Century*. Medieval Cultures vol. 28. Minneapolis, MN: University of Minnesota Press, 2001.

Sollers, Philippe. *Logiques*. Collection Tel Quel. Paris: Editions du Seuil, 1968.

Soupault, Philippe. "Déposition." *Les Cahiers du mois* 21–22 (June 1926): 149–61.

Spenser, Edmund, Thomas P. Roche, and C. Patrick O'Donnell. *Edmund Spenser, the Faerie Queene*. The English Poets. New Haven: Yale University Press, 1981.

Springer, Norman. "The Language of Literary Openings: Hemingway's *Cat in the Rain*." In *Narrative Poetics: Innovations, Limits, Challenges*, edited by James Phelan, 103–13. Columbus, OH: Center for Comparative Studies in the Humanities, 1987.

Stafford, Fiona J. *Starting Lines in Scottish, Irish and English Poetry: From Burns to Heaney*. Oxford: Oxford University Press, 2000.

Stanzel, Franz Karl. *A Theory of Narrative*. Translated by Charlotte Goedsche. Cambridge: Cambridge University Press, 1984.

Stein, Gertrude. *Ida: A Novel*. Lanham, MD: Cooper Square Publishers, 1971 [1941].

Steiner, George. *Grammars of Creation*. London: Faber and Faber, 2001.

Sternberg, Meir. *Expositional Modes and Temporal Ordering in Fiction*. Baltimore, MD: Johns Hopkins University Press, 1978.

Sterne, Laurence. *The Life and Opinions of Tristram Shandy*. London: Penguin, 1967 [1759].

Stevick, Philip. "Beginnings." In *The Chapter in Fiction: Theories of Narrative Division*, 75–86. Syracuse: Syracuse University Press, 1970.

Strowski, Fortunat. "Le Valérysme contre le roman." *La Renaissance: Politique, littéraire, artistique* (2 May 1925): 16–18.

———. "Pour le valérysme." *La Renaissance: Politique, littéraire, artistique* (23 May 1925): 12–13.

Svevo, Italo. *La coscienza di Zeno*. Bologna: L. Cappelli, 1923.

Thibaudet, Albert. "Réflexions sur la littérature – du surréalisme." *Nouvelle Revue Française* XXIV, no. 138 (1925).

Todorov, Tzvetan. *Introduction to Poetics*. Brighton: The Harvester Press, 1981.

Topia, André. "Incipit joyciens. Le fœtus et le dictionnaire." In *L'incipit. Actes du colloque De Poitiers 29–30 mars 1996*, edited by Liliane Louvel. Poitiers: La Licorne, 1997.

Torgovnick, Marianna. *Closure in the Novel*. Princeton, NJ: Princeton University Press, 1981.

Trollope, Anthony. *Is He Popenjoy?* New York: Elibron Classics, 2005 [1879].

Trollope, Anthony. *The Duke's Children*. The Centenary Edition of Anthony Trollope's Palliser Novels. Oxford and New York: Oxford University Press, 1983 [1880].

Twain, Mark. *Adventures of Huckleberry Finn (Tom Sawyer's Comrade)*. New York: C.L. Webster and Company, 1885.

Tynjanov, Jurij. "On Literary Evolution." In *Readings in Russian Poetics: Formalist and Structuralist Views*, edited by Ladislav Matejka and Krystyna Pomorska, 66–78. Ann Arbor: Michigan Slavic Publications, 1978.

Uspenski, Boris. "Poétique de la composition." *Poétique* 9 (1972): 124–34.

Valéry, Paul. *Alphabet*. Paris: LGF – Livre de Poche, 1999.

———. *Cahiers*. Vol. I. Paris: C.N.R.S.

———. *Cahiers*. Vol. V. Paris: C.N.R.S.

———. *Cahiers*. Vol. XXIII. Paris: C.N.R.S.

———. "Commencement d'orphée." In *Lake Collection 9.2*, TccMs, 1p.: University of Texas at Austin, Harry Ransom Center, 1921.

———. *Ego Scriptor. Poèmes et petits poèmes abstraits*. Paris: NRF Gallimard, 1992.

———. *Œuvres*. Pléiade. Edited by Jean Hytier, vol. I. Paris: Gallimard, 1957.

———. *Œuvres*. Pléiade. Edited by Jean Hytier, vol. II, Paris: Gallimard, 1960.

Vallès, Jules. *L'enfant*. Paris: Le Siècle, 1878.

van Dijk, Teun Adrianus. "Pragmatics and Poetics." In *Pragmatics of Language and Literature*, edited by Teun Adrianus van Dijk, 23–57. North-Holland Studies in Theoretical Poetics 2. Amsterdam and New York: North-Holland Pub. Co./ American Elsevier Pub. Co., 1976.

Veit, Carola. "The Evolution of Samuel Beckett's 'Nouvelle Écriture'." In *Commencements du roman: Conférences du séminaire de littérature comparée de L'université de la Sorbonne Nouvelle*, edited by Jean Bessière, 159–75. Paris: Honoré Champion, 2001.

Verrier, Jean. *Les Débuts de romans*. Paris: Bertrand-Lacoste, 1992.

Vogeleer, Svetlana. "Le Concept de point de vue et son application aux phrases existentielles qui ouvrent un texte narratif." *Le Langage et l'homme* XXII, no. 1 (1987): 26–32.

Vollman, Rolf. "Was war am Anfang?" *Die Zeit*, 2000.

Walser, Martin. "Erfahrungen mit ersten Sätzen oder Aller Anfang ist schwer." In *Vormittag eines Schriftstellers*, 151–62. Frankfurt: Suhrkamp, 1994.

Watt, Ian. "The First Paragraph of *The Ambassadors*: An Explication." In *Henry James: The Ambassadors*. New York, NY: Norton, 1994.

Weaver, Bruce L. *Novel Openers: First Sentences of 11,000 Fictional Works, Topically Arranged with Subject, Keyword, Author, and Title Indexing*. Jefferson, NC: McFarland & Co., 1995.

Wellek, René. *Concepts of Criticism*. New Haven, CT: Yale University Press, 1963.

Welsh, Alexander. "Opening and Closing *Les Misérables*." In *Narrative Endings*, edited by Alexander Welsh. Special issue, *Nineteenth-Century Fiction* 33, no. 1 (1978): 8–23.

Westermann, Claus. *Biblischer Kommentar. Altes Testament: Genesis 1–11*. Neukirchen-Vluyn: Neukirchener Verlag, 1974.

White, Hayden. "Criticism as Cultural Politics." *Diacritics* 6, no. 3 (1976): 8–13.

Whitlock, Baird W. *From These Beginnings: Openings of Fifty Major Literary Works*. New York, NY: Schocken, 1985.

Woolf, Virginia. *To the Lighthouse*. London: L. & V. Woolf at the Hogarth Press, 1927.

Woolf, Virginia. *Mrs Dalloway*. New York: Harcourt Brace and Company, 1925.

Woolf, Virginia. *The Waves*. Annotated and edited by Molly Hite and Mark Hussey. A Harvest Book. Orlando, FL: Harcourt, 2006.

Yeschua, Silvio. "La Marquise sortit à cinq heures." In *Valéry, le roman et l'œuvre à faire*, 157–60. Paris: Minard, 1976.

Zmegac, Viktor. "Zum Problem des Erzähleinsatzes bei Thomas Mann." *Filologija (Zagreb)* 4 (1964): 205–19.

Zola, Émile. *Œuvres Complètes*. Paris: Cercle du livre précieux, 1966.

INDEX